Risk Management *for insurers*

Second Edition

Risk Management for Insurers

Risk Control, Economic Capital and Solvency II

Second Edition

by René Doff

Published by Risk Books, a Division of Incisive Financial Publishing Ltd

Haymarket House
28–29 Haymarket
London SW1Y 4RX
Tel: + 44 (0)207 484 9700
Fax: + 44 (0)207 484 9797
E-mail: books@incisivemedia.com
Sites: www.riskbooks.com
www.incisivemedia.com

© 2011 Incisive Media Investments Ltd.

ISBN 978 1 906348 61 8

British Library Cataloguing in Publication Data
A catalogue record for this book is available from the British Library

Publisher: Nick Carver
Comissioning Editor: Sarah Hastings
Editorial Development: Jade Mitchell
Managing Editor: Lewis O'Sullivan
Designer: Lisa Ling

Typeset by Tricolour Design, Sudbury, Suffolk

Printed and bound in the UK by Berforts Group Ltd

Contents

About the Author

René Doff has worked in banking for a number of years, and been a risk manager since 2000. Within Rabobank, the largest bank in the Netherlands, he was involved in Basel II and economic capital implementations. Since 2005, he has been working in insurance, especially in the Eureko Group, the largest insurance company in the Netherlands. He has been involved in risk management implementation and Solvency II and, in that position, set up and chaired the Dutch Solvency II working group. In 2006 and 2007, he worked for the European Insurance Federation (CEA), one of the leading parties in the Solvency II debate. Since 2007, René has been involved in risk management and Solvency II implementation of Eureko's Dutch and international insurance business.

René Doff has a background in finance, business administration and mathematics. In 2006, he earned his PhD on risk management for insurers. He is a regular speaker at international conferences, publishes regularly in academic and practitioner journals and has written a number of books. In the Netherlands, *Risk Management for Insurers* (2006) and *Economic Capital and Risk Management in Banking* (2004) are considered as standard works on risk management in that country. The first edition of this book, *Risk Management for Insurers* (2007), has proven to be just as successful.

Preface

In 2007, I published a book on risk management for insurers. Its foreword was written by Jos Streppel, the then chief financial officer (CFO) of Aegon and an industry leader on risk management and fair value. He mentioned that the insurance industry was going through turbulent times and undergoing a wide range of developments. How could we have known then that turbulence of a totally different magnitude was coming our way?

In the meantime, the insurance industry has weathered a severe financial crisis that put virtually all insurance companies across the globe under stress. Some insurers faced capital shortages, others experienced solvency erosion and reorganised the risks within their company. This put risk management firmly on the agenda of executive boards of all insurers. CFOs and chief risk officers (CROs) worked day and night to ensure that companies got back on their feet, while explaining to financial stakeholders how they managed it.

In the meantime, Solvency II has approached its implementation date at top speed. Since the publication of the first edition of this book, the Solvency II Framework Directive has been published and approved, providing more guidance on the specifics of the regulation. Further guidance has come from the European Insurance and Occupational Pensions Authority (EIOPA) in the form of the Quantitative Impact Study 5 (QIS5) technical specifications and other consultative documents. Insurers have been working hard to implement all these regulatory requirements to a level that satisfies supervisor's criteria.

Jos Streppel also remarked that risk managers are important people within an insurance company. The financial crisis and the consequential focus on risk and risk management indicate that they have become even more important and the demands on them have increased since. However, the risk manager does not work in isolation. Attention for risk management has increased to such an extent that the risk manager has a significant audience. What is the best way to explain all the activities of the risk manager in their daily work? And how should they convince their colleagues to take risks seriously?

The good news is that the risk manager has a coherent risk framework to use: economic capital is the overarching method to measure and steer risks throughout the organisation. Also, Solvency II is based on this method. Economic capital is the key financial parameter to measure risks, to be balanced against long-term value creation.

This book will explain how economic capital fits into a coherent risk management framework. Jos Streppel highlighted in the first edition how important it is for insurance employees throughout the organisation to understand this economic capital framework. He emphasised a mutual exchange of views based on economic capital to improve decision-making on risks and value.

After the success of the first edition, I felt it necessary to update the book to include new developments in the Solvency II debate, as well as the ramifications of the financial crisis. These two aspects will further enhance insurance companies' perspectives on risk management and the way in which a company creates value. Therefore, the reader will find here a totally new chapter on the financial crisis, explaining its origins and impact on insurance companies. Obviously, the Solvency II chapter has been updated to take into account the new status. In order to further enhance learning from the banking industry, a new chapter on Basel III has also been included. This book reiterates that risk management is more than a set of actuarial calculations – the outcomes should be actively used by decision-makers, including the executive board or management team. However, that alone is not sufficient. Solvency II requires companies to set up an adequate risk organisation. A new chapter addresses how this can be achieved.

I think the success of the first edition was mainly due to the simple and clear explanation of the technical concepts, using examples whenever possible. This has remained the same for this edition. Although many more industry participants have become familiar with Solvency II as a main industry driver for change, still relatively few people outside the technical area have mastered the concept sufficiently to help drive developments of the models and their application in insurers' decision-making processes. To that end, a book like this continues to fulfil the needs of the insurance industry. And, to be honest, relatively few books like this exist. For that reason I am grateful to help you, as a reader, to enhance the insurance landscape.

Summer 2011
René Doff

1

Introduction

Risk management is at the core of the insurance business. While this has been the case for some time, its importance has started to change. This increasing importance of risk management was already an ongoing process due to a better understanding of insurance companies' risks, but it had accelerated even more by the time the financial crisis began in 2008. The financial crisis has been deeply debated and its impact on global economies will be permanent. One key theme that remains is that a better and wider understanding of the risks of financial institutions is required – and that this understanding needs to be developed throughout the industry. This book will address these changes and explain the new concepts being used in modern and best-practice risk management. It will also discuss in depth the new developments that are taking place in the regulatory arena.

THE RISING IMPORTANCE OF RISK MANAGEMENT
Risk has become more and more important over the past decades. There are five basic reasons for this.

First, the insurance industry has undergone a process of deregulation. Prior to this, regulations clearly set out the rules of the game for insurance companies. The development of gradual deregulation allowed them to take on more risks and explore the competitive edges of the market.

Second, there has been a number of privatisation waves; for

example, the life market is heavily stimulated by tax-favourable treatment in order for governments to be able to reduce state pensions. Similarly, health insurance is being privatised in a number of countries. Eastern and Central Europe is another example that comes to mind easily, but only a couple of years ago the health system in the Netherlands was also fundamentally restructured and further privatised. Other developing countries are gradually privatising parts of the insurance market, be it life, non-life or health. This has increased the competitive forces in the insurance market. The drive for competitive prices and market share has led to falling premiums, which have had to be compensated for by taking on investment risks. In life insurance, competitive forces have also led to universal life and unit-linked products (see Chapter 3).

Third, insurance firms are acting more and more across borders. International competition has also caused some of them to pursue new risks. At the same time, cross-border transactions are an important way to spread (and hence reduce) risks. However, this also made many firms vulnerable to new global risks – such as the terrorist attacks of 9/11 in 2001, Katrina in the US in 2005 and the Japanese tsunami in 2011.

Fourth, capital markets have become more volatile over the past few years. Part of this volatility can be attributed to more efficient and globalised markets. As a result of the move towards fair valuation of assets (see Chapter 7), volatility in asset portfolios is having a direct impact on insurance companies – or, to understand it better: volatility has become more visible. In addition, investment strategies have become a more important source of return for companies in search of a better overall return. There are many reasons behind this, one of which is the competition to outperform competitors on the stock markets in the search to please shareholders. This explains part of the move towards more complex investment strategies. The globalisation of the capital markets and the internationalisation of the insurance industry has made underwriting and investment activities more interdependent than before. This places additional importance on investment strategy as a source of risks. All this implies that insurance has become more fragile to disruptions of the international capital markets, such as the global financial crisis of 2008 (see Chapter 6).

Lastly, as the importance of these risks grew over time, they also caused problems: risks can hurt. In the late 1990s, the number of insurer insolvencies grew significantly. Some failures hit policy-holders while others, fortunately, did not. However, the failures uncovered the risks for many institutions and attracted attention from regulators. The increasing attention resulted in some major regulatory reforms, as will be discussed in Chapters 7 and 8.

As a result, insurance companies changed the way in which they dealt with risks. The European Insurance Federation CEA showed that around 80% of European insurance companies are either in the process of upgrading their risk management practices or have just gone through such a process. This clearly highlights the importance of risk management.

NEW METHODOLOGIES AND TECHNOLOGIES

The way in which risks are being managed in insurance companies is undergoing a revolutionary change. Insurance companies have always assessed risks, for instance by distinguishing geographical areas in motor insurance or incorporating age into life insurance premiums. However, advances in technology have provided op-portunities to exploit the full use of quantitative techniques. This is how mathematics entered the field of risk management in the mid-1990s. It started in the banking industry, especially in invest-ment banking, and quickly covered commercial banking as well. Insurance followed in the late 1990s and early 2000s. These devel-opments also caught the eye of the supervisors, who consequently incorporated the innovative techniques in their regulatory frame-works. Basel II in the banking industry has been the predominant example of this, triggering many discussions. In 2010, Basel III was issued in banking. Again, insurance regulations followed closely behind, as we will see in Chapter 8 of this book. Along with the increasing insight into the risks of the insurance companies, super-visors realised the disadvantages of the supervisory framework that used to be in place where risk and supervisory capital require-ments were insufficiently related and even included inverse incen-tives. This happened in multiple countries across the globe, such as the UK, Switzerland and the Netherlands – who redesigned their frameworks in the period 2004–05. Non-European countries such as Australia and Canada have also upgraded their supervision. Solvency II is the major reform of European insurance regulations, acting as an example for the fundamental redesign of insurance supervision for many countries. The insurance industry, as well as supervisors, considers Solvency II a unique opportunity to incorporate all risk management developments into the new regulatory framework.

THE RISING STAR OF THE RISK MANAGER

In addition to those developments, financial institutions became aware that if risks and risk management were to be so important, they needed to be incorporated into the management control framework of the institution. This was not without problems. An old quote from *Euromoney* magazine is often cited, because it successfully highlights the identity boost of the risk manager:

> "First he sat in the back seat and then he had his foot on the brake, now he has got one hand on the steering wheel! Is there no end to the risk manager's advancement into every aspect of risk-taking in a financial firm? Next, he'll be right there in the driving seat..." (*Euromoney*, February 1998)

This quote is anecdotal for the way in which (financial) risk information is included in the day-to-day management of the company. It gave the incentive to companies to implement embedded value, economic capital and risk-adjusted return on capital (RAROC) into their management control frameworks. New words are starting to enter management reports, including many abbreviations and technical terms. While terminology, definitions and acronyms may differ from company to company, their common denominator is the aim to measure long-term value by balancing risk and reward.

Creating long-term value by balancing risk and reward is exactly what bridges the gap between financial companies and financial markets. The concept is central to an investment strategy, especially since the famous portfolio theories of Markowitz in the 1950s. Now, the new risk management technologies that will be described in depth in this book provide opportunities to do exactly the same in insurance companies.

In addition, corporate governance scandals such as Enron and

WorldCom have shown how vulnerable an organisation is when risks are not adequately addressed. Sarbanes–Oxley (SOX) and equivalent rules have emphasised the importance for enterprise-wide risk management (ERM) frameworks. We will examine that in more detail in Chapter 11, although it will also be touched upon in Chapter 5 when operational risk will be discussed.

All this emphasises the role of risk management in the day-to-day operations of the business. Achieving this, however, is not easy. To that end, many insurance companies have set up risk management programmes to implement modern risk management frameworks. Additionally, governance structures are put into place that result in setting up risk management departments and the appointment of chief risk officers (CROs). Whilst some CROs report to the chief financial officer (CFO), others have a position in the executive board (Chapter 11). All in all, risk management as a profession is on the rise.

SOME EVIDENCE

Now, are these risks really as important as they are thought to be? The answer to this must be a resounding yes. A global consulting firm concluded that, in the aftermath of the equity crisis of 2002–03, European life insurance companies were faced with an aggregate capital shortfall of €100 billion.[1] This has been partially confirmed by the companies themselves, who have de-risked their equity exposures significantly since 2003. However, the significance of financial risks continues to show, as was seen in the financial crisis of 2008. At one moment equity markets were considered the key area for risk management attention, at another moment even government bond markets drew massive attention (PIGS countries, see Chapter 6). One could add to this an impressive pile of newspaper articles about the financial losses during the capital market crises. All this shows the importance of proper risk management and that careful decision-making processes based on risk and return will eventually pay off.

During the financial crisis, capital was scarce for all financial institutions, both banks and insurers. This was at a time that financial institutions were strongly in need of capital. At the same time, both assets were difficult to value since there was hardly a market. Insurance liabilities have been incorrectly valued due to the stringent valuation rules. These rules are now under debate in the projects Solvency II and IFRS4 Phase II. This will lead to a redesign of valuation methodologies for insurance liabilities, an area that caused difficulties during the crisis.

In a sense, banking and insurance bear many similarities. However, the same report highlights that banks' capital productivity has been more than 30% higher than insurance companies' capital productivity (11.7% vs 8.7%), as can be seen from Figure 1.1. In particular, the way in which insurance companies handle risks is an area of performance improvement. All this emphasises how important it is that insurance companies properly take into account their risk profiles and address this in their management control frameworks.

Figure 1.1 Capital productivity in European banks and insurers 1987–2002*

*In this graph, life and non-life insurers are combined: this is because in practice many European insurers are composites, and de-facto cross-subsidisation makes it difficult to fully separate publicly disclosed profitability between Life and Non-Life.

Source: Datastream, MOW, 2004

The findings in Figure 1.1 are relevant because the banking and insurance industries have increasingly converged. Banks and insurance firms compete for the same shareholders and for the same consumers (bank deposits and mutual funds versus life insurance products). This implies that, if insurance companies want to remain competitive, they will need to improve their capital efficiency. This is an extremely challenging task for many insurance companies that are already finding themselves in competitive and mature markets. Additionally, insurance products are generally more complex and less liquid. In any case, they cannot (yet) be easily traded on secondary markets, unlike most banking products. We have however also seen the drawbacks of massive reselling on secondary markets (see Chapter 6).

Moreover, banks and insurance companies are increasingly combined in one firm: a financial conglomerate (FICO). At the same time, a reversed development has also taken place where some FICOs plan to disintegrate, such as ING. These FICOs are important players in the financial industry as they account for roughly 30% of deposits and 20% of insurance premiums in Europe. In smaller markets, they even hold market shares of more than 50%. It is important to recognise that, from the perspective of a FICO, it is desirable to be able to compare the risks involved in the two business lines (banking and insurance). To that end, risk should be an element of the management control framework of a FICO.

A LANGUAGE PROBLEM

With risk management being at the core of the insurance business, and having the risk manager at the steering wheel, it should be a topic of relevance for a wide audience within the insurance industry. A wide audience is required to understand the fundamentals of modern risk management. Solvency II requires companies using internal models that key decision-makers understand well the fundamentals of the risk models. At the same time, the risk management arena is crowded with highly specialised staff, such as actuaries, mathematicians and financial controllers. In their day-to-day work, they build risk models and implement systems to measure risks as accurately as possible. The technical nature makes it difficult for non-technically oriented people such as managers to follow the debate and to interpret the outcomes of the calculations.

This book aims to fill the gap between the quantitative details of the risk models and the managerial consequences of the outcomes; there is a role for both parties. Managers will need to accept that risk is a core of their business and that the modern quantitative methodologies can be valuable tools to run their businesses in a more enhanced way. Risk managers will need to be able to explain the risk models in an extremely simple manner. KISS (keep it simple, stupid!) should be the risk manager's mantra.

With that in mind, this book will explain the modern risk management spectrum and provide an overview of risk measurement methodologies. It aims at assisting all the people within the insurance industry who want to better understand the field of risk management. It will help the reader to understand the concept of risk, as it emphasises the relevance of the outcomes of the risk measurement methodologies.

OUTLINE OF THE BOOK

The principle idea of this book is that risk and capital are inherently tied together. As capital is the buffer with which to absorb risks and the amount of available capital within a firm is limited, the risk profile is translated into the amount of capital required to absorb that level of risk. To that end, there are two capital requirements. First, there is an internal capital requirement because the company sets limits to its own risk profile. This is to safeguard long-term continuity. The objective is to maximise value creation, conditional to this internal capital requirement. The internal capital requirement is also called economic capital because it is based on economic principles. Second, in its role as protector of policyholders, the supervisor aims to limit excessive risk taking by insurance companies in order to stabilise the financial system. Chapter 2 explores these concepts in more detail.

This book identifies seven major risk types, which will be fully considered in Chapters 3, 4 and 5. For each risk type it will be discussed what the risks are exactly, how they can be measured and then managed. These chapters will also focus on the structure of the risk models and the methodologies used to calculate economic capital.

Although risks have always been recognised and identified by insurers, they have not always been thought of with the same level of seriousness. Crises have come and gone, albeit more frequently and severe over time. The equity and interest rate crisis in the early 2000s was considered relatively severe by many financial institutions. It might be fair to designate it as a wake-up call for many institutions. However, the shock that went through the financial markets in 2008 wiped out every previous crisis. Or, actually, what happened were a wave of shocks, varying from liquidity to equity, interest rates and government bond markets. A book on risk management would be incomplete without a proper analysis of this financial crisis and lessons learned. It would be impossible to understand everything after reading only one book, but Chapter 6 at least draws together the most important conclusions.

As indicated, supervisors have an important role in representing the stakes of the policyholders. Chapter 7 will explore the developments in supervision. In Europe, Solvency II will drastically redesign the supervisory rules for regulatory capital for insurance companies – Chapter 8 will elaborate on this and highlight the key changes in the landscape of the insurance industry. This is relevant since Solvency II serves as a global example of insurance supervision, and hence it is good to understand it and its consequences. We will see in Chapter 6 how the financial crisis also hit the banks. Solvency II heavily draws upon the experience in banking and Basel II. Chapter 9 will therefore explain the banking regulation, as it serves as an important example. Of course, the chapter will also elaborate on Basel III, the latest update of the supervisory framework for banking.

Chapter 10 will then discuss in detail how the economic capital outcomes of all these risk models need to be interpreted. Most importantly, it considers how they should be incorporated into the management control framework of the insurance company in its aim to manage value creation by balancing risk and reward. The chapter includes many practical numerical examples based on a hypothetical case study.

Chapter 11 will examine how risk management could be implemented in insurance companies from an organisational perspective. Questions such as how to organise corporate governance, and what is the role and position of the CRO will be answered. Although quite different from previous chapters – where technical issues are addressed – it is key to identify the challenges in implementing risk management organisationally. Also, an adequate risk management organisation should be able to leverage the technical implementation of the quantitative measures such as economic capital.

Finally, Chapter 12 will bring all the strands together, and provide a summary and some conclusions.

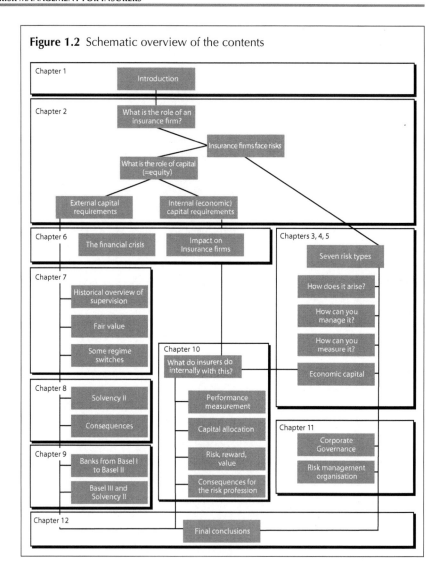

Figure 1.2 Schematic overview of the contents

1   See Mercer Oliver Wyman, "Life at the end of the tunnel? The capital crisis in the European life sector", 2004.

2

The Insurer as a Financial Institution

This chapter describes the function of the insurer as a financial institution. Equity capital has a special role within financial institutions, and thus also within insurance companies; therein, risks and risk management have a central position. In addition, supervision will also be discussed in this chapter.

WHAT IS AN INSURER?

The insurer is a financial institution. The key product of the insurer is the promise to make financial compensation at some moment in the future, depending on the type of product. The fact that products of financial institutions are not tangible (they do not "manufacture" anything) has resulted in their becoming the subject of academic discussion. Why do insurers actually exist? The reason why an individual person needs insurance is obvious: they obtain security and are covered for certain risks – for instance, one's house burning down. Even if there is only a small probability, an individual does not have the financial means to reconstruct the house all over again; therefore, they need to cover that risk.

But, even then, the question remains: why do insurance companies exist? An entire village or residential area could, for instance, mutually agree that each resident helps with the reconstruction of burnt-down houses. A great advantage is that, after a fire, each resident will only have to pay a small amount, the damage being shared between all residents. We call this the principle of solidarity:

people help each other. The total expected damage cost is smaller for each resident. The probability of all the houses in the village burning down simultaneously (and the entire village having to reconstruct all the houses all over again) is, after all, smaller than the probability of one specific house burning down. This is the pooling principle: by adding up several risks, the total risk decreases. By making agreements among a group of individuals, taking out fire insurance with a financial institution becomes superfluous.

Within a small, well-organised group of participants such construction could work well. As a matter of fact, this is how many mutual insurers started. However, the "pooling principle" indicates that the total risk decreases as the group of participants increases. As such, there is a need to have the largest group of participants possible. In practice, not every insured object is identical nor is every risk as high, which is why the risk needs to be estimated in advance. Insurers have the necessary experience and knowledge for these estimations, and dispose of the necessary economies of scale to do so efficiently. Besides, the total risk decreases best by spreading the risks; for instance, sharing the risks among property owners from different villages instead of only among owners from the same village. Spreading is a key element of insurance – spreading over geographical locations, sectors, types of objects and so on. Insurers can apply this spreading method better than individuals because of their economies of scale. Insurers' economies of scale include two different advantages: efficient use of expertise and the good possibility of risk spreading.

The phenomena of adverse selection and moral hazard play an important part in insurance and insurers. Adverse selection means that persons most in need of risk coverage will be the ones to turn to an insurer. A perfectly healthy person has less need for medical insurance than someone with bad health. For the insurer, this involves fewer possibilities for risk spreading. Moral hazard is the phenomenon that people tend to be less careful once they have taken out insurance because the damage will be compensated for anyway.[1] Both adverse selection and moral hazard involve costs for the group of insured due to screening of new and existing clients. An insurer obtains economies of scale for these costs.

An insurer could concentrate on the "settlement" of the compensation: making sure that each participant contributes when damage occurs, so costs are spread among the participants. However, that is not efficient. Therefore, the insured pay a premium upfront from which the insurer can subsequently pay compensation. The insurer knows whether the premium has been sufficient only in due course. After all, the claim payments are uncertain and risky. We call this the inverse exploitation cycle. This also involves a risk for the insurer. For example, if there are more damages than expected then the premium has not been sufficient and the insurer will have to bear the costs involved. Mostly, it cannot subsequently require a "supplementary payment" from clients. The risk for the insurer is central to this book.

Thus, we have introduced a few reasons why insurance companies exist. The most important reasons are efficient use and economies of scale concerning expertise, possibilities of risk spreading and the ability to charge premiums in advance and pay compensation afterwards. This last part, however, implies the insurer runs risks as well.

Traditionally, many insurance companies started in the legal form of a mutual or cooperative. These legal forms have members rather than shareholders. A simple form of a mutual or cooperative is when all inhabitants of a certain community agree to compensate each others' losses in the case of an event occurring. Many mutual insurance companies are deeply rooted in a certain community, either regionally oriented or professionally. Mutuals tend to be more strongly related to their client base than stock-listed companies, since the clients are also their members and hence they determine the strategy of the company. This is different from stock-listed companies where shareholders determine the strategy. Examples of this are insurance mutuals relating to trade organisations, predominantly in the farming sector. These mutuals have traditionally expanded into the retail insurance markets and, as a matter of fact, they receive a wide client base. Over time, however, many mutuals turned themselves into stock-listed companies during the last decades of the 20th Century. This is because that was a period of extensive growth and mutuals can issue capital less easily than stock-listed companies. At the same time, mutuals could have a large reserve of retained earnings since they cannot issue dividends to shareholders. In Europe, mutuals represent roughly 25% of the market in terms of premium volume, and there are 1,600 European mutual insurance companies.

We mostly divide the insurance business into life and non-life insurance. Apart from that, health insurance is sometimes considered to be a separate category. As to its characteristics and risk management techniques, health insurance is a hybrid form of life and non-life insurance. Therefore, health is not treated separately in this book.

Non-life insurance promises a policyholder future compensation for damage suffered from previously agreed incidents. Life insurance promises a policyholder future compensation (or several) upon death or simply at a certain age. It mostly covers a much longer period than non-life insurance. For a long time, the life and non-life industries within the insurance sector have been two relatively separate worlds. This is partially due to past regulations and backgrounds and the long-term nature of life insurance. This book will argue, however, that the principles of economic capital apply to both and, therefore, risk management for life and non-life insurance is closely related.

> **PANEL 2.1 HISTORICAL ORIGIN OF INSURANCE**
> The precursor of life insurance in Europe dates from Ancient Greece in approximately 200BC. Against a fixed deposit, residents of the Greek city-state Milete could obtain a monthly lifelong compensation. Upon death, the rest of the deposit went to the city council. The premium (deposit) depended on the age of the "insured person". The Romans had an insurance called collegia, where compensation was granted upon death. Although this collegia was originally intended to finance the funeral ceremony, the rest was used as provision for the surviving relatives. It was, in reality, a term assurance. For collegia the premium also depended on one's age. For the Greek as well as the Roman insurance, financial problems within the government were the underlying motivation. The premium was mostly meant to cover an acute financial problem of the state. After the Dutch scientist Johan de Witt developed mortality tables in the 17th Century, there were opportunities for real life insurers to propose a premium depending on age. Not until the 19th Century did the first modern life insurers appear.
> The principle of non-life insurance goes back to ancient China, where merchants divided their merchandise among their ships. When one ship perished, the merchants then bore the damage together. Such

initiatives remained until the era of industrialisation, often institutionalised through mutual companies. The value of insured objects was relatively low. However, transport insurance was often traded in an exchange market. The famous Lloyd's is a good example of this. From 1696, Edward Lloyd's coffee house kept a list of ships arriving and leaving, their cargoes and the dangers of the intended routes. Thus, the coffee house was the place par excellence where insurance agents traded. They carried insurance policies with them on which merchants only needed to write their names – hence the name "underwriter". With the success of the coffee house, Lloyd's List became more and more institutionalised as an insurance exchange market.

Due to the growth of welfare in times of industrialisation, more non-life insurers gradually appeared in the 19th Century. They developed into the insurance companies as we know them today.

THE BUSINESS ECONOMICS OF INSURANCE COMPANIES

The world of insurance has specific accounting rules. Therefore, an insurance balance sheet cannot simply be compared with the balance sheet of a non-financial institution. In non-financial institutions, the liability side of the balance sheet (the financing of assets) stands relatively detached from the primary process / product of the particular company. Financing is at the service of the core activity (asset side of the balance sheet). For an insurer, this is actually the other way around. Granting insurance automatically involves creating technical provisions. Technical provisions are also indicated by the slightly more general term "insurance liabilities". An insurance policy promises compensation to the policyholder in the future. In order to comply with this obligation, the insurer makes up an early-stage provision called technical provision. The technical provisions of an insurer are the largest liability item on the balance sheet. Because of that reason, the technical provisions are a topic of supervision – as will see be seen later in this book.

The technical provision of a life insurance policy is created directly at the sale. This is the "money box" from which the agreed compensation will be paid in the future. Concerning non-life insurance, a provision is made when a claim is reported[2] but the compensation is uncertain. With non-life insurance, it is not clear if compensation will actually take place and how high that compensation will amount to exactly. In life insurance, it is certain that each person will die some day, but the moment and amount of compensation is uncertain. Or, when the amount of compensation is pre-determined, it is uncertain in advance how much of that amount will already be provisioned from the premium payments. For a long time, this uncertainty has been covered by "prudence" when establishing the technical provisions. The prudence margin is implicitly hidden in the technical provisions. The actuary, as a qualified entity for the establishment of the technical provision, handles mortality or claim expectations with sufficient care. The actuary uses statistical techniques for the prudence margin. The annual accounts of an insurance company always include a statement of the chief actuary or qualifying actuary on the adequacy of the technical provisions.

The assets of the insurer consist of investments; different to those within some non-financial institutions, the assets are actually at the service of the liabilities. Premiums are invested in several ways. The four main forms are bonds, mortgages, shares and real estate as well as, additionally, "commodities" and derivatives. We also speak of fixed income, referring to bonds and mortgages. The objective of investment is obtaining a reliable return, which is partially returned to policyholders in the form of lower premiums or higher claim payments. For that matter, insurers are relatively careful investors and often take into account a long time horizon and provide a well-spread investment portfolio. This is necessary – after all, investing is mostly at the service of future compensations to policyholders, which cannot be endangered. Therefore, investments are matched as well as possible to these obligations. When an insurer promises to pay out a certain amount in 30 years' time (eg, via an annuity), the premiums have to be invested in order for this amount to be released after that period of 30 years.

The third balance-sheet item is the equity capital: the balance of the assets (investments) minus the debts (mainly technical provisions). The capital roughly consists of share capital and reserves. Additionally, insurers can add the subordinated debt capital (for instance, self-issued bonds) to the equity capital under certain conditions. In addition to being a residual item on the balance sheet, the equity capital is the final safety net for risks: it serves as the ultimate buffer to absorb risks. When setbacks within claim amounts turn out so big that even prudence in the technical provision is not sufficient, one needs to break into the equity capital.

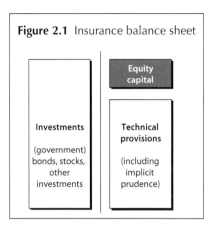

Figure 2.1 Insurance balance sheet

THE RISK FOR THE INSURER

When interpreting the term "risk", we explicitly choose the perspective of the insurer. What is the risk for the insurer? Suppose that an average[3] of 1 in 1,000 cars suffers total loss annually. According to the law of large numbers, the premium of each insurance policy contains a risk premium of one-thousandth of the value (next to cost charges, for instance). When each year exactly 10 out of 10,000 insured cars suffer total loss, does that involve "risk"? No, definitely not. The total claims can be compensated for from the risk premium of all obtained premiums. For individual clients there is uncertainty, but for the insurer itself there is none.

In practice, the claim pattern appears to be unstable. In one year, the claims may be higher than another. In the long run, the risk premium will be sufficient to cover the average claim amounts, but in some years it can turn out badly. Then it is firstly covered by prudence in the technical provisions, and finally by the capital. The same applies to risks in the investment portfolio: if there are setbacks there, the capital serves as the buffer and absorbs them.

Risk is defined as "the phenomenon where results can be worse than expected". The total risk spectrum is usually divided into several risk categories. Several classifications are possible, but the one below was created as the market standard (see Figure 2.2). Many of the definitions refer to a possible decrease in value. This refers to a decrease in the value of the capital due to the risks addressed.

❏ Life risk: the risk of decreases in value due to different mortality than expected or due to a change in the mortality expectation.
❏ Non-life risk: the risk of decreases in value by different or higher claims than expected or by changes in the expectation over time.
❏ Market risk: the risk of decreases in value by changes in market variables, such as interest rates, share prices, exchange rates, real estate prices and the like. This also includes asset and liability management (ALM).[4]
❏ Credit risk: the risk of decreases in value when counterparties are not capable of fulfilling their obligations or when there are changes in the credit standing of counterparties.
❏ Liquidity risk: the risk of unexpected or unexpectedly high payments, where complying with the obligations involves a loss.
❏ Operational risk: the risk of losses due to shortcomings in internal processes, people, systems or external events.
❏ Business risk: the risk of losses due to changes in the competitive environment or internal flexibility.

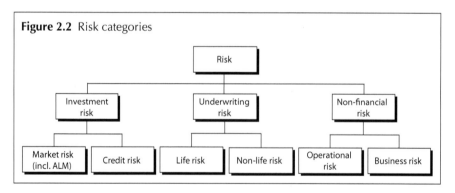

Figure 2.2 Risk categories

Market risks have consequences for both investments and technical provisions. However, in practice, the risks are addressed via the investment portfolio. Therefore, we place market risks under investment risks (see Figure 2.2). The combination of market risks and credit risks is also called financial risks. As this could imply other risks not having financial consequences, in this book we prefer the term investment risks.

Liquidity risk is not included in Figure 2.2 because, in general, insurers do not reserve any economic capital for it. The adequate measurement of liquidity risk is still in its early stages, and we will come back to that in Chapter 4. However, as will be seen in Chapter 6, the financial crisis of 2008 was based to a large extent on liquidity risk. The attention paid to operational risk is growing, as will be addressed in Chapter 5. Therefore, economic capital is often reserved for operational risk, although measuring methods are still being developed.

In general, risks can be treated in three ways (see Figure 2.3). First, you can control the risk: risk control. Risk control involves observing the risks actively and, if necessary, taking measures in order to restrict losses. Second, the consequences of the risk can be covered financially: risk financing. The emphasis here is not on the event itself, but on the financial consequences. Reinsurance is an example of risk financing. Third, the risk can be reduced: risk reduction. The most obvious measure is stopping the risky activity in question, but that is not always advisable or possible. In that case, diversification, or risk spreading, is a very good alternative. Measuring risks is necessary for risk financing and risk reduction.

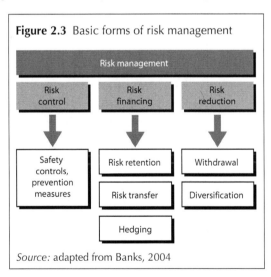

Figure 2.3 Basic forms of risk management

Source: adapted from Banks, 2004

Holding capital, which will be treated later in this chapter, falls under the category of risk financing, as the insurer retains the risk itself. The insurer can also control and/or influence the risk profile. A higher risk often involves a higher return in the long-term and a lower risk involves a lower return. A higher risk also implies a less-firm promise by the insurer to policyholders that they will receive their promised compensation in the future. Although the various risks differ from each other, they have a similar impact on policyholders. Therefore, the risk profile is an important control variable for the insurer.

PANEL 2.2 DIFFERENT DEFINITIONS OF THE CONCEPT OF RISK

There are different definitions of risk: in the insurance world "probability times impact" or "frequency times severity" is often used. Statistically, this multiplication produces the expected value; for instance, how many claims are expected annually? The field of risk management actually focuses on the fluctuations around this expectation. Within large portfolios, most fluctuations disappear due to diversification. The question is if there is really a genuine risk attached to it for the insurer. This book specifically focuses on the remaining risk for the insurer. In Chapters 3, 4 and 5, the risk categories will be treated in depth.

The most famous definition of risk is: risk is the probability of losses. As this refers only to negative effects, we call this a pure risk. Examples of pure risk are an earthquake, theft of goods or the loss of clients.

In financial markets, however, a speculative perception of risk is more common. Both positive and negative effects are addressed. As there is a probability of stocks decreasing in value, investors run a risk with purchase. However, this is compensated for by the expectation of an increase in value or because there is a periodical return (eg, a dividend or interest). We call this a speculative risk. A commonly used term in speculative risk is volatility. Volatility implies that there are certain fluctuations (of value) around an average. Investments that fluctuate strongly around the average involve more risk than investments with a stable pattern. Generally, we say that a more speculative risk produces extra return. On the contrary, we can expect that when we are deluded by high returns, there will probably be a snag in it somewhere. Speculative risk and return are two sides of the same coin.

INSURANCE SUPERVISION

For a national economy, it is important that policyholders can put their trust in receiving their promised compensation in the future. When an insurer goes bankrupt, the trust in all insurers can be badly damaged. The result is no one dares to take on insurance anymore, which causes damage to an economy. Therefore, there is insurance supervision. Banking supervision has historically been more developed than insurance supervision due to the consequences of a possible systemic crisis when a bank goes bankrupt. Banks do much business with each other, meaning the bankruptcy of one bank could lead to spillover effects. This interdependence is not so high between insurers.

The insurance company, as mentioned, undergoes an "inverse exploitation cycle" (see page 13). The moment when clients pay premiums is very distant from the moment when insurers will pay out possible compensation. This is inconvenient for the insurer, as it does not know upfront if the premium will be sufficient, as well as for clients as they simply have to trust the insurer will meet its future obligations. This means that the client will have to estimate the current (financial) solvency of an insurer, and also (even harder) the willingness of the insurer to stay solvent over time. The insurer could simply adapt its financial situation once it has received all the premiums from clients, before it makes any claim payments. A policyholder has no influence on this. This trust is the most important foundation of a financial institution. Therefore, trust in the insurance industry is a paramount theme for insurers. And, to be honest, the financial industry as a whole has experienced loss of trust by the public due to the massive losses during the financial crisis of 2008. Dating from that period, it is interesting to note the developments of unit-linked life products where clients were promised high returns, but faced increasing losses. Here, clients also lost trust in the insurance industry to honour future claim payments. Rebuilding this trust is an important theme in the industry. Supervision can help building that trust, since supervisors are an independent party in this debate.

Each individual could thoroughly investigate the insurer's (financial) state of affairs. However, that is not efficient, as each policyholder would then have to invent his own wheel. In addition, due to the specific accounting rules, insurers are complex and opaque to outsiders. Thus, not everybody has the necessary expertise to judge the financial situation of an insurance company. The supervision of insurers is therefore assigned to a supervisor.

Some insurance products are mandatory by law, especially third-party liability insurance. In order to gain market share, there could be an incentive for insurance companies to set a premium that is too low to be economically viable. Of course, this could harm policyholders. To avoid undesirable consequences for policyholders, insurance supervisors used to monitor the adequacy of premiums. However, supervisors have deregulated premium rates and monitored insurance companies by looking at technical provisions and minimum capital requirements.

It is common to distinguish between prudential supervision and market-conduct supervision. The former involves supervising the insurer's financial conditions, such as minimum capital requirements and technical provisions. The latter involves supervising market practices to prevent situations such as churning. In some countries, there are separate bodies for these two sorts of supervision; in others, they are combined. In addition to insurance companies, banks are also supervised. In many countries, supervision of banks and insurers is combined into one single institution.

At the time of writing, solvency requirements for insurers are crudely determined in most countries. The European framework dates from the 1970s, although some threshold amounts were updated in 2003. In Chapters 7 and 8, we will look in more depth at the supervisory rules and Solvency II. Here we note that the traditional solvency regulations are not risk sensitive and even contain inverse incentives for insurance companies.

THE ROLE OF CAPITAL

We can identify three main reasons why insurers hold a capital buffer. First, capital is set aside to absorb extreme unexpected losses caused by the risks involved, which guarantees long-term continuity. When the insurer assumes that its activities will be profitable, it will want to guarantee their continuity. Besides, without continuity the insurer could not obtain future profits, meaning that there has to be sufficient capital to cover unexpected losses, otherwise no expected future profits can be obtained. This is an internally pursued reason for holding capital. We refer to this form of minimum capital requirement as economic capital, to point to the economic grounds for holding capital. However, too much capital could be too expensive and endanger profitability. The economic capital concept is usually associated with statistical calculations to establish the minimum capital buffer as exactly as possible. From Chapter 3 onwards, we will expand upon the calculations of economic capital for the different risk categories in much more detail.

Second, rating agencies such as Moody's and Standard & Poor's are in the line of the internal solvency requirements. In order to be active on the capital markets, insurers are evaluated by such rating agencies. When they establish a rating, they also look at the financial aspects of the insurer and the amount of capital plays a great role in this. When the insurer drops below certain limits, it could have consequences for their rating. This happened for many insurance companies during the financial crisis of 2008 (see Chapter 6). As it is important for insurers to have a certain rating, the amount of capital also serves as precondition for this rating. In this book, we view the rating agencies in conjunction with the internal solvency requirement, although at the time of writing rating agencies have less-detailed models than the insurers' internal models for economic capital. However, rating agencies increasingly rely on companies' own economic capital models for information.

Third, insurance supervisors require a minimum capital buffer, which serves to protect policyholders and thus protect the stability of the economic system (see Figure 2.4). The minimum capital requirement is one of the means used for that purpose. This external capital requirement is also referred to by the terms statutory capital and regulatory capital, which translates into the term capital charge. There have been capital requirements for years, although these have been reviewed in several countries (including through Solvency II, see Chapter 8). Capital requirements also apply to banks, and these have also been revised under the frameworks for Basel II and Basel III.

Both the internal and external solvency requirements are compared to the available capital. Although the establishment and practical details of both kinds of capital (economic versus regulatory capital) differ, the reasons behind them are identical. In both cases, they involve a capital buffer that has to be able to absorb possible losses caused by risks. The insurer will thus hold sufficient capital to cover the highest of the internal and external solvency requirements.

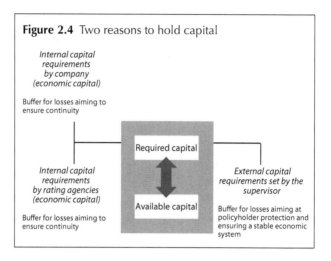

Figure 2.4 Two reasons to hold capital

Internal capital requirements by company (economic capital)

Buffer for losses aiming to ensure continuity

Internal capital requirements by rating agencies (economic capital)

Buffer for losses aiming to ensure continuity

Required capital

Available capital

External capital requirements set by the supervisor

Buffer for losses aiming at policyholder protection and ensuring a stable economic system

A PARADIGM SHIFT: FAIR VALUE

For a long time, risks were particularly reflected in the technical provisions. Although the capital was the ultimate buffer for the risk, there was no emphasis on precisely establishing the minimum amount of capital. Additionally, the rules for establishing technical provisions were different between countries, particularly concerning the level of implicit prudence. This is unimportant as long as insurers operate on a mainly national basis. Since the 1990s, however, internationalisation has become widespread. Consequently, differences between countries could turn out to have a negative impact for insurers.

One important development is fair value. Fair value, or market value, is gradually becoming the standard method for the valuation of financial instruments and also applies to insurance liabilities. The idea behind it is that financial instruments change in value during their term and the traditional purchase value no longer provides a true reflection. In the 1990s, several debacles took place when institutions suddenly went bankrupt because the actual value of assets was way below the purchase value, or the liabilities were actually higher than accounting values (see also Chapter 7).

Fair value is "the amount for which an asset could be exchanged or a liability be settled between knowledgeable, willing parties in an arm's-length transaction". This involves the price that parties, who are well informed and willing to make transactions, are prepared to pay for an asset or debt. For insurance products, there are valuation models to establish the fair value. In general, the net present value (NPV) of the future cashflows is used. The discount rate is the risk-free interest rate; for instance, the interest rate derived from government bonds. In Chapters 7 and 8, we will expand upon the calculation method. In Chapters 3 and 10, we will see that the concept of embedded value is a precursor of fair value.

In comparison to fair value, the traditional valuation method is more prudent. The technical provisions have to be "sufficiently adequate" to comply with future liabilities. In other words, traditionally insurers aimed to have an amount of technical provisions such that it would always be sufficient to honour clients claim payments. Fair value focuses on "exactly adequate", which is more difficult to determine, although it does give a much better reflection of the true liabilities.

When technical provisions are valued fairly, an objective reflection of the expected future obligations is obtained and additional prudence is no longer included in the technical provisions. Therefore, it is necessary to pay explicit attention to the amount of capital as a buffer against risks. Thus, the establishment of the minimum capital buffer is more important when we apply fair value to technical provisions.

Table 2.1 Differences between the traditional and fair-value methodologies

	Traditional paradigm	Fair value paradigm
Technical provisions	Sufficiently for future policyholder claim payments; Determine future cash flows prudently; Discounting with fixed rate (life) or not discounting at all (non-life)	The exact value of future policyholder claim payments; Determine future cash flows realistically; Discounting with yield curve (life and non-life)
Risks	Reflected in implicit levels of prudence in technical provisions	Reflected in the capital requirements
Role of solvency requirements	Crude method, supplements technical provisions	Refined method, central in risk assessment

PANEL 2.3 FAIR VALUE AND THE DISCOUNT RATE

As discussed, a central part of fair-value calculations is discounting the future cash flows. This holds for life as well as for non-life technical provisions. The discount rate of traditional embedded value was a certain discount rate that reflected the total return on investments in a prudent way. This is consistent with the theory of the capital asset pricing model (CAPM). However, more modern theories look into market-consistent pricing, where risks are addressed separately and the relevant discount rate is the risk-free interest rate. Government bonds are considered to be risk free, at least the government bonds of most western economies (see Chapter 6 on the credit risk of government bonds during the financial crisis). The disadvantage of government bonds is that most government bonds have long maturities, eg, 10 years. A full and representative government bond curve does not exist. For shorter-term cash flows, a different discount rate should be chosen. The alternative is to choose the interbank swap curve as the relevant discount rate. The interbank swap curve consists of interest rates that are used in transactions between banks in a normally deep and liquid market. The advantage of this is that interest rates exist for a wide array of maturities, both extremely short term (three months) and longer term. In the Solvency II regulations, also the interbank swap curve is used (see Chapter 8).

VALUE-AT-RISK

Value-at-risk (VaR) has become the overarching technique for measuring risks. It originated in the 1990s when banks' trading activities gradually included complex products that were sensitive to all kinds of price changes in the market, ie, risks. These were denoted by the Greeks, such as delta, gamma, vega and rho. With these complex trading products becoming more important, it became equally crucial to explain all these risks to non-technical people (such as managers). To that end, VaR was developed; VaR expresses the risk as one number, which makes it easy to understand.

VaR is the "most likely" maximum loss in value (in monetary amounts such as euros or dollars) that can happen to a portfolio of instruments. The term "most likely" is derived by using statistical techniques, ie, the confidence interval. For a statistical confidence interval of 99%, we can say that in 1 out of 100 times the loss will be worse than the VaR number. This is equivalent to 2.5 days per year, given 250 trading days per year. Next to the confidence interval, the holding period is important: do we look at the "most likely" maximum loss in a one-day or one-month time interval? The original VaR applications often used a one-day or a 10-day period because this is the period normally required to liquidate a certain risky position. For most products, one day is sufficient, but under stressful conditions some products need more liquidation time. We have seen in the period of 2008–11 that, for some assets, longer periods are needed to liquidate in times of stress. For instance, during the first months of 2011, there was hardly a demand for Greek government bonds. As a result, even when sellers would accept a large loss, no buyers were willing to buy at that price. The same holds for the period in 2008 when short-term funds became scarce on the capital markets due to investors' fear of hidden risk exposures in counterparties.

As will be seen in the next section, the concept of economic capital is derived from VaR. However, the confidence level is significantly higher than 99% – for instance, 99.50% or 99.95%. This is derived from the credit rating of the institution itself. The holding period is also much greater; typically one year. This is because other risks are less liquid than market risks in banks' trading portfolios. This will also be discussed in more detail in the following sections.

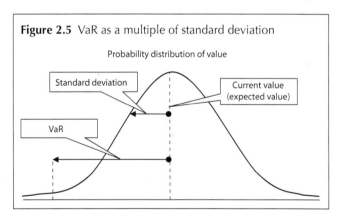

Figure 2.5 VaR as a multiple of standard deviation

The VaR technique assumes that the price changes over time follow a normal probability distribution (or a distribution that is related to the normal distribution). The normal probability distribution is derived from two variables: the mean and the standard deviation. These two variables are easily calculated from observable market prices. For the normal probability distribution, it holds that 2.3 times the standard distribution is the 99% confidence level.

If the $VaR_{99\%, 1\ day}$ of a transaction €5 million, this implies that a bank on average expects to lose not more than €5 million in 99 out of 100 trading days.

In addition to the regular VaR for an entire portfolio, companies also calculate the marginal VaR of a certain sub-portfolios. The marginal VaR provides the amount of VaR that is added to the total VaR by adding the specific portfolio.

Three methods are used to derive the VaR, varying in complexity and each having its own pros and cons. One disadvantage they all have in common is that they represent only one number. Therefore, VaR analysis, in practice, is amended by stress-testing. The three methods are as follows.

Analytic variance/covariance approach: this assumes that market returns are log-normally distributed. This means that the logarithms of the returns are normally distributed. Hence, the two central parameters (average, standard deviation) can be relatively easily derived from a historical dataset. Using these parameters, the VaR is calculated by subtracting from the average a multiple of the standard deviation, depending on the desired confidence level. As indicated above, 2.3 times the standard deviation refers to a 99% confidence level. This approach is sometimes also called parametric VaR. Its main advantage is that this approach is extremely simple. Unfortunately, this simplicity comes at the cost of less sensitivity to "fat tails", ie, extreme market events.

Historical simulation approach: this uses real, observed market prices of the past period to derive the maximum loss. Therefore, it is necessary to have sufficient historical data available. From the historical dataset of, for instance, 500 trading days, sorted in ascending order, one can derive the 99% confidence level by taking out the five largest losses. The remaining largest number is the VaR of 99%. The approach is relatively simple and aggregation across markets is also possible. The disadvantage is that extreme events are not captured as long as they are not included in the dataset. Most importantly, it is necessary to analyse a sufficiently long historical dataset.

Monte Carlo simulation approach: this estimates probability distributions based on historical data to derive the VaR. The probability distributions are used to simulate randomly the value of the portfolio over the specified time horizon (eg, 10 days). With sufficient simulation outcomes, we can construct a hypothetical time series as described above. Thus the VaR can also be derived relatively easily. The advantage of this approach is its accuracy. However, it is also computationally complex, because all kinds of interdependencies must be modelled.

As indicated, VaR represents the worst-case loss. Assuming that the equity capital position is exactly the VaR, a loss larger than the VaR amount would trigger the insolvency of the firm. Thus, VaR indicates the point of insolvency. To some extent, it is also interesting to know what the loss is to policyholders in the case of insolvency. VaR does not take that into account, but tail-VaR does. Tail-VaR is the average loss in the case of insolvency (see Figure 2.6). VaR is calculated as the cut-off point in a probability distribution, whereas tail-VaR is calculated as the area of a probability distribution beyond the cut-off point. For portfolios with an identical VaR outcome, the tail-VaR can differ significantly because one portfolio includes fat tails and the other does not. Other terms for the concept of tail-VaR are expected policyholder deficit (EPD) or expected shortfall.

Tail-VaR has conceptually attractive characteristics, for instance that the tail-VaR of two combined portfolios is always equal or less than the sum of the two separate tail-VaR outcomes. In theoretical cases, this requirement does not hold for the VaR measure. Whilst theoretically more correct, tail-VaR is also more complex to calculate. Therefore, most insurance companies apply VaR in practice in their risk models rather than tail-VaR.

Figure 2.6 VaR and tail-VaR

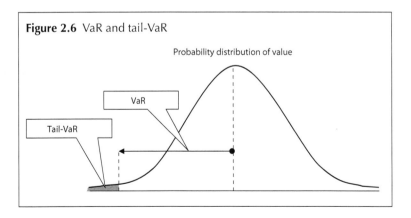

ECONOMIC CAPITAL

As has been noted, economic capital is the minimum capital available for potential calculated setbacks. How can insurers determine their minimum capital position? Let us take the non-life risk as an example. Issuing non-life insurance automatically results in reported claims. The premium contains a risk premium to compensate for the average long-term claim amounts (apart from a cost component and a profit charge). Over a long period, a portfolio is profitable, as the premium covers the claim amounts. Statistically, we also call this the expected loss or best-estimate loss. However, in a certain year, the claim amounts can be higher than the expectation. We call the deviations from the expectation the unexpected loss. When the claim amounts are lower than expected, the rest of the obtained risk premiums can be reserved for more adverse times. When the claim amounts are suddenly higher than expected, the insurer, however, needs to have a sufficient buffer to cover this setback: economic capital. When the claim amounts are even higher than the buffer, the insurer goes economically bankrupt: the capital turns out to be negative.

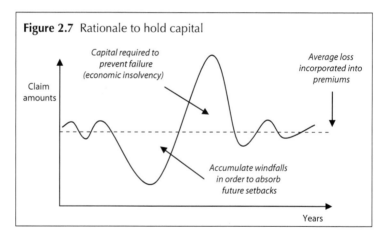

Figure 2.7 Rationale to hold capital

The insurer holds a minimum capital buffer to cover very high claim amounts and thus reduce the likelihood of its own bankruptcy. The actuaries of the insurer, using their experience of claim amounts, create a probability distribution of the possible volume of claims. Small claims occur relatively often, but are not devastating for an insurer. Generally, these can simply be covered by regular profit. Higher claims are less frequent, but could involve major consequences. Unexpected high losses involve consequences for the profit and capital position, which will be affected in the following order:

❑ first, the planned profit disappears (partially);
❑ then, the capital evaporates slowly but surely; and
❑ finally, the losses hit the providers of liabilities (policyholders and others).

In order to prevent the policyholders[5] from being affected by such extreme claim amounts, the insurer will determine its capital buffer to such an extent that policyholders, at least, will not be harmed. As mentioned, probability distributions are used to establish the minimum size of the capital buffer. In Figure 2.8, such a probability distribution is shown where the profit (loss) is compared with the probability of this profit (loss) actually occurring. For this illustration, a normal probability distribution is used, although in practice all kinds of probability distributions are used. Figure 2.8 shows this insurer is expecting a positive profit, as the highest probability is situated to the right of "zero". However, there is a slight probability of an extreme unexpected loss, as shown on the left side of the chart. In order to avoid extreme unexpected losses involving consequences for policyholders, economic capital needs to be set aside.

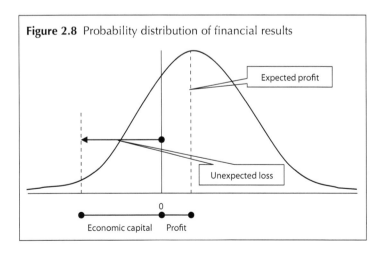

Figure 2.8 Probability distribution of financial results

For the insurer, it is not economically profitable to cover all possible losses with equity capital. The insurer allows for losses to occur that could lead to bankruptcy in an extreme situation. The probability of bankruptcy is very small (actually, it is better to speak of probability of default; see Chapter 4 on credit risk). A probability of bankruptcy of 0.05%[6] indicates, for instance, that the insurer allows there to be, statistically, a chance of 1 in 2,000 that it will go bankrupt. Statistically, losses can exceed the economic capital only once in 2,000 years, which implies that in 99.95% of the cases there is a sufficient capital buffer to cover the losses over a certain period of time (often one year). We also call this a confidence interval of 99.95%. Similarly to the confidence interval concept, the term "return period" is used in the reinsurance industry. A confidence interval of 99.95% is equal to a return period of 2,000 (years), as a bankruptcy occurs only once in 2,000 years.

Beside the confidence interval, the time horizon is also important. A really extreme claim amount varies if we look at one particular day, month or year. In one year, more or higher claim amounts can occur than in one day. At the same time, insurers have more time to absorb high claim amounts in one year than in one day. Often, a time horizon of one year is chosen. This seems contradictory to the long-term horizon of life insurance, which can run up to a period of 30 years, for instance. Here, the one-year horizon does not indicate that after one year no further losses are expected, but that it is assumed that the management of the insurer in question can take measures within a period of one year to address the crisis situation, for example, reducing other risk positions or attracting additional capital.

The ratings of the well-known external rating agencies such as Moody's and Standard & Poor's (see Chapter 4) can also be translated into certain probabilities of bankruptcy. A bankruptcy probability of 1 in 2,000 concurs, for instance, with the A+ rating of Moody's and A+ of Standard & Poor's. For capital markets, ratings are an instrument used more often than bankruptcy probabilities. Therefore, the rating ambition of insurers is often used as a basis to determine the bankruptcy probability. On the basis of the rating ambition, the corresponding confidence interval is chosen from the probability distribution. An insurer that aims for an A+ rating thus chooses a 99.95% confidence interval from the probability distribution. This is represented in Figure 2.9. An insurer aiming for an A rating allows itself to have a bankruptcy probability of 0.07%. On the left side of the chart, this company looks for the point where the probability of extreme unexpected losses equals exactly 0.07%. The confidence interval then is 99.93%.

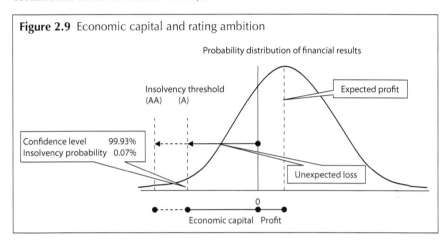

Figure 2.9 Economic capital and rating ambition

Thus, a company with an AA rating (for identical activities) holds relatively more capital than an A-rated company, but less than an insurer with an AAA rating, which also concurs with the risk perception of the market. The bankruptcy probability of an AA-rated company is, after all, smaller than that of an A-rated company.

On the basis of the preceding, we now come to the following definition of economic capital:

> Economic capital is the minimum capital buffer needed to cover all unexpected losses that can be caused by the different risks to which the insurer is exposed within a certain time horizon, and the confidence interval that corresponds to the internal rating ambition.

Earlier, this book described expected and unexpected loss in terms of claim amounts, which is translated into accounting terms. The same counts for fair-value terms. This book has also discussed expected value, often also called best estimate value. The equivalent of unexpected loss is the value at a certain confidence interval. This is often called the worst-case value. From now on, the terms best estimate and worst case will be used in this book.

How does the insurer calculate economic capital? The most common method is to create risk models per risk category, as described earlier in the chapter when discussing the risks for the insurer. For each risk category, there are separate models (these will be discussed in Chapters 3, 4 and 5). The results are then aggregated, taking into account diversification. Diversification is the phenomenon whereby different risks partially offset each other. The result of this analysis is an outcome in terms of economic capital per risk category. The advantage is that the insurer has economic capital outcomes on a level where those outcomes can be steered, ie, per risk type. This way, the market risk and non-life risk can be controlled separately. Therefore, having separate economic capital figures is preferable. Aggregation has to take place carefully. Diversification plays an important part here and will be looked at again in Chapter 10.

Another method is the so-called dynamic financial analysis (DFA), in which all risk components are modelled simultaneously. One big model is created for all the risk drivers, such as non-life claims, share prices and interest rates. Therefore, a DFA model has only one outcome: the total economic capital on the aggregated level of a modelled unit (for instance, a business unit). The disadvantage of this method is that it cannot be arranged in an orderly manner. That aside, in a DFA model the underlying risk categories are no longer separately visible either. This is impractical when steering the risk profile. Some parties with such DFA models gradually move towards separate economic capital models per risk category. A great advantage of DFA models is that related risks are also modelled simultaneously.

PANEL 2.4 ECONOMIC CAPITAL FOR THE EXPECTED PROFIT?
Earlier, it was indicated that the economic capital is calculated as the difference between the worst-case loss and the expected loss. The idea is that the expected loss is already calculated in the premium proposition and the worst-case loss is covered by economic capital. To draw a parallel with the fair-value framework, the economic capital is calculated as the difference between the worst-case value and the expected value. However, the expectation is to make a profit, otherwise, in principle it would not be financially attractive to sell that particular policy.

If the expectation is to make a profit in terms of value, it is assumed that the value will be higher within a year from now.

By calculating the economic capital as worst-case value minus expected value (both in a year's time), the insurer holds economic capital over the expected profit. An extreme, and probably only theoretical, example clarifies this: suppose that the insurer always makes a profit in terms of fair value, but that profit can fluctuate. In other words, the value over one year is always higher than the present value. However, how much higher exactly is uncertain. Does this insurer need to hold economic capital for that purpose? The insurer cannot go bankrupt and thus holding economic capital probably goes against intuition.

Advocates say that the insurer should set aside economic capital here, because the management has based its business plans on the expected profit. Each setback regarding the expectation needs to be compensated for in the economic capital to ensure business plans can continue. Opponents take it to mean that the management will swiftly adapt its plans and that there will be no capital necessary as long as there is no probability of loss (in terms of value). The authorities are not absolutely unanimous in their judgement. However, in this book, the meaning is that it is not sensible to hold economic capital for an expected increase in value. Therefore, this book calculates economic capital as the difference between the worst-case value and the expected value or zero.

Another possible solution is to calculate economic capital over expected profit, but nevertheless and at the same time treat the expected profit as an additional capital buffer.

CONCLUSION

This chapter describes the functions of the insurer. Insurance involves accepting and absorbing risks. A policyholder needs to trust that there will be sufficient buffers to cover this risk adequately and hence that the insurer will fulfil its liabilities. Therefore, insurance supervisors are put in place to monitor the insurance industry. An important component of this supervision is the solvency requirement: each insurer has to reserve a minimum amount of capital. Chapters 7 and 8 will discuss the supervision of insurers and some relevant developments more thoroughly.

Apart from that, the insurer wants to maintain a minimum amount of capital itself due to its own risk profile and because the market requires it to do so. We call this buffer economic capital.

Statistical models play a role in establishing the economic capital for each risk type. These will be examined in the Chapters 3, 4 and 5. Chapter 10 discusses the application of economic capital in the field of management control.

1   This last effect is sometimes resolved by introducing a deductible for the policyholder.
2   Apart from the so-called IBNR provision (see Chapter 3).
3   Here we use the statistical term "expectation". For instance, we expect that 1 in 1,000 cars will suffer total loss.
4   ALM will be treated thoroughly in Chapter 4.
5   Or other providers of capital; it is not unusual for an insurer at group level to issue other forms of capital, such as subordinated debt, as a supplement to equity capital.
6   $1/2000 = 0.0005 = 0.05\%$.

Underwriting Risks: Life Risk and Non-Life Risk

This chapter describes the underwriting risks. For a long time, the life and non-life industries were two relatively separate worlds, as their day-to-day practice differs and each has its own historical roots and legal backgrounds. Therefore, they will be described separately in this chapter. However, it will be shown that the control and calculation of economic capital for the life and non-life industry are closely related.

LIFE INSURANCE PRODUCTS

Life insurance is insurance that is coupled to the death or simple longevity of a person. It is an agreement to pay out a certain sum of money or value at a certain moment in the future. There is great diversity in life products and it would be beyond the scope of this book to run through all forms, so what follows is a short review.

Traditional life insurance products include endowment assurance, term assurance, life annuities and other hybrids. Pure endowment assurances pay out an amount when the person is still alive at a previously agreed moment, while term assurance provides a payment when a person dies before an agreed moment. Annuities pay out a series of amounts during a certain time period – for instance, until death. Modern insurance products include investment insurances, unit-linked and universal life products. These are much more like structured investment products, where the actual investment risk is for the policyholder. Unit-linked and universal life products, in particular, often allow for flexible premium and benefit payments. Often minimum return guarantees are provided with these products, which also involves risks for the insurer. For a long time, traditional life insurance products also included a high guaranteed rate of return. The client may not perceive this to be a guaranteed return, just as a fixed future benefit. However, the underlying fundamentals of the insurance product require the calculations of the future benefit to be based on a fixed rate of return on investments.

PANEL 3.1 PENSIONS... SPECIAL FORM OF LIFE INSURANCE

In principle, pensions are also a form of life insurance. After a number of years of premium payments, the insured receives lifelong compensation after they have reached pensionable age (typically 63 or 65 years old). Upon death, compensation to the widow/widower often follows as well. The basic principles are comparable to those for life insurance. There are collective pension insurance products presented by insurance companies and pension funds. Pension funds involve special regulations and the contracts are different to those for individual life insurances. In addition, the contract partner of the pension fund is often a sponsor company providing the pensions for many employees instead of for individuals. Compared to traditional and individual life insurance, the duration of the pension liabilities is higher, typically 30 years or more. Due to this long time horizon, inflation becomes a more dominant (and hence more important) issue. Inflation at 2% over a 30-year time horizon is a total price increase of over 80%. Or, in other words, this needs to be incorporated in the investment strategy of the pension fund – by no means a simple task. Only since the late 2000s, inflation-linked bonds have become available on the capital markets that protect assets against inflation. To have a little amount of flexibility over this long time horizon, pension contracts often comprise clauses on conditional indexation and adaptation of the benefits to inflation.

As will be discussed here, life risk is highly relevant for pension funds. The ageing effect of the post-WWII population has definitely set the agenda for many pension funds. How will the pension fund continue to be able to compensate the benefits of pensioners when their expected age increases over time? And continues to increase! The reasons for this vary widely, from better health systems to better working conditions. However, the consequence is that the expected life expectancy has increased by almost 20 years in the last century.

The pensions industry has specific characteristics, but this book will not pay separate attention to pensions. However, what follows is highly

---

applicable to collective pension insurance, as the methods used by and basic principles for the insurer are comparable to those of life insurance. One element that differs is the supervision on pension funds, which seems to be more nationally oriented than supervision of the insurance industry (Solvency II, see Chapter 8).

WHAT IS LIFE RISK?

At the sale of a life insurance policy, the insurer runs the risk of the insured dying too soon or "too late". Life risk involves the time of death in relation to the expected time of death. Each human being will die some day, only the moment when is uncertain.

With a lifelong annuity, the insured receives a series of benefit payments upon reaching a previously agreed age in compensation for one or more premium payments. The sum of the premium payments and the corresponding investment returns have to be sufficient for the benefit payments. When the insured lives longer than expected, more benefits have to be paid than expected. This is a risk for the insurer – longevity risk. An endowment assurance involves a mortality risk: it is disadvantageous for the insurer if the insured dies sooner than expected. Depending on the composition of the portfolio, a higher mortality rate, rather than a lower rate, can be disadvantageous. Sometimes mortality risk is used as the general equivalent of life risk. However, it is preferable to make a distinction between mortality and longevity risk, and to use life risk as the overarching term.

Life risk is not a theoretical concept; insurers suffer the actual consequences of life risk. Think of epidemics such as Aids, or even pandemics such as Spanish flu, SARS and bird flu. In the late 1980s, it seemed that Aids could have enormous effects on life expectancy. Many researchers analysed several possible scenarios: what might be the influence of Aids on mortality rates? In Africa, the consequences of HIV and Aids are enormous, with an infection rate of 30% in some countries. This has decreased the life expectancy in these countries to an age of around 30 years. Ageing has also been the subject of discussions, as it too involves consequences for life risk. Let us assume a simple life annuity that pays €100 every year to a person from age 65 until death. In the 1990s, life expectancy was around 80 years, hence around 15 payments would need to be made. The NPV of these payments against a 2% discount rate is about €1360, so with a price of €1500 this makes a nice €140 profit in absence of costs (almost 10% profit margin). However, in the meantime, it has turned out that life expectancy has increased to about 85 years. This means that 20 rather than 15 annual payments will need to be made, with an NPV of over €1700. Instead of a nice €140 profit, the contact faces a €200 loss. This is a simple example of how ageing will impact life insurance products. Apart from this, ageing has large consequences for the structure of social security systems, health provision and the structure of the economy – not all of which will be discussed here.

PANEL 3.2 SPANISH FLU

Spanish flu is a classic example of a pandemic – it was a very aggressive variant of the influenza virus and caused the deaths of between 20 and 40 million people. The disease spread worldwide in only a few months. It was first discovered in the US in March 1918. In Spring 1919, the Spanish flu disappeared again. Many countries were still experiencing censorship due to the First World War. Only in Spain, which had remained neutral, did the press pay attention to the pandemic, hence the name.

It is estimated that 2.5–5.0% of the global population died as a result of the pandemic, with 20% of the people suffering from the disease to some extent. Approximately half of the American casualties in Europe died as a result of Spanish flu, not from fighting the enemy. In total, 28% of the US population suffered, as well as 200,000 British and 400,000 French casualties. The flu caused problems across the entire globe, from the US to Europe and Asia.

Symptoms included high fever, muscle pain and a sore throat. Gradually so much energy was lost that people could no longer eat or drink. People aged 20–40 years old were particularly affected, as opposed to a normal flu wave, where older people are more vulnerable. To this day, the exact cause remains unknown.

Life assurance involves the risk that investment returns may be falling short when the client receives benefit payments. This is called investment risk and it will be discussed in Chapter 4. This chapter will focus on the risk caused by changes in mortality rates, both longevity and mortality effects.

Life risk is the risk of decreases in value due to different mortality than expected or due to a change in the mortality expectation.

Life risk is divided into three components:

❏ volatility risk: the risk of "regular" fluctuations in mortality under normal circumstances, including its extreme peaks;
❏ trend risk: the risk of the currently estimated trend (such as expected mortality developments) changing and the insurer making the wrong estimates for the future; and
❏ calamity risk: the risk of disasters or calamities (eg, war, epidemic) with an incidentally high mortality rate.

The trend risk component is sometimes divided into a parameter risk and a model risk. The trend risk reveals itself when risk managers estimate statistical risk models of mortality developments. The parameter risk is the risk that the wrong parameters are used, although the basic model is correct. The model risk is the risk where the basic statistical model is incorrect. For instance, a normal probability distribution is used, while the mortality does not appear to be normally distributed.

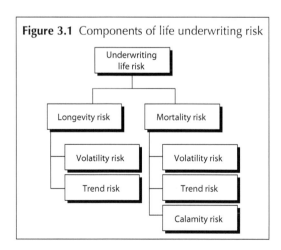

Figure 3.1 Components of life underwriting risk

CONTROLLING LIFE RISK

An insurer has no influence over the moment of death of an individual client. On a portfolio basis, however, the underwriting policy is an important instrument for either accepting or not accepting certain risks. Aside from that, there are also insurers who encourage their clients to adopt a healthy lifestyle, for instance, through discounts at gym membership. There are even insurance firms that specialise in smokers. This portfolio composition can reduce the mortality risk, although it is also used as a commercial instrument.

This chapter has already concluded that longevity risks and mortality risks have a simultaneous existence. With good distribution in the portfolio, an insurer can succeed in making these partially offset each other. A person dies sooner or later than expected, but only one of these possibilities will apply.

Reinsurance is a good instrument with which influence the life risk. Reinsurers take over part of the risk in exchange for a premium. Reinsurance is applied more widely in the non-life industry (this is described in more detail later in the chapter).

A variant of risk control is securitising a part of the insurance liabilities. This refers to actually selling the risk to the capital markets. As this occurs in large blocks of business, such transactions are not possible for all insurers. This is a relatively new concept and the markets are still not well developed. Also, the turmoil experienced by the securitisation market during 2008 (see Chapter 6) has certainly not done these developments any good. However, transactions continue to take place in a number of countries, including the UK.

Some life products include guaranteed returns and additional profit sharing clauses. In some markets, such as so-called with-profit products or participating contracts, form a substantial part of the market. For instance, in 2003 they amounted to over 30% of the liabilities of stock-listed companies and over 50% of the mutual insurance business. With-profit contracts promise a conditional return on top of the guaranteed benefit. Often these with-profit clauses are to the discretion of the insurance companies' management. The additional return, called a bonus payment, depends on the overall profit of the company or on a certain block of assets. This profit is then distributed (shared) across a so-called cohort of business. Because the insurance company expects to make a profit, it also expects to pay profit sharing, which should of course be recognised in the technical provisions. However, if financial setbacks occur, the company could cut bonuses. Hence, these elements of technical provisions act as a risk-absorption buffer, even if they cannot be classified as (equity) capital.

The profit-sharing contracts provide the insurance company with flexibility to share a part of the risk with the policyholders. However, once a certain track record of profit sharing has been built up, a company cannot easily cut profit sharing (for instance, due to supervisory interventions). This means that, while the payments are strictly conditional, they are in fact unconditional – and this limits the risk absorption of the technical provisions. The variety of profit-sharing clauses is enormous; moreover, differences exist between countries and regions. For instance, for some products in Germany and Austria the company is allowed to change profit sharing without notifying policyholders, whereas this is not possible in the UK.

Mostly, this risk-absorbing nature of insurance liabilities is used to cover investment risks because those risks are dominant in modern life insurance contracts. However, with-profit business can also be used to control life underwriting risks.

MEASURING LIFE RISK

Fluctuations in mortality rates are relatively small, especially in developed countries, where the mortality rate is relatively stable (decreasing) from year to year. However, annual small changes in mortality rates can involve major consequences over the entire duration of a life insurance portfolio (for instance, 30 years).

Mortality tables are the most appropriate instrument with which to measure life expectancy and the life risk. Several agencies regularly publish mortality tables, such as the actuarial associations. Additionally, an insurer keeps track of the mortality development of its own portfolio and the difference between expected and actual mortality rates. Naturally, there is a difference between longevity risk and mortality risk.

Mortality tables are based on actuarial models of mortality statistics. Internationally, the so-called Lee–Carter model is the standard, although there are quite a number of variants. The Lee–Carter model is a statistical model that estimates the mortality rate for each age group. Insurers and pension funds use this model to analyse mortality and longevity trends. The Lee–Carter model observes a certain trend for the average increase in age and assumes that this trend will continue. In practice, we can see that the speed in which people get older increases. The ageing effect has not proved constant over time. Therefore, variants on the Lee–Carter model also exist.

There are many sources of public mortality tables – for instance, from national actuarial societies, national bureaus for statistics and even some governmental departments publish mortality tables. In the UK, the government's actuarial department used to publish mortality tables, but that responsibility has been transferred to the Office of National Statistics. In the US, the Centers for Disease Control and Prevention publishes mortality tables. Other examples are the Canadian Human Mortality Database, the China Life Insurance Mortality Table (published by the Chinese Supervisor CIRC) and the mortality tables of the Dutch Actuarial Association.

The mortality table of the Dutch Actuarial Association is publicly accessible and reviewed every five years. The Actuarial Association distinguishes data for the entire male population (EMP) and the entire female population (EFP). Table 3.1 represents a part of these tables. The mortality table indicates per age group how many people are still alive when 10 million are born and what the mortality probability is. In Table 3.1, it can be seen that out of 10 million male babies (age zero) only 9,932 million three-year-olds and 8,797 million 61-year-olds are left. Likewise, the table shows that 64-year-old women have a 0.918% probability of dying at that age (q_x), as $(8,999,177 - 8,916,565)/8,999,177 = 0.00918 = 0.918\%$.

Based on the mortality table, the insurer determines the technical provisions. If mortality rates change, an additional technical provision may have to be created. In the period 1980–90, many sensitivity analyses were made that analysed how an epidemic such as Aids could have an impact on mortality developments. As a result, the impact of Aids on technical provisions was distilled.

Apart from the mortality rates, there is the principle of embedded value for life insurers: the embedded value represents the value of a portfolio of life insurance products (Chapter 10 will discuss embedded value in greater depth). As risk management especially focuses on the economic value, the consequences of risks for the embedded value are often taken as a starting point.

Table 3.1 Mortality table

Men (EMP 1995–2000)			Women (EFP 1995–2000)		
Age	q_x rounded	l_x rounded	Age	q_x rounded	l_x rounded
0	0.00584	10,000,000	0	0.00469	10,000,000
1	0.00050	9,941,605	1	0.00042	9,953,124
2	0.00038	9,936,638	2	0.00027	9,948,959
3	0.00025	9,932,858	3	0.00019	9,946,316
. . .			. . .		
60	0.01118	8,897,261	60	0.00633	9,266,737
61	0.01256	8,797,766	61	0.00696	9,208,033
62	0.01415	8,687,264	62	0.00760	9,143,967
63	0.01593	8,564,307	63	0.00830	9,074,464
64	0.01791	8,427,871	64	0.00918	8,999,177
65	0.01995	8,276,947	65	0.01012	8,916,565
. . .			. . .		
90	0.22047	881,226	90	0.16976	2,282,766
91	0.23617	686,946	91	0.18776	1,895,244
92	0.25135	524,709	92	0.20678	1,539,390
93	0.26920	392,822	93	0.22707	1,221,082

Source: Dutch Actuarial Association

The traditional principle of embedded value does not sufficiently take the risk into account because not all risk components are incorporated well. Therefore, successors such as European embedded value and market-consistent embedded value have improved the concept. This will be examined again in Chapter 10. Chapter 7 describes regulation in the field of fair value. At this moment, it should be noted that fair value and market-consistent embedded value are in line with each other.

ECONOMIC CAPITAL FOR LIFE RISK

The calculation for the economic capital of life risk is based on the fair value of the insurance liabilities. That is the NPV of all future cash flows, in this case discounted with the risk-free interest rate curve (eg, deduced from government bonds). The idea behind economic capital is: how much capital does one need in order to cover an extremely high increase in the fair value of insurance obligations? The model therefore calculates the fair value for two mortality assumptions: first for the expected mortality rate, which gives the so-called best estimate fair value; then for an extreme mortality rate, which gives the worst-case fair value. The extreme mortality is the mortality that corresponds to the chosen confidence interval, for instance 99.95%. The difference between this is the economic capital (see Figure 3.2).

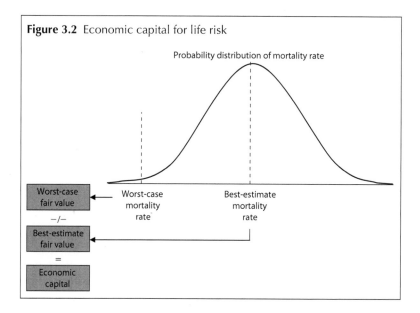

Figure 3.2 Economic capital for life risk

Naturally, economic capital is calculated for each component of life risk and for both longevity risk and mortality risk. As such, five components per insurance portfolio are created: (1) longevity volatility risk; (2) longevity trend risk; (3) mortality volatility risk; (4) mortality trend risk; and (5) mortality calamity risk. In theory, the longevity calamity risk would also have to be determined because sudden incidents causing a sudden increase in the life expectancy are also possible, eg, a new medicine to treat serious diseases such as cancer or Aids being developed. At the time, the invention of penicillin also caused an increase in life expectancy. In practice, however, insurers do not calculate economic capital for longevity calamity risk. The possible assumption may be that calamity risk is higher for mortality risk than for longevity risk anyway.

The volatility risk is determined based on fluctuations in the mortality tables. On the policy level, a risk model estimates the expected probability and the worst-case probability of an insured person dying. Some insurers use a standard probability distribution to determine the worst-case mortality table, while others dispose of a simulation model. For both situations, the model calculates the value of the benefit payment, taking into account the available technical provision. If the technical provision is sufficient, the insurer suffers no loss. The economic capital is the difference between the worst-case value and the expected value of the benefit payment to the insured. On the portfolio level, diversification is taken into account. This analysis is carried out for longevity and mortality risks.

The trend risk is determined by analysing the developments (trends) in mortality tables. The models for trend risk observe the expected mortality trends and their possible deviations. On the basis of statistical regression techniques, the insurer determines the worst-case deviation of the expected trend. Statistical regression is a technique producing forecasts based on indicators from the past. The model for trend risk determines the value of the insurance liabilities in expected mortality tables and in a worst-case trend. Here, the economic capital is also the difference between the expectation and the worst-case value. This analysis is carried out for longevity and mortality risks.

Determining the economic capital for calamity risk is not straightforward. There are both simple and very complex approaches. Simple methods could involve a simple factor-approach – for instance, by multiplying the technical provisions by a standard factor, or applying the volatility of the mortality twice or three times. This is more a matter of belief than science. More complex approaches are based on simulations of extreme events – for instance, the Spanish flu or specially developed scenarios. There are also insurers that simulate an extreme mortality on the basis of statistical techniques (extreme value theory). It is complex to generate sufficient data to enable adequate stochastic modelling on the extreme events, especially for life mortality tables.

When the insurer has calculated these five components per portfolio, it determines the total economic capital of that portfolio by taking into account diversification in the aggregation process. Naturally, mortality risk and longevity risk mostly offset each other. Then, the sum of several portfolios is determined, also taking diversification into account.

PANEL 3.3 DETERMINISTIC AND STOCHASTIC RISK MODELLING
There is a difference between deterministic and stochastic risk modelling. Deterministic is a term that refers to the situation where the parameters are known to the calculations, ie no probability distributions are used within the calculations. For life risk, the insurer could simply calculate the expected life mortality tables and the worst-case mortality tables and then determine the value of technical provisions only using these two outcomes. The probability distribution of life expectancy does not enter into the calculations of the technical provisions. This is called a deterministic model.

Stochastic modelling involves much more probabilities. The entire probability distribution of the mortality tables is used to make a model of the technical provisions. Based on this model, the economic capital is determined. Potentially certain effects in the mortality table will result in the highest economic capital relating to a different mortality set than the worst-case mortality table used in the deterministic model. It goes without saying that stochastic modelling is much more complex than deterministic calculations.

The separation between deterministic and stochastic holds for all risk types, both life and non-life, but also for the financial and non-financial risks that we will discuss in Chapters 4 and 5 respectively. Over time, as expertise and risk modelling grows more advanced, more and more risk models will become stochastic.

NON-LIFE INSURANCE PRODUCTS

Non-life insurance is insurance where the insurer promises to compensate a certain loss, which is different to the previously discussed life insurance where the compensation does not depend on the suffered loss. There is a high level of diversity in non-life insurance. Property insurance covers the losses to buildings and inventory caused by a variety of incidents. Motor insurance covers the loss of vehicles due to traffic incidents, but also due to weather conditions (eg, the holes in car roofs caused by a hail storm). Liability insurance covers the losses of third parties for which the insured is liable. There are many more forms of non-life insurance that would reasonably fit in this chapter, such as transportation, marine and credit insurance, but they will not all be reviewed here. The Solvency II Directive (see Chapter 8) includes a list of all identified non-life insurance categories.

The essence of non-life insurance is that the policy conditions include a very clear description of the loss to which the coverage applies. For some incidents that are explicitly excluded in the policy conditions, there could be a special coverage on a national level. For instance, this applies to a terrorism risk where national terrorism pools exist to cover the losses of acts of terrorism that go beyond the ability of insurance companies to cover. Another example is catastrophe or earthquake pools. One speaks of deductibles within the insurance contract when the loss is compensated only from a certain initial threshold amount onwards. Losses that fall below that threshold are not compensated. There could be thresholds on an annual basis or on a case basis. Most non-life insurance policies have a one-year duration period, but in practice most of the policyholders renew their policies annually.

In non-life insurance, the insurer establishes a technical provision at the moment of the reported claim (for "incurred but not reported", IBNR, see below). The claim manager makes an estimate of the loss. During the claim handling process, the estimate might be adapted. When such a process takes very long there are several estimate adjustments. Products with a longer period to settle are called long-tail products – for instance, personal liability insurance. Short-tail products such as fire are settled relatively fast. During the estimation phase, large adjustments can follow, especially for liability claims. This is because the estimate for the total claim amount may change over time due to a better insight in the actual claim, but also due to legal interpretations and even court case rulings.. As such, technical provision can fluctuate because it only becomes clear whether the provision taken is adequate upon completion of the claim-handling process. A possible surplus is also called "run-off result". A structural run-off result of a certain underwriting department can be a sign of (too) prudent estimates.

The IBNR provision is a specific technical provision. During the year, the accountant and the actuary make up the balance of the claim reports together and judge how much technical provision is needed. When the annual accounts are closed – for instance, on December 31 – a total review has to be created on that date. However, it is possible that in the period previous to the closure, incidents occurred for which claims were not yet reported. For that purpose, additional technical provisions are taken, such as the IBNR provision. On the basis of past experience, the actuary creates an estimate based on which a part of the premium is reserved as IBNR provision.

WHAT IS NON-LIFE RISK?

Non-life risk fuels one's imagination: in the summer of 2005, Hurricane Katrina had enormous consequences in the US. In 1999, the storm Lothar caused huge unexpected losses in the north of France. In January 2007, a heavy storm measuring 12 on the Beaufort scale disrupted economic and social life in much of north-west Europe in one day. In late 2010, heavy snowfall forced air and land traffic to a standstill in northern Europe and parts of the US. Weather conditions are not the only ones involving non-life risk, eg, in the terrorist attacks in 2001 (New York), 2004 (Madrid) and 2005 (London) and the Chernobyl disaster. Also lava eruptions from the Icelandic volcanoes blocked air traffic in parts of the northern hemisphere in mid 2010 for a number of weeks.

It is obvious that the occurrence of claims is the key business of a non-life insurer. As such, non-life risk is not the phenomenon of claims occurring, but that more or larger claims occur than expected and additional technical provisions might have to be taken at the expense of capital.

> Non-life risk is the risk of decreases in value by different or higher claims than expected or by changes in the expectation over time.

We distinguish three components in the non-life risk:

❑ Premium risk: the risk that, in the current year, more and/or larger claim amounts are reported than expected (this is can also be called current year risk);
❑ Reserve risk: the risk that additional technical provisions for previous years' reported claims are necessary (this is can also be called prior-year risk or run-off risk); and
❑ Catastrophe risk: the risk of large-scale catastrophes, such as natural disasters.

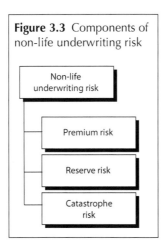

Figure 3.3 Components of non-life underwriting risk

The difference between premium risk and reserve risk is the run-off of reported claims. The reserve risk is especially important for long-tail claim reports such as liability insurance. For physical injury, an unexpected complication can appear after a few years and the additional loss amounts then falls under reserve risk. Jurisprudence can also play a part here: in a certain case, a lawsuit may prove a higher compensation claim is appropriate, which then also applies to other comparable cases. Therefore, an insurer has to take additional technical provisions for those other cases.

In fact, catastrophe risk could also be seen as an extreme case of regular premium risk. In practice, special models are available to estimate catastrophes – for instance, on the basis of meteorological and seismographic data. These models do better justice to the specific situation of catastrophes. Therefore, catastrophe risk is considered a separate category.

CONTROLLING NON-LIFE RISK

Both insured and insurers benefit from restricting the loss. Therefore, insurers try to encourage their clients to reduce the probability of incidents and decrease the volume of loss. There are several possibilities for this. This section will discuss preventive measures, underwriting policy and policy conditions, scenario analyses, reinsurance and alternative risk transfer (ART) techniques.

An obvious measure for loss control is prevention: smoke detectors, fire extinguishers, lightning rods, etc. There are preventative measures to prevent the incident (such as lightning rods), but also to restrict the direct loss (such as fire extinguishers) and to restrict the indirect loss (such as providing escape routes). Prevention is important to both the insurer and the insured. Although it is clearly also used as a commercial instrument, some insurers are known to use prevention as a tool for controlling non-life risk. Apart from the instrumental side of it, it also creates client awareness and, as such, prevention is a good tool to control non-life risk.

An instrument that is at least as important for controlling risks is the underwriting policy, by which the insurer can determine in advance which cases it wants to insure. As such, the underwriting policy is an important policy document. It contains, among other things, instructions regarding a maximum insurable sum or value or the sector where the client is active, such as geographical regions, etc. Policy conditions also offer a form of risk control; the exclusion of terrorism and flooding risks in some countries is a good example. Naturally, the insurer also has rules for certain concentrations; although each individual building in a street might fit well within the underwriting criteria, it could well be that insuring an entire street is undesirable.

A natural instrument for controlling non-life risk is portfolio composition. A specialised portfolio is prone to more concentration risk than a well-diversified portfolio. This holds not only for geographical diversification, but more importantly for spreading the types of insurance products. For instance, this implies a healthy mix between motor and property insurance, as well as a mix between retail and small business insurance, etc.

A useful instrument for analysing the aggregated risks is scenario analysis. It could happen that insurers (or departments therein) are not sufficiently aware of the risks within a certain portfolio. For instance, are the consequences of extreme frost or snowfall known? Are underwriters sufficiently aware of the potential collapse of building roofs under a heavy weight of snow? The bird flu scenario has stimulated minds among some insurers. A scenario analysis is, in fact, nothing but a structuralised brainstorming session (which is actually different to a quantitative scenario analysis). However, that particular structure can be useful when it involves complicated questions arising in risk management.

Reinsurance is a good instrument for risk control. Reinsurers are actually insurers for the primary insurance industry: they take over part of the risk in exchange for a premium, called the cession. Reinsurers mutually take over risks, known as retrocession. There are numerous reinsurance constructions. So-called facultative reinsurance concerns the reinsurance coverage per case/object, while the risks automatically move over to the reinsurer when a "treaty" has been closed. Within both categories, there are numerous reinsurance forms. The most famous are the proportional reinsurance and excess-of-loss (XOL) contracts (see Figure 3.4). In proportional reinsurance (such as quota share, or QS contracts), the reinsurer takes a proportional part of the claim amounts for its account and receives a proportional part of the premium in exchange. These contracts involve "sharing mutually". XOL contracts are meant to cover extreme losses. The reinsurer compensates large-scale losses, or when the annual total exceeds a certain amount. XOL contracts have a specific retention level and coverage. Retention is a kind of deductible for the insurer. The reinsurer will compensate only once that level has been exceeded. When a loss exceeds coverage limit, the costs involved are for the insurer instead of the reinsurer. In practice, an insurer deals with several reinsurers. The total reinsurance coverage is made up of several "layers", each placed within a different party.

Apart from reinsurance, other instruments are also becoming available gradually on the capital markets – for example, cat bonds (catastrophe bonds), weather derivatives or contingent forms of capital. A cat bond is a bond whereby the interest repayments or redemption depend on possible catastrophes. By issuing these bonds, the insurer creates financial flexibility in case of a catastrophe. Weather derivatives are financial instruments paying a certain amount depending on the weather conditions. As such, there are weather derivatives with compensation when the average daily temperature is below or above a certain threshold temperature, or when a certain wind speed is reached. For a crop insurer, this could be a useful method to cover the risk involved in an unsuccessful harvest. Contingent capital is, for instance, an agreement with certain investors from which an insurer can issue shares against a profitable rate at the time of a catastrophe, also creating financial flexibility for the insurer. Such instruments are the so-called ART products. The use of ART is not yet widespread, but is gradually increasing.

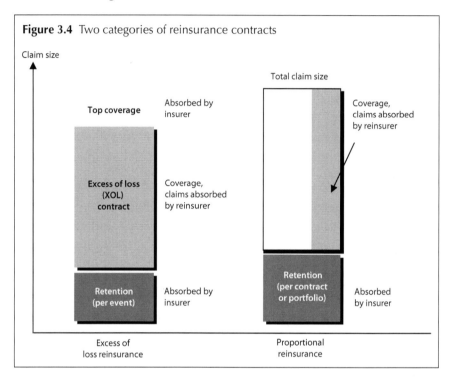

Figure 3.4 Two categories of reinsurance contracts

Captives are also included among ART products, but have a specific character. A captive is a type of internal reinsurance company where results can be spread over a period of time under certain conditions. This provides breathing space for the financial processing of large-scale losses. However, because it is, in fact, an internal reinsurance company, the losses are not really economically transferred to an external party. Rather, the captive is used to smooth losses over time. Besides, the use of captives is often based on fiscal reasons.

PANEL 3.4 REINSURANCE EXAMPLES

An insurer has an industrial zone in its portfolio that has been insured for a sum of €100 million, at a premium of €10 million. The insurer has €4 million available to purchase a reinsurance contract and can choose between an XOL or a QS contract.

The XOL contract has an attachment point (ie, retention level) of €5 million and a coverage of €50 million. This means that losses from €5 million upwards are covered up to the amount of €55 million. The QS contract covers as standard 40% of the claim amount in exchange for 40% of the premium income.

Suppose that a heavy storm takes place, producing a total claim amount of €30 million. Table 3.2 indicates how big the loss is and how much the reinsurance contract would cover. In a XOL contract, the insurer itself only needs to bear €5 million (retention level). The reinsurer refunds the remaining €25 million. In a QS contract, the insurer must bear €18 million, because only €12 million (ie, 40% of €30 million) falls under the reinsurance.

Table 3.2 Coverage of two reinsurance contracts for one major storm (€ millions)

	XOL	QS
Total claim amount	€30	€30
Reinsurance cover	€25	€12
Remaining loss for insurer	€5	€18

Suppose that instead of one heavy storm taking place within a certain year, 30 smaller storms with a loss of €1 million per storm occur (see Table 3.3). Each time, the claim amount would fall under the retention threshold of the XOL contract and the insurer would then have to bear the full €30 million. The QS contract covers €12 million of the loss (ie, 40% of €30 million) and the insurer would have to bear the remaining €18 million.

Table 3.3 Coverage of two reinsurance contracts for multiple smaller storms (€ millions)

	XOL	QS
Total claim amount	€30	€30
Reinsurance cover	€0	€12
Remaining loss for insurer	€30	€18

Thus, a XOL contract is a particularly good instrument to cover risks of major incidents, while a QS contract can cover a larger amount of smaller losses.

MEASURING NON-LIFE RISK

The claim ratio is used as an indicator for the non-life risk. The claim ratio is the total claim amounts divided by the premium, expressed as a percentage. In fact, a claim ratio indicates whether the premium is adequate to cover the claims. When the claim ratio is higher than 100%, loss takes place. In addition, there is also the combined ratio: the sum of the costs and the claim amounts as a percentage of the premium. This gives a more complete view of the profitability, although it troubles the image of the claim amounts alone.

The claim ratio itself is not a real risk indicator, but the development over time can give an idea of the risk. The fluctuation of the claim ratio is a risk indicator, although the claim ratio barely gives an insight into the probability of extreme events. Besides, it could create a nominator effect: when an insurer increases the premiums, the claim ratio decreases. However, this does not reveal anything about any large claims occurring or not. Nevertheless, a claim ratio of 60% does offer a little more comfort regarding profitability than a claim ratio of 85%.

Premium risk

Creating probability distributions is a good instrument for obtaining an insight into the non-life risk. This applies to premium risk in particular. On the basis of historical data, the actuary determines the probability distribution of claims, thereby distinguishing small and large claims. For the small claims, the actuary creates a probability distribution of the total claim amount. For the larger losses, they will often determine a separate probability distribution for the frequency of claims (ie, the probability of large losses occurring) and the size of the claims. The actuary uses these distributions to determine the economic capital, among other things.

Reserve risk

The so-called loss triangle is an important instrument by which to estimate the run-off pattern of claim reports. These run-off patterns are important for reserve risk. The loss triangle makes a difference according to the accident year and development year. The accident year is the year during which a certain event took place. In the following years (the development years), it gradually becomes clear how big this claim amount will become. This is especially relevant for liability insurance for which a long period of time can be involved. Over time, there will be a much better insight in how the loss triangle will develop. Panel 3.5 gives an example of a loss triangle. The loss triangle distinguishes an accident year and a development year. However, in accounting the calendar year is observed and these figures are expressed "on the diagonal" of the loss triangle. The 2011 accounting year reveals all losses from the 2011 accident year that are situated in the first development year, as well as losses from 2010 in the second development year, etc.

PANEL 3.5 LOSS TRIANGLE

Suppose that an insurer has registered all losses from a portfolio since 2005. In 2005, it received €100 million worth of claims of the policies in that year. One year later, this insurer received an additional €50 million claim amounts from the policies from 2005, but also €103 million on account of newly sold policies in 2006. As more history from previous years gradually becomes available, the form of the loss triangle is created. In time, the loss triangle in Table 3.4 arises, where the insurer is certain of the upper half (shown in black) and the lower half is still unknown (shown in grey). The insurer is now at the beginning of calendar year 2010; in calendar year 2009, it received a total of €233 million in claims (149 + 37 + 32 + 10 + 5 = 233).

Table 3.4 Run-off triangle (€ millions)

		Development				Total Claim	Premium Received
2005	€ 100	€ 50	€ 30	€ 10	€ 5	€ 195	€ 200
2006	€ 103	€ 51	€ 31	€ 10	€ 5	€ 200	€ 210
2007	€ 106	€ 53	€ 32	€ 11	€ 5	€ 207	€ 230
2008	€ 73	€ 37	€ 22	€ 7	€ 4	€ 143	€ 190
2009	€ 149	€ 74	€ 45	€ 15	€ 7	€ 290	€ 240
2010	€ 154	€ 77	€ 46	€ 15	€ 8	€ 300	€ 255

Accident Year

The question now is: how many claim amounts are expected in 2010

---

from the previous years? For that purpose, the insurer looks at the relation between the consecutive years. On average, the relation between the first and the second development year is 2:1. In 2010, €74 million is expected (ie, 1/2 multiplied by €149 million) of claims from 2009. Using this method, the insurer can complete the entire loss triangle.

There are many methods to complete the loss triangle. The most advanced insurers often use the following methods, depending on the available data required to do the calculations:

❑ Expected loss ratio method;
❑ chain ladder method;
❑ Bornhuetter–Freguson method; and
❑ Brosius method.

When the actuary uses the loss triangle to establish the technical provision, they use the expected run-off patterns. They observe what the statistical expectation is per accident year, coming from the average run-off pattern over time. We call this the best-estimate claim amount per accident year. The actuary then determines the claim amount using a certain level of prudence. However, using modern software packages, it is also possible to run a more advanced analysis of the run-off pattern. Some software packages estimate the predefined number of confidence levels, such as 50% (best estimate), 75%, 90% and 99%. This way, for example, it is possible to calculate the worst-case run-off at a confidence interval of 99.95%. As such, two loss triangles are created: a loss triangle including the best-estimate claim amount per accident year and one showing the worst-case claim amount per accident year. More advanced systems allow insurers to estimate the entire loss distribution of the run-off. This results in a model of the technical provisions based on the entire loss distribution where the worst-case loss can be determined more directly. Again, the former is called a deterministic model, whereas the latter is called a stochastic model (see Panel 3.3).

One element that has received attention in the actuarial profession is the inflation effect in non-life claims. This is especially relevant in long-tail business because it takes a long time before claims are finally settled. Hence, in addition to the traditional loss triangles, companies also take into account inflation effects. Traditionally, the non-life technical provisions were based on non-discounted cash flows, and even then determined prudently. Not discounting future cash flows implies additional (hidden) prudence in the technical provisions. Nowadays, fair value of technical provisions requires insurers to discount all future cash flows, which takes into account inflation. In principle, this is not too much different from the techniques used in life insurance, except for the fact that non-life actuaries have less experience with it. In addition, of course, fair-value technical provisions are based on realistic estimates of future cash flows rather than prudently determined cash flows.

Catastrophe risk

Measuring catastrophe risk is complex. Several reinsurers, specialists in catastrophe risk, have commercial models for catastrophes. Well-known models are RMS, EQE and AIR, but reinsurers also have self-developed models. Most of the large non-life insurers use such models in their analyses. Also, non-life insurers may rely on the outcomes of models from the large reinsurers, such as the market leader Swiss Re. They predict the probability of catastrophes and the loss caused by a catastrophe. The models are based on geographical, seismographical and meteorological information. The user can see at a detailed level what the loss could be if, for instance, a hurricane took place in a certain region.

Catastrophe risk can also be measured using scenario analysis. Insurers simulate historical events such as hurricane Katrina, tsunamis like the ones in Japan or Indonesia or other historical events. An insurer estimates the impact on the portfolio if a catastrophe like these would happen in a specific geographical area. Of course, the outcomes are dependent on the choice of the scenario, but it proves very helpful in pointing out sensitivities.

ECONOMIC CAPITAL FOR NON-LIFE RISK

We have divided the non-life risk into three components: premium, reserve and catastrophe risk. For each component, there are separate methods to determine the economic capital. The components are aggregated taking into account diversification.

The economic capital for premium risk is based on probability distributions of the claim probability and the claim amount. The actuary often creates separate probability distributions for small and large events, as discussed above. Mostly, the premium risk is not normally distributed. At the level of policy, however, there is a high probability that no claim will take place and, if then there is a claim, there is a certain volume but a very small probability of the loss being enormous. For the estimate of the claim probability, a so-called poisson, or negative binominal, distribution is often used and for the claim amount a so-called lognormal or a gamma distribution is used.

On the basis of statistical simulation, the insurer can "join" these two probability distributions in one total probability distribution for the annual volume of the claims for the insurer. A simulation generates many random observations for the loss frequency based on the probability distributions. This is comparable to throwing a dice. For instance, if the simulation indicates that for a certain policy three claims occur yearly, a loss amount is simulated per simulated claim. This is yet another random observation from the probability distribution of the claim amount. A simulation contains many random observations – for instance, 100,000 – that can then also be represented in a probability distribution by arranging them in ascending order. This is the stochastic model as described in Panel 3.3.

The economic capital for premium risk can then be determined by reading off the desired confidence level in this overall probability distribution – for instance, 99.95%. This reflects the total claim amount in a worst-case year. As it still includes the "best estimate", this still needs to be deducted. The best-estimate claim amount can also easily be read off from the probability distribution, the 50% confidence interval. The economic capital for premium risk is the worst-case claim amount minus the best-estimate claim amount (see Figure 3.5).

The economic capital for reserve risk is based on the loss triangles. Most of the standard software programs for loss triangles calculate, on the basis of the underlying data, what the expected run-off is, and what the run-off pattern is in an extreme scenario (ie, based on a certain confidence interval). For both scenarios, the insurer calculates what the value (fair value) of the future liabilities will be, using the NPV method. The fair value of the worst-case scenario is higher than the fair value of the best-estimate run-off. The economic capital for reserve risk is then easily calculated by subtracting these two fair values from each other (see Figure 3.6). Figure 3.6 shows a deterministic model. Stochastic models for reserve risk are similar to the premium risk model in Figure 3.5.

Figure 3.5 Economic capital for premium risk

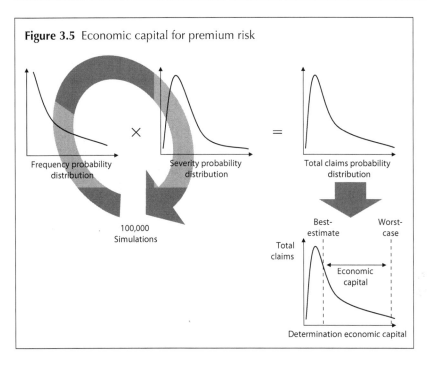

Figure 3.6 Economic capital for reserve risk

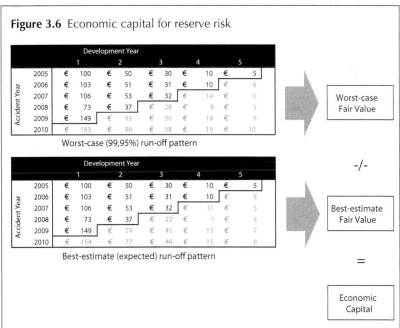

The economic capital for catastrophe risk is determined by special catastrophe risk models and software, for which simulations are also used. In this way, the insurer determines the expected claim amounts and the worst-case claim amounts due to catastrophes. The economic capital is again the difference between these two values.

CONCLUSION

This chapter has described the underwriting risks, life risk and non-life risk. The products were discussed briefly, as well as the methods to control and measure the risk; the calculation method of the economic capital was also thoroughly described. For both risk categories, fair value is used for the calculation of economic capital. As discussed, fair value can be a paradigm shift, especially for non-life actuaries that traditionally have been less used to discounting future cash flows. Economic capital has been explained based on deterministic and stochastic models.

4

Investment Risks:
Market, Credit and Liquidity Risk

This chapter will discuss investment risks, which are also known as financial risks. These risks mostly arise from the investment process of insurers, but some are also due to underwriting activities. The credit risk of reinsurers is one example. An important risk in insurance is interest rate risk, having impact on both the liability and asset side of the insurers' balance sheets. We will see in this chapter how so-called asset and liability management takes place to address this risk. This chapter will also address three main investment risks: market risk, credit risk and liquidity risk, including the main sub-risks. As in the previous chapter, we will start by explaining each risk before going into detail on how to control and measure the risk. For each risk, this chapter will explore the relevant economic capital models. Liquidity risk is a special risk type, as will be seen later in this chapter, because economic capital is a less-suitable method for addressing liquidity risk. We will start, however, with market and credit risk.

WHAT IS MARKET RISK?
An insurer invests its technical provisions and its equity capital as part of its primary function as a financial institution. The investment process is at the service of the core activity as an insurer, ie, providing insurance products. Although investments are generally perceived as "risky", that is not necessarily the case. One can also invest in government bonds – something that insurers definitely

do. At the same time, we have seen in the late 2000s that government bonds are not completely risk free either during the sovereign bond crisis. Chapter 6 explores the financial crisis in more detail. No insurer invests its total investment portfolio in stocks – traditionally believed to be the most risky asset category. All in all, we can be sure that fluctuations on the financial markets can have consequences for insurers. This phenomenon is called market risk.

Market risk is the risk of decreases in value by changes in market variables, such as the interest rates, equity prices, exchange rates, real estate prices and the like. This also includes ALM.

Most of the assets of an insurer consist of bonds and equity (see Figure 4.1). Fixed income investments are assets with a fixed interest rate: government bonds, corporate bonds and mortgages. Other assets such as shares and real estate investments do not have agreed returns in advance and generally involve more risk than fixed income investments. The expected return on these assets is, however, higher because they include a compensation for that risk. We see that equity investments in both Europe and the US are roughly 25% of the portfolio. Fixed income portfolios in the US are relatively greater than in Europe, but that is partly compensated by a lower share of mortgage loans. Within Europe, however, there are major differences in the asset allocation per country. This is due to the different insurance products, as well as differences in local regulations within Europe. With the introduction of Solvency II, it is expected that these differences will gradually disappear.

Apart from the above-mentioned asset categories, insurers often have derivatives such as options and swaps in the portfolio to cover risks. This kind of coverage of market risks is called hedging. Although these derivatives are complex products, the ability to introduce these effectively is gradually increasing. Besides, financial market parties are increasingly anticipating the needs of insurers and offering special derivatives. Examples are inflation-linked or mortality bonds.

The investment process of an insurer is not a stand-alone process. Rather, it is linked to the underwriting process, because the profile of the insurance liabilities is an important driver. An insurer invests in such a way that assets are sufficient to cover the future liabilities. In other words: the assets are chosen in such a way that the cash flows from investments are matched as well as possible to the benefit payments to policyholders, ie, the technical provisions. However, assets are not usually allocated to individual insurance policies on a one-to-one basis. The investment process takes place on an aggregated level and it is thus possible to benefit from economies of scale.

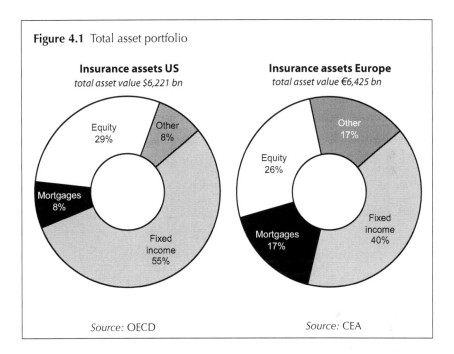

Figure 4.1 Total asset portfolio

Insurance assets US
total asset value $6,221 bn

Equity 29%
Other 8%
Mortgages 8%
Fixed income 55%

Source: OECD

Insurance assets Europe
total asset value €6,425 bn

Other 17%
Equity 26%
Mortgages 17%
Fixed income 40%

Source: CEA

The value of the investments is subject to the fluctuations of financial markets, despite the fact that the investments are matched to the technical provisions. If the liabilities are perfectly "matched" (Panel 4.1 expands on the term), these fluctuations have no consequences for the insurer as a whole. The decreases (increases) in value of the investments are equal to the decreases (increases) in value of the technical provisions. However, when there is a mismatch, the insurer runs market risks.

Market risk is the risk of decreases in value by changes in the market variables such as interest rates, share prices, exchange rates, real estate prices and the like. This also includes asset and liability management (ALM).

We can divide market risk into several subcategories, parallel to the market variables (interest rates, equity prices, foreign exchange rates, etc). This classification depends on the investment portfolio of the insurer. Below are a few commonly used categories.

Interest rate risk
The risk of decreases in value due to changes in the interest rates. Matching is of particular importance here, as the interest rate has an effect on the value of both the assets and the liabilities.

Equity risk
The risk of decreases in value due to changes in the equity prices.

Currency risk
The risk of decreases in value due to changes in the foreign exchange rates. This is also called foreign exchange (FX) risk.

Inflation risk
The risk of decreases in value due to changes in the inflation expectations.

Real estate risk
The risk of decreases in value due to changes in real estate prices. This is also called property risk.

Private equity risk
The risk of decreases in value due to changes in the private equity markets. Although private equity is, in fact, a component of equity risk, it is considered separately due to its specific character.

Credit spread risk
The risk of decreases in value due to changes in the credit spread. The credit spread is an extra compensation as a part of the interest rates of corporate bonds on top of government bond interest rates. As such, this gives a reflection of the capital market's general senti-ment of corporate bonds. Chapter 6 will highlight that the credit spread played an important role during the financial crisis, both the bond credit spread, but also the credit spread on a number of gov-

ernment bonds (such as Greece). Credit spread risk is sometimes incorrectly seen as a component of the credit risk. However, the credit spread risk is determined by capital market sentiment and not by the situation of one individual counterparty, such as credit risk.

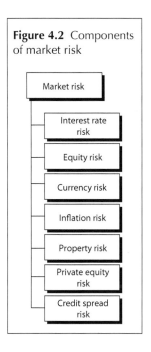

Figure 4.2 Components of market risk

Interest rate risk is an important market risk category because interest rate changes impact both assets and liabilities. Interest rates have impact on the value of bonds and other fixed income securities because they are their major value driver. Also, they have an impact on insurance liabilities as many insurance products include guaranteed returns (ie, a fixed guaranteed interest rate). This effect is easily explained: in the valuation process future policyholder benefits are discounted (NPV) by a discount rate, ie, an interest rate. If interest rates increase, the value of liabilities decreases, which is positive for the insurance company, assuming that assets do not change. As indicated, assets values do change when interest rates fluctuate. If asset values do not change in tandem, the insurance firm as a whole may face a loss (or profit).

Generally, products with a longer duration are more affected by interest rate changes. This holds for both assets and liabilities. For most of the life insurers, the duration of the assets is lower than the duration of liabilities. Hence, an interest rate decrease results in a decrease of total value. In addition to this, many insurance products include all kinds of embedded options and guarantees: for example, settlement options that allow clients to choose between a lump sum benefit or annuity or lapse/surrender options that allow policyholders to cancel the policy in advance of the maturity date. Obviously, the minimum guaranteed rate is itself an important option. These characteristics are extremely sensitive to interest rate changes. As a result, the value of an insurance portfolio does not change proportionally to interest rate changes (this phenomenon is called convexity).

Normally, the interest rate curve has an upward slope: 10-year rates are higher than five-year rates. A parallel shift in the yield curve keeps the slope intact, eg, both 10-year and five-year rates change with 100 basis points. However, in practice yield curves do not always change in a parallel way. In an extreme (but absolutely not theoretical) instance, the yield curve can be flat (equal interest rates for all maturities) or even inverse (higher rates for short maturities). Many of these interest rate changes occurred during the financial turmoil that started in 2008.

These interest rate changes can have real impact on insurance companies, depending on the mismatch position. A prominent example of interest rate risk is the failure of the Japanese company Nissan Mutual Life in 1997. At that time, the company had 1.2 million policyholders and roughly US$17 billion of assets. Nissan Mutual Life had sold guaranteed annuities of up to 5.5% without hedging the interest rate risk. During the low interest rate period in the 1990s, the company faced enormous difficulties in honouring the guaranteed rates. Finally, the Minister of Finance had to close the company, resulting in the first insurance company bankruptcy in five decades. Total losses amounted to US$2.5 billion. Other examples exist as well, since many insurers faced high losses due to the low interest rate environment after 2008, when investment strategies were unable to meet the guarantees issued at policyholders. Chapter 6 will explore the impact of the financial crisis on insurers in more detail. However, it has already been mentioned that many insurers faced extreme losses due to the turmoil in the global financial markets. This is called market risk.

CONTROLLING MARKET RISK

The most important instrument for controlling market risk is creating a good investment plan, in line with the analyses of the ALM department. Often there are several investment plans. The strategic investment plan indicates how much market risk the company wants to take, what the allocation (in terms of percentage) to the different asset categories is (fixed-income, equity), what the maximum mismatch can be, etc. In the tactical investment plan, different sectors are chosen: geographical, business sectors and so on. Similarly, the actual investments are indicated in the operational investment plan: individual bonds and shares.

Asset and liability management (ALM) contains two components. Firstly, ALM stems from an analysis of the profile of insurance liabilities. The ALM department derives the cash flow pattern of the insurance portfolio from the production systems, the emphasis thereby being on outgoing cash flows and benefit payments to clients. Secondly, ALM works out a strategic investment mix that meets the preconditions such as a maximum mismatch, a minimum solvency to be maintained and a maximum risk exposure (in terms of economic capital). Another term for ALM is ALM study, a periodical investigation of these two components.

We have already indicated in Chapter 3 that profit sharing is an important instrument for controlling risks. While initially developed as a commercial tool to attract more customers by providing additional return on top of the guaranteed rate, participating contracts are also a useful instrument for mitigating part of the market risks to clients.

Although a mismatch can be undesirable, insurers often deliberately choose to create one in order to generate additional return. That this also involves an additional risk needs no further explanation, and controlling this risk is the key duty of the investment department.

In practice, most insurers outsource the day-to-day management of the investment policy to (internal) asset managers. These parties then receive a mandate that gives them the freedom to operate with the aim of maximising the investment return. Naturally, the ALM insights (strategic investment mix, based on the ALM studies) constitute the preconditions of the mandate. There are also limits for certain asset categories, as stipulated in the investment plan.

PANEL 4.1 TWO MATCHING PRINCIPLES

Matching is the process of aligning the asset portfolio to the profile of the insurance liabilities, ie, technical provisions. This is to ensure that the insurer can have at its disposal the cash flows from the asset portfolio when cash flows are needed for the underwriting and claim processes. By doing so, the objective is also to align asset returns and client return requirements, including the risk sensitivities of the two. There are basically two principles for matching investments and liabilities. In cash flow matching, assets are chosen for which the cash flows exactly follow the cash flows of the insurance liabilities. A 10-year annuity is matched to a bond with a 10-year maturity. Cash flow matching is generally considered the "safest" strategy, but it is not possible for all products. Guaranteed returns or profit-sharing are, for instance, difficult to match using the cash flow matching principle. A major obstacle to cash flow matching is the uncertainty in liabilities due to underwriting risks. Also, in cases where cash flow matching is possible, it might not be desirable. Cash flow matching reduces financial flexibility for the insurer to pursue potential investment opportunities that arise – for instance, because the company has certain interest rate expectations.

Duration matching is more value based, rather than focusing on each of the individual cash flows. In duration matching, investments are found where the interest rate sensitivity of investments and insurance liabilities is identical. When the interest rates change, investments and liabilities experience the same effects and the consequence for the insurer is nil on balance. Therefore, this strategy is also called immunisation. The central risk measure is the modified duration, which indicates to what extent an instrument decreases in value if the interest rate increases by 1%. A bond with a modified duration of 5 decreases by 5% in market value when the interest rate increases by 1%. However, this measure only holds for smaller interest rate changes.

$$\frac{\Delta market\ value}{market\ value} = modified\ duration \times \Delta interest\ rate$$

In the investment mandate, certain "benchmarks" are often referred to. For each investment portfolio, it is indicated which benchmark needs to be followed, for instance the FTSE index or MSCI index. There are many composed indexes that can serve as a benchmark for the asset manager. The "tracking error" indicates to what extent the investor deviates from their benchmark. As the asset manager specialises in investment, they also dispose of a detailed risk management system. The establishment and monitoring of limits and tracking errors are also included in the systems. This means that the investment manager has to rebalance the portfolio as soon as the difference between the actual portfolio and the benchmark breaches a certain threshold, the maximum tracking error. In some cases, rebalancing is done relatively quick and simple, whereas in other cases it may be impossible (whenever the market does not allow to sell or buy at a certain cost). Also, it may be undesirable to rebalance directly, for instance, when there is an intentional strategy to deviate temporarily from the general market. Economic capital plays a similar role in the entire investment system of the asset manager, since it can also serve as a general limit to the risk portfolio.

PANEL 4.2 INSURERS AND OPTIONS

Options are a very important component of ALM. Not so much because insurers invest a lot in options, but because (mainly, but not only, life) insurance products include many option-like constructions: embedded options. These include interest rate guarantees, repayment options and unconditional profit sharing and bonuses. At the time of issuing an insurance product, options may seem worthless. But during the often long term, options can definitely reach high values. The interest rate sensitivity (duration) of these embedded options is often high and therefore they deserve special attention from the ALM department. Only since the early 2000s, options have received attention, both from a practical as well as an academic perspective. Before that, awareness that guarantees included risks was relatively low. Also, the guarantees were badly recorded in the underwriting systems and databases. Therefore, insurers were unaware that options actually existed, let alone that they might/should be attached values before the time of claim payments. The fact that life insurance products (and hence the guarantees) have a long time to maturity makes an option even more costly in terms of risk and capital. We will see in Chapter 8 that Solvency II also pays explicit attention to embedded options.

MEASURING MARKET RISK

In the past, the tracking error was the central risk measure and the difference between the actual investment portfolio and the benchmark was specifically observed. Nowadays, there is more emphasis on the mismatch between investments and insurance liabilities. The total (fair value) balance sheet of the insurer is central to measuring the mismatch of assets and liabilities valued using market-consistent methods (ie, fair value). For insurance liabilities in particular, the calculation of the market-consistent value is complex, because the accounting system is not based on fair value. Embedded options are also explicitly identified and separately valued in the risk management system.

In the market-value balance sheet, capital is the closing gap between insurance liabilities (ie, technical provisions) and assets. Simple scenarios for interest rates, equity prices, foreign exchange rates or other variables can be created with special software. Two types of scenarios are involved: historical and simulation scenarios. Historical scenarios, which are developments that actually took place, display the possible consequences for the present balance sheet: eg, what would happen if the stock market crisis of 1998 took place again? And what would the balance sheet look like in such a situation? A similar exercise is running imaginary scenarios: a set of events that are likely to occur but not identical to something that happened in the past. Before the 2000s, it was considered to be unlikely that interest rates would be low in periods that assets returns were also low (classical economic theory). This could be an imaginary scenario. Also, a 10-year period of extremely low interest rates and market illiquidity is an example of this. Again, the insurer identifies the effect on current and future balance sheet and the potential risk measures to take. In scenarios based on simulations, statistical models are used to estimate, eg, the future interest developments based on current knowledge of the interest rate structure. From the recent history, a probability distribution for the entire future yield curve and other risk parameters is extracted. The simulation works similarly to the simulation described in the previous chapter: from the probability distribution, the model draws 100,000 observations (eg, 100,000 times a potential yield curve) with which the balance sheet is recalculated. Using this outcome, the simulation basically generates 100,000 potential future balance sheets. This is really a new probability distribution of the balance sheet from which conclusions can be drawn regarding risk vulnerability and sensitivity.

PANEL 4.3 REPLICATING PORTFOLIO

A specific technique is the principle of replicating portfolio. In this principle, an imaginary investment portfolio is created that is identical to the insurance liabilities (ie, the technical provisions), without taking the underwriting risks into consideration. The technical provisions are actually replicated with an imaginary asset portfolio, specifically consisting of bonds and options. The market risk is measured by the effects of interest rates, equity or other scenarios applied to both investment portfolios: the actual asset portfolio and the replicating portfolio. As both portfolios consist of known investment instruments, there are standard methods available to value them. When, in a certain scenario – for instance, an interest rate scenario – the two portfolios equally increase or decrease in value, there is no market risk for that market variable. When the portfolios do not increase or decrease identically, there is a market risk.

ECONOMIC CAPITAL FOR MARKET RISK

In order to establish the economic capital for market risk, the replicating portfolio and statistical simulations methods are used. In the replicating portfolio method, the risk manager creates an imaginary investment portfolio generating exactly the same cash flows as the insurance liabilities. Underwriting risks are not taken into account and the calculation starts from the expected mortality rates and the claim amounts. In this way, the risk manager separates the underwriting risk from the market risks.

The next step in the calculation is generating scenarios. There is a separate scenario for each risk component, such as interest rate risk, equity risk, etc. Statistical models are developed to generate scenarios. In the field of interest risk especially, there are widely accepted statistical models where the risk manager only needs to estimate the parameters on the basis of historical interest rates. These statistical risk models can simply extrapolate a possible future interest rate curve multiple times from the present interest rate curve – for instance, 100,000 times. For each risk component there is a separate model, which in turn generates scenarios. Some software packages even perform combined analyses.

The total model determines the value per scenario of the replicating portfolio (for instance, 100,000 times per risk component) and the value of the actual investment portfolio. The difference is the value of the equity capital, projected one year ahead. With all these possible future values of capital, the insurer can make a statistical probability distribution again. It is most probable that capital will increase in value in one year's time, but there is a small probability of the capital of the insurer dramatically decreasing in value.

In this probability distribution, the desired confidence interval and, hence, the worst-case value can easily be read off. For instance, a desired rating of A+ equals 99.95%. With 100,000 observations, the 99.95% confidence interval is the 50th observation if they are ranged in ascending order. The expected value (best estimate) is the middle observation. The economic capital is then calculated from the difference between the expected (best estimate) value and the worst-case value (see Figure 4.3).

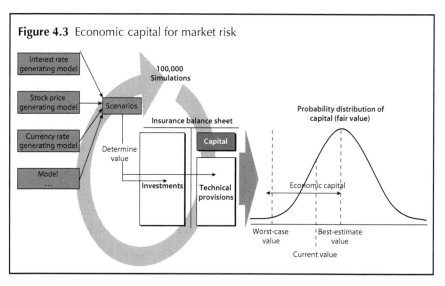

Figure 4.3 Economic capital for market risk

WHAT IS CREDIT RISK?

Apart from fluctuations in financial markets as a whole (market risk), the investment portfolio is obviously also sensitive to the state of individual assets. When one certain investment is not repaid, the insurer suffers a loss immediately. This is most obvious for bonds, which make up a significant part of the asset portfolio. When a bond issuer does not repay the bond at maturity, a direct loss arises. However, bond values also change when the issuer is downgraded due to changes in the ability to repay the loan. Other credit risk exposures in the investment portfolio arise with derivatives, because the counterparty in the derivative transaction alsoi needs to honour the obligation when due. This is called credit risk.

> Credit risk is the risk of decreases in value when counterparties are not capable of fulfilling their obligations or when there are changes in the credit standing of counterparties.

The investment portfolio of insurers consists largely of bonds. Should they be only government bonds, the insurer would run no credit risk: it is certain that the bonds will be repaid at the end of the maturity. Most western governments are considered very solvent and hence perceived risk-free. The governments of emerging markets are, however, less solvent. For instance, during the 2002 crisis in Argentina, the government defaulted on its interest payments and repayment of the government bonds. Another example is the government bond crisis, where the market had serious doubts that a number of European governments would be able to repay the bonds due to high budgetary deficits (see Chapter 6). Greece seems to be the most dominant example where, at the time of writing, discussions are ongoing about whether or not the Greek government should default or restructure its debt position. In either case, investors will face a loss, either the total or a partial value of the bonds.

However, in order to obtain a higher return, insurers also invest in corporate bonds that involve more credit risks: a corporate could fail to pay its interest payments or repayments or even both, which would saddle the investor. To compensate for such risks, the interest on corporate bonds is higher than on government bonds. Corporate bonds mostly account for the largest part of the total credit risk of the insurer, even though the balance sheet consists of only a smaller part of corporate bonds.

Another source of credit risk is the mortgage portfolio, another important component in the investment portfolio. In the life insurance industry in particular, mortgages are often granted in conjunction with life insurance. A mortgage is a loan where real estate property is taken as collateral. It often involves individuals, with a house as the pledge, but it can also involve real estate, such as offices and shopping areas. As the collateral has sufficient value, the credit risk is restricted. If the mortgager (ie, the client) is unable to repay, the mortgagee (the insurer) has the right to sell the house. At times of high increases in the property market, such as during the late 1990s and early 2000s, the credit risk on mortgages was considered almost nil. In the late 2000s credit risk on mortgages increased in some markets, contributing to this was the decrease in housing prices and as a consequence house owners could not repay their mortgages.

However, when property prices decrease, as could occur as a correction to a real estate bubble, credit losses can take place in the mortgage portfolio. For instance, after a period of growth US housing prices decreased during the late 1990s and then exploded again in the early 2000s. Another example of real estate price corrections was in the Japanese market, where just before the turn of the century about US$20 trillion of property value was erased in Japan: some private property prices decreased by 90% after a couple of year and some commercial real estate property top locations even decreased by 99% in value.

Reinsurance can also be a source of credit risk. It could be that a counterparty in a reinsurance contract cannot fulfil its obligations at the moment when the money is actually needed – for instance, after a catastrophe. The loss from a catastrophe can be enormous, as can the credit risk. In addition, insurers are more often using derivatives to cover and hedge risk positions. It is important to guarantee that the counterparty in the derivative contract will pay up when necessary. The insurer also runs a credit risk here, meaning the risk that the counterparty may not comply with its obligations.

Credit risk is sometimes also related to the insurer's risk of clients who do not pay their premium. Strictly, a client is not insured when they do not pay any premium and the insurer does not have to pay compensation when there is a claim. There is no credit risk either. In practice, insurers are fair when defaulting clients are involved; therefore, the debtor administration keeps close track of the payment delays. As the individual amounts are often much smaller than the credit risk in the bond portfolio, mostly no economic capital is calculated for this risk. Another type of credit risk occurs in the case of brokers and agents that need to transfer premiums received from clients to the central bank accounts of the insurer.

The components of credit risk that were discussed here are represented in Figure 4.4.

Figure 4.4 Components of credit risk

CONTROLLING CREDIT RISK

As with all risks, spreading is the key to credit risk control – and it applies to all components of credit risk. The bond portfolio is a widely diversified portfolio. There are limits for individual counterparties, geographical regions, rating categories, business sectors, etc. These are stipulated in the investment mandates and also thoroughly controlled by the asset manager. As such, a concentration of the credit risk is prevented.

The same applies to the reinsurance policy. For instance, it will state limits for spreading by the reinsurers involved and the maximum coverage per reinsurer. For that purpose, credit rating is often used. In addition, the reinsurer is thoroughly analysed before doing business. Collateral is the instrument that is used to control the credit risk on mortgages; it is an extremely efficient instrument, as losses on mortgages are almost nil.

MEASURING CREDIT RISK

The set of instruments for measuring credit risk is highly developed within the banking industry. This is necessary, as banks grant private credits that cannot simply be traded. This is very different for insurers, who have predominantly liquid marketable bonds and mortgages in the portfolio. This means that insurers, more than banks, will be subject to small changes in the financial position of the counterparty. An insurer will then sell the bond, whereas a bank does not have that possibility for private loans.

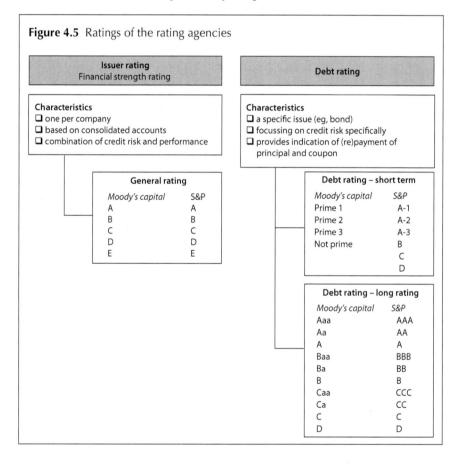

Figure 4.5 Ratings of the rating agencies

The credit rating is central in measuring credit risk. A selected number of major international agencies judge the financial solidity of market parties and publish their judgement through a type of report called a rating. These rating agencies base their judgement on a variety of information on the company: financial ratios, profitability, solvency and liquidity, as well as more qualitative aspects such as market position, client groups and management quality. The most well-known ratings are provided by the rating agencies Moody's and Standard & Poor's (S&P) (see Figure 4.5). Other rating agencies are Fitch Ratings, AM Best, Dun and Bradstreet and Dominion. The rating agencies publish different kinds of ratings. A difference is made between a rating for the enterprise as a whole (issuer rating) and the rating of an individual debt (debt rating). In the last category, a difference is again made between short-term and long-term debt.

The good thing about rating is that rating agencies review their ratings regularly, mostly every year. An insurer does not constantly have to keep an eye on the bond portfolio itself to see if it is still solvent. Rating agencies assess the credit quality of each individual bond in the portfolio. That does not prevent the insurer from using its common sense in investment decisions and during portfolio monitoring. During the financial crisis (see Chapter 6), but also before the importance and power of the rating agencies in the entire financial system became more visible, this was recognised as a problem. After all, financial participants structure their financial market products in such a way that it could qualify for a certain rating. Also, the rating is a trigger that determines the value of financial instruments to a large extent. Rating agencies received massive criticism during the crisis, when many financial instruments were downgraded. A delicate fact is, of course, that the companies that issue the investment pay the rating agencies to grant a rating, potentially creating conflicts of interests. In supervisory systems, the rating could determine the solvency requirement that an insurer (or bank) should set aside, both in Solvency II and Basel III (see Chapters 8 and 9 respectively). This urges that insurers should have their own separate view on the credit risk of counterparties, including a detailed credit analysis. That this could be translated in a rating only has advantages, since it provides a common language for market participants.

The credit rating is also translated into the probability of a counterparty defaulting within one year, called the probability of default

(PD). An A+ rating is equal to a PD of 0.05%. Table 4.1 shows how ratings and PD are related.

Table 4.1 Ratings and historic default rates

Agency				Ratings			
Moody's	Aaa	Aa	A	Baa	Ba	B	Caa
S&P	AAA	AA	A	BBB	BB	B	CCC
PD (in %)	0.01	0.03	0.07	0.20	1.10	3.50	16.00

In the banking sector, three parameters are often used to measure the credit risk. For each parameter, statistical risk models are available, depending on the specific counterparty or loan.

Probability of default
Probability of bankruptcy, expressed as a probability percentage.

Loss given default (LGD)
The loss when the counterparty is defaulting, expressed as a percentage of the outstanding amount. If there is collateral, the LGD decreases.

Exposure at default (EAD)
The outstanding amount at the time of default of a counterparty, expressed as a currency. The EAD is usually the total notional of the loan, but not necessarily; eg, additional credit lines, current accounts, etc.

These parameters are central to credit risk models. Insurers would rather focus on the external ratings than on internally calculated PD, LGD and EAD. Internal parameters are also less important for the bond portfolio. However, for private loans, these parameters are relevant.

ECONOMIC CAPITAL FOR CREDIT RISK
There are roughly two methods available to determine the economic capital for credit risk. The first method is in line with the banking in-

struments and calculates the "worst case" and the expected credit loss on the basis of the three parameters (PD, LGD and EAD) mentioned above. The advantage of this method is the concordance with the banking principles, which are well developed and widely accepted.

The expected credit loss is calculated by multiplying the three parameters by each other. The worst-case credit loss is determined by a square-root formula. In line with the definition, economic capital for an individual bond is the difference between the expected and the worst-case credit loss[1] (see formula below). When establishing the economic capital for a bond portfolio, diversification is taken into account.

$$Economic\ capital = \underbrace{LGD \times EAD \times \sqrt{PD \times (1-PD)}}_{=\ worst\text{-}case\ loss} - \underbrace{LGD \times EAD \times PD}_{-\ best\ estimate\ loss}$$

The second method uses a simulation. The insurer creates risk models to determine the value of the bond portfolio and the three risk parameters (PD, LGD and EAD) are input. Additionally, the phenomenon called rating migration is taken into account. This is where the rating of counterparties can change from year to year. Through simulation, the model calculates the value of the bond portfolio in a large number of scenarios. On this basis, a probability distribution is derived (as also described in the section on market risk). The economic capital is then determined analogously: the difference between the worst-case value and the expected value.

WHAT IS LIQUIDITY RISK?
An insurer needs liquid assets (cash) to pay out the policyholder benefits. Simultaneously, it also receives liquid assets in the form of premiums. These two cash flows are mostly unequal. As liquid assets produce less return than investments in bonds; for instance, an insurer strives to have sufficient liquid assets available – not too many, but definitely not too little!

When an insurer suddenly or unexpectedly has to pay more benefits than expected, there could be insufficient liquid assets – for instance, after a heavy storm or the unexpected first snowfall of the year. The claims need to be paid as soon as possible, so the insurer must free up liquid assets by selling part of its assets, possibly at an unfavourable moment. This can lead to financial losses. Whenever the market is low at the time the insurer needs to sell assets, it will face a loss. But what if there is actually no demand at all for this type of asset at that time? The insurer may decrease its price even further, but that is completely ineffective: there are no buyers. This situation occurred in a number of ways during the financial crisis, as will be seen in Chapter 6.

The insurer naturally aims to prevent defaulting on its clients as much as possible. If the client does not receive the expected compensation because the insurer has liquidity problems, confidence in the insurance company could be in danger, even if it is solvent.[2] Not all clients can distinguish this, which is understandable. If confidence is endangered, several clients could cancel their insurance, with disastrous consequences. Life insurance would have to be repaid immediately and, for non-life insurance, clients would demand part of their premiums. These consequences justify prevention of liquidity problems.

Liquidity issues in the financial markets usually happen when there are large financial market disruptions, such as natural disasters causing big insurance claims, downgrading of large companies and major unexpected regulatory changes. These may be based on facts, but also on rumours – financial markets are sensitive to new information and speculation. These could potentially create market disruptions and cash in- or outflows.

In addition to equity capital, a number of large insurers issued subordinated bonds to serve as a buffer to absorb losses. These bonds have a certain maturity and, for shorter maturities, the insurer may assume that they are rolled over quite simply: a bond at maturity is repaid with the proceeds from a new bond. This happens not only with regular subordinated bonds, but also in complex securitisation transactions. What would happen if there is no appetite for the new issued bond in the market? The insurer will need to repay the first bond, without having the new bond available. In other words: the insurer will need to have liquid assets at hand to withstand this.

This has highlighted a number of important issues:

❑ liquidity and solvency are not identical – a perfectly solvent insurance company may have large liquidity problems;
❑ timing of payments is paramount to facing liquidity risk;
❑ market sentiment plays a big role in liquidity risk; and
❑ liquidity risk not only impacts assets, but also liabilities.

We define liquidity risk as follows.

> Liquidity risk is the risk of unexpected or unexpectedly high payments, where complying with the liabilities involves a loss.

For a bank, the liquidity risk is much more dominant than it is for insurers. Bank deposits are claimable[3] on demand for a large part, as opposed to the technical provisions of the life insurer. The insurance liabilities of non-life insurers could suddenly have to be paid. For insurers, being less strongly intertwined than banks, there is less probability of the problems of one insurer having spill-over effects to another insurer.

We can distinguish market liquidity risk and funding liquidity risk. Market liquidity risk is the phenomenon that less liquidity is available in the market. This could be because there is no appetite to buy or sell assets. As a consequence, the insurer needs to find access to different funds to honour payments in order to prevent default on these payments. Often it relates to different assets. Funding liquidity risk is the phenomenon that an insurer cannot roll-over its assets or liabilities (mostly liabilities). Consequentially, assets need to be freed up to fill the gaps or other liabilities need to be defaulted on. Ultimately, the liability holders are at risk here. Often, market liquidity problems exacerbate funding liquidity problems. Conceptually, there is no difference between the payment of a claim to policyholders when due and an interest/principal payment to investors. However, the impact of harming policyholders is mostly considered to be greater than for investors. Besides, contracts with investors could potentially have clauses regarding subordination.

How is liquidity risk managed within the insurance company? The treasury department monitors cash flows on a day-to-day basis and uses liquid assets as efficiently as possible in the form of short-term and liquid investments. The treasury department identifies the liquidity of each balance sheet item, both now and on future dates (eg, 12 or 24 months ahead). For each balance sheet item, it is assessed how liquid it is by the capital markets and whether or not (un)expected payments could arise. This includes claim behaviour, but also lapses and prepayments. It is also important whether future cash flows can be expected to arise from current contracts. Also, payments due to operational costs (salaries, office rents) are taken into account. Financial contracts, such as derivatives, securitisations or special funding structures, could include so-called triggers that cause additional payments. A simple example is a derivative transaction where more collateral is required. Naturally, this process results in a large liquidity buffer to pay out unexpected non-life claims. In general, there are liquidity limits to the asset portfolio.

Of course, a way of addressing liquidity risk is holding a liquidity buffer as part of the assets. In times of stress, however, this might not be sufficient. Another potential means of generating liquidity in times of stress is through contingent liquidity – either contingent capital or loans. Contingent liquidity is a financial contract that enables a company to access financial resources in times of crisis. An example is a contract where a third party supplies additional capital or a subordinated loan after the solvency ratio drops below a certain level. It is critical to arrange these contracts in non-crisis situations, because during a crisis investors are normally less prepared to provide funds. This was also seen during the financial crisis that started in 2008 (see Chapter 6) when companies in financial problems could not access the capital markets for funding or capital. Governments finally had to bail out a number of institutions, including the world's largest insurer at that time, AIG.

Measuring liquidity risk is not that simple. In the insurance industry, there are no standard measurements for liquidity risk. Nor is economic capital calculated for liquidity risk. The reason is that economic capital is focused on the solvency position. Previously, it was remarked that a perfectly solvent institution can also have liquidity problems. Some experts even stated that liquidity risk is much more dangerous than solvency risk (ie, all other risks). In other words: liquidity risk is either totally in control or totally out of control and life threatening. The underlying message is that liquidity risk can manifest itself via the joint occurrence of all other risks.

The size of the liquidity buffer is an important measure of liquidity risk, but more interesting is to run scenarios to assess the liquidity profile of the company under stress. This is similar to historical and imaginary market risk scenarios, except for the fact that the focus is on liquidity rather than solvency. Often during market crises, a shock in (market) liquidity arises. To that end, many potential liquidity scenarios are available to companies. It was also noted that liquidity risk is closely related to other risks. Good management of other risks can prevent liquidity problems. This alone is not sufficient, however. Specific attention to liquidity risk is required, including a detailed liquidity analysis.

CONCLUSION

This chapter described the risks relating to the activities of insurers on financial markets. In market risk, the sensitivity to interest rates and equity prices is generally dominant whereas, in credit risk, the bond portfolio is the most important point of attention for many insurers. The chapter examined the origin of risks, and how they can be managed and measured. In the calculation of economic capital, a structure of simulation models was described. It concluded with a discussion of how liquidity risk differs from the other investment risks and how insurers address this. Chapter 6 will later describe how many of the issues discussed in this chapter manifested themselves during the financial crisis.

1   In the banking sector, this is called unexpected loss (UL).
2   A company is solvent if there is sufficient capital (ie, assets exceed policyholder liabilities) and is liquid if it can honour the claimable payments requested.
3   Additionally, the banking system includes a "lender of last resort" (often the central bank), from which banks can immediately borrow liquid assets under conditions in case of a liquidity crisis.

5

Non-Financial Risks: Operational and Business Risk

This chapter will discuss non-financial risks: operational and business risks. We call these non-financial not so much because they cannot have financial impact, but rather to point out that they are different from the investment and underwriting risks addressed in the two previous chapters. Non-financial risks are not less important, on the contrary. However, non-financial risks are faced in the same way by non-financial institutions (such as shops or factories), whereas investment and underwriting risks are typically only a challenge for the financial industry. The focus on non-financial risks began for the banking industry at the time when they were aiming to get a better understanding of the full risk spectrum. Over time, insurers have also adopted the approaches developed by the banks. One thing should therefore become clear from reading this chapter: non-financial risks are much more difficult to capture in economic capital than the risks of the two previous chapters.

WHAT IS OPERATIONAL RISK?

Not so long ago, operational risk was still defined as "everything but market and credit risk". For many years, operational risk was a catch-all for all kinds of incident that did not fit into a determined risk category. It was, by its nature, a wide-ranging concept. Since the discussion on capital requirements for operational risk within the context of Basel II,[1] the need for a specific definition has grown, which has restricted the concept. This partially resulted in operational risk gaining more attention in the insurance industry. Additionally, a number of events led to more attention being paid to this new issue.

> Operational risk is the risk of losses due to inadequate or failed internal processes, people or systems, or due to external events.

The definition above already indicates that this is still a wide subject, affecting a major part of the industry. It is not a new focus for insurers, although its relative importance is increasing due to growing computerisation, numerous mergers and acquisitions, and the impact of globalisation. On the basis of a few examples, it will be shown that operational risk remains a wide ranging.

Some of the most tangible examples of operational risk hitting the headlines include the cases of the Prudential in the US, HIH Insurance in Australia and the accounting scandals at Enron, WorldCom and Ahold. Apart from these, there were several smaller incidents which also gained press attention, as private clients were directly involved and had to suffer negative consequences. One example was the incorrect connection of IT systems at ING, whereby clients did not receive the return guarantees promised in the contracts.

The case of ING falls under the category of "losses due to shortcomings in systems" and was caused by an IT problem. In 2005, ING admitted publicly that an error had been discovered in its production systems: the IT system for the quotations and the final policy administration were not connected correctly. As a consequence, quotations to clients contained guarantees that ultimately were not included in the final policy, or at least were not administered as such: clients received less return than had been promised to them. Eventually, ING did compensate its clients. It also took some necessary additional measures because, by coincidence, the market interest rate at that moment was lower than the guaranteed interest rate. If the market rate had been higher, there probably would have been no problems.

An incidental circumstance is that the error had already been discovered internally a few years earlier, causing negative publicity. The question is: what damage has this caused to ING's reputation, and how many clients will take their insurance business elsewhere? Such an effect is not easily measurable and, even if it could be, it would probably not be registered as "operational loss".

Prudential is one of the biggest US financial institutions, with major insurance operations across the globe. The Prudential affair falls under the denominator "churning", and is a form of human failure. Prudential faced a loss of more than US$2 billion as a result of churning in the US during the 1990s. Churning is the practice whereby clients are deliberately encouraged to buy expensive products in order to generate high commissions and fees. Partially, this is also what happened with subprime mortgages in the US (see Chapter 6). In 1996, regulators discovered that Prudential was aware of these practices and had even promoted the wrongdoers. This eventually led to a lawsuit in 1997 based on losses faced by more than 10 million policyholders.

It is assumed that the actual loss faced by the policyholders was even higher than the ultimate US$2 billion claim. In addition, the reputational damage is extremely hard to assess. Even if Prudential had not lost the court case, it would have suffered reputational damage. However, in such a case it is unclear whether any "operational risk loss" would have occurred in the accounts as a result of this scandal.

In 2001, HIH Insurance Group (Health International Holdings) collapsed after a period of aggressive growth in the 1990s. This failure is said to be Australia's largest ever bankruptcy. The company was founded in the 1960s and, after a period of stable growth, extended its operations across Australian borders and rapidly increased its market share in the country. Most notably, it acquired a large Australian competitor, FAI Insurance. In 2001, however, HIH had to announce it was going into liquidation. This was attributed to aggressive growth, underpricing strategies and reserving problems, complex reinsurance agreements and unclear delegation of authorities.

It is obvious that failure of a major insurance company causes losses to the insurance market. While it is very difficult to determine the extent of these losses, it is important to assess the true underlying causes. Most probably, there are multiple, interrelated causes, but such an analysis could prevent new cases from occurring.

Below are a few crucial features of operational risks:

❏ operational risk is a wide-ranging concept;
❏ the damage as a consequence of operational risk is often only

partially quantifiable – the so-called indirect losses, damage to reputation and opportunity losses, are not, or, are barely measurable or attributable to one single incident (eg, Prudential and ING);

❏ operational risk and the damage involved can be influenced to a large extent by insurers (all mentioned examples); and

❏ operational risk has a big overlap with other risk areas, such as underwriting and investment risks. A large number of losses are caused by a combination of operational risk and other risks (eg, ING and HIH).

As discussed, one of the main features of operational risk is that it can be highly influenced by the company. Insurers have two possibilities here: risk control and risk financing (see also Figure 2.3, page 19). Risk control includes taking internal measures in order to prevent risks or restrict the loss. Risk financing consists of transferring the risk to a third party. The most well-known form of risk financing is insurance, but holding capital (economic capital) to cover losses is also a form of financing.

Although parts of operational risk can and will be financed, it is not optimal to finance all operational risks. Preventing losses will often be cheaper than insurance against losses or setting aside relatively expensive capital. Therefore, the emphasis will always be on risk management. However, much attention is paid to measuring operational risk, as this is a precondition for the financing of this risk.

CONTROLLING OPERATIONAL RISK
The measures that insurers can take to reduce operational risk are numerous. This chapter will now consider some examples of measures that can be taken in order to illustrate that everyone is involved in operational risk control.

Administrative organisation/internal control
In order to control human errors and fraud, the set-up of the administrative organisation and internal control is crucial. The most famous aspect of administrative organisation/internal control (AO/IC) is the four-eyes principle. Processes relating to approvals, claims handling and payments can often only be achieved when

two people are involved and take responsibility for the payment. With this further control, many frauds and mistakes can be prevented. Administrative organisation can be programmed into systems by giving people restricted access to systems or, for instance, by programming input/verification control on outgoing payments. Another option is the distribution of tasks among different departments and/or work with signatures.

Physical security
In order to protect companies against external incidents such as fire, theft, external fraud or hold-ups, physical security can play an important part. Placing cameras, providing escape routes, and installing sprinkler systems and fire extinguishers can already prevent many problems and limit the loss in the case of such events.

Business continuity
When an incident takes place, an insurer cannot always afford to cease activities temporarily. When no temporary payments can be made, the consequences for policyholders can be disastrous. For system deviation possibilities, extra generators in case of power failure and data back-ups, in particular, are important. Many insurers create special procedures, the so-called business continuity procedures (BCP) or business continuity management (BCM), so that direct action can be taken when systems or other components of the business process are unavailable, without disturbing the primary processes. If an entire department needs to be transferred to another location, many aspects have to be organised in a short period of time: accommodation, transport, facilities such as telephones and computers, access to relevant IT systems, etc. A BCP/BCM policy stipulates in advance important agreements that enable swift action to be taken in critical situations.

Workplace conditions
Workplace conditions often have a big influence on absenteeism and the number of workers affected by illness or disability. As illness is a form of human "failure" and the costs can be extremely high when people end up disabled, this also forms part of operational risk control. For insurers in particular, the existing danger is of a rising num-

ber of cases of RSI. Therefore, much attention is being paid to the organisation of individual workstations for employees.

Risk awareness

The basis of operational risk control is the risk awareness of why certain measures are important. These include why you should not give personal passwords to colleagues, when you should warn a client of the risks they are taking, why identification of a client is important and what can go wrong when you spread processes across two or more departments.

A control self-assessment (also called risk self-assessment) has always been the favourite instrument for operational risk control at the process level. Control self-assessments focus on risk awareness and better knowledge of the process of which someone is part. Employees from different steps of the same process gather in workshops in order to brainstorm on weaknesses, risks and potential improvements. Peoples' involvement in the identification of risks also results in their involvement and buy-in when mitigating these risks.

Although self-assessments are time-intensive, they are often introduced where the potential for improvements to the risk control is significant. The major disadvantage of self-assessments is that their results are not (or are barely) quantitatively translatable. In measuring operational risk, this instrument has never been able to play an important part. Thus, it is not applied in isolation, but is seen as more of an amendment to the statistical methods used by some large insurers. In fact, the idea of self-assessment is also the basis of the scorecard method (see page 98). Both instruments are based on the knowledge and experience of key people in the process.

Risk governance and organisation

A modern insurer cannot do without a good risk organisation. This involves clear allocation of tasks and responsibilities and controls on how these are used. Separation of certain duties in order to avoid conflicts of interest may seem obvious, but in practice this rule seems to be violated easily. For instance, a commercial manager determining the price of a product when they are only rewarded based on the number of sold products rather than the total technical result of the product. Or the investment manager who sets the limits of assets categories and determines the operational asset strategy. This all requires a good governance system. In many of operational risk scandals that reached the media, corporate governance was a key issue: who controls the company on behalf of the shareholders? Is the supervisory board sufficiently able to challenge and control the top executives? However, this is valid within the company as well. How is the head of a certain department challenged and how do decisions take place within the organisation? We will address risk management organisation in more detail in Chapter 11.

It is common to identify three lines of defence within the organisation. The first line of defence is management itself. Operational management is responsible for making decisions and ensuring that the total risk profile is within limits. The second line is typically an advisory body that supports line management to measure and manage risks. Developing risk measurement methodologies falls within this activity, such as an economic capital model. Drafting risk policies is another support activity for setting boundaries to limit the risk in operational departments. The risk management department typically has the role of second line of defence. The third line of defence is an independent unit that checks whether business units comply with the company's risk policies and identify where certain risks are out of control. This unit is typically internal audit, reporting directly to the top management, and often also to the company's board of directors.

The corporate governance discussion was intensified by the introduction of the Sarbanes–Oxley (SOX) regulation in the US, requiring that directors of stock-listed companies explicitly state that the information supplied to the market (eg, annual accounts) is reliable and accurate. While most people would agree with the objective of the SOX regulation, the way in which that objective was to be achieved received a lot of criticism. Companies complying with SOX have to document intensively and rigidly the risks in their internal processes and the measures taken to address these risks. Since SOX is rule-based, a company does not have the freedom to adapt the documentation and evidence requirements to company-specific situations. Indeed, complying with SOX is time consuming and doubt could be cast on whether documenting alone improves risk processes. In some cases, it has caused in intensive bureaucracy of documentation. At the same time, it has forced insurers to identify the key risks in the operational processes leading to the information in the annual accounts. After the first implementation in the early 2000s, companies are now improving the SOX processes in order to make them more efficient and practicable.

When the control of operational risks are compared with the control of, for instance, investment risks, one can see that operational risk is controlled on a lower level in the organisation. Operational risk does not involve limits and policy committees, but operational measures. Operational risk is also difficult to aggregate. In fact, each individual employee has to be aware of operational risks and think about controlling them, whereas controlling investment risk is covered by a few key specialists. Therefore, it is not surprising that line management is the crucial link in controlling operational risks.

However, in the late 2000s, more attention had been paid to operational risks at higher levels within the organisation. Whereas an integrated group policy for controlling operational risks was exceptional some years ago, it is now becoming – at least for the big, internationally operating insurers – generally accepted. Central aggregation of data and consolidated management reporting of operational risks is also being addressed.

Within insurers, one can distinguish four supporting departments that are involved, each from another discipline, in the reporting and analysis of operational risks.

❏ The internal audit department identifies, on the basis of so-called "operational audits", "compliance audits" and "IT audits", weaknesses in processes or systems and advises on what measures should be taken. The internal audit department also informs the board of directors and the supervisory board of any detected shortcomings.
❏ The compliance department, specialising in insider trading, fraud and integrity (regulations), performs a supervisory function and also reports directly to the board of directors. Within each relevant business unit or department, a person is charged with the tasks of "compliance officer". This person has to be able to report independently at any time.

❑ The (management) control department informs the higher management of major operational risks through management reports.
❑ The risk management department compiles risk data and draws up reports on risks and losses.

The activities and objectives of the last two departments have an important overlap, as the risk management process is comparable to the process of management control.

None of the above-mentioned departments play the most important part in the risk control process. Line management is ultimately responsible, and thus is the most important player in managing and controlling operational risk.

MEASURING OPERATIONAL RISK

Although operational risk is not a new risk category, measuring this risk only started in the 2000s. The need to measure operational risk arose from the banking sector. The same applies to the translation of this measurement data to economic capital. In the period before 1999, only a few banks specialised in the measurement of operational risk. Since then, measuring operational risk has developed rapidly due to Basel II (see Chapter 9). Insurers have followed banks, although they have not always been as developed as banks in their measurement methodologies for operational risk.

In measuring operational risk in terms of economic capital, three components play a main role: operational loss data, scorecards and self-assessments, and key risk indicators (KRIs) and key control indicators (KCIs). These components can be combined accordingly (see Figure 5.1). Often, one of the above-mentioned components is dominant and the remaining components are used supplementarily. Some insurers use loss data as a basis for their economic capital calculations and amend that with scorecards, self-assessments and KRIs or KCIs. Others rely more on scorecards and self-assessments for their economic capital calculations and validate the results with loss data and KRIs or KCIs. In this regard, operational risk differs from other risk categories (for instance, market risk), where one general standard method is applied.

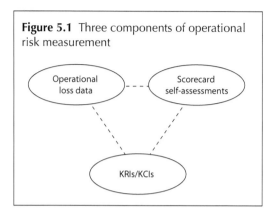

Figure 5.1 Three components of operational risk measurement

To categorise operational losses, a classification of event types has been developed. This classification is useful in operational loss data modelling and scorecards. It is often used as a basis to design the databases that are required for data collection. It seems logical that events related to fraud occur with a different frequency than system failures, for instance. Also, when relating the events to causes and potential measures, the classification is useful. After all, fraud is to be prevented and detected in a different way than system failures. Within each event type, there are multiple sub-types. The main types are:

❑ internal fraud;
❑ external fraud;
❑ employment practices and workplace safety;
❑ clients, products and business practices;
❑ damage to physical assets;
❑ business disruptions and system failures; and
❑ execution, delivery and process management.

Operational loss data

When all operational losses are entered into a database, extreme losses can be estimated on the basis of a statistical distribution function. Often losses are categorised into the event types mentioned above and activities – business lines such as life, non-life and asset management. When all loss data on incidents are compiled well and allocated into the correct categories, multiple probability distributions of operational losses can be estimated. In practice, insurers combine categories in order to restrict the number of probability distributions.

Losses as a result of operational risk are, in general, not normally distributed. Therefore, one or more of the alternative probability distribution functions are more applicable. However, the insurer still needs to calculate the parameters. In some cases, probability distributions for the frequency and impact of the loss are estimated separately.

Fortunately, not many dramatic incidents occur among insurers. Therefore, there is not always sufficient data available to estimate a reliable probability distribution. To estimate a probability distribution, a large number of data points are necessary (both small and big events). In order to resolve the data problem, external loss data is also used. The Association of British Insurers (ABI) set up an initiative to collect operational risk loss data in 2005, called Operational Risk Consortium (ORIC). All members submit their own data to a central database that collects and categorises all data anonymously. All members can use the outcomes to make their own operational risk model. In total, about 2,500 large losses have been collected. Roughly 25 insurance companies are now members of this initiative.

In addition, some companies use the methods developed within their banking unit within a financial conglomerate (combination of a bank and an insurer). When using external data, it should be observed that there are big differences in the risk control environments of different organisations. This is reflected in greater or less operational losses suffered. Therefore, combining data from different companies is less simple than it seems at first sight. Each organisation needs to compile a good mix of internal and external data points used to estimate the probability distributions. The criteria of what constitutes a good mix between internal and external data points could very well differ per company as well.

The economic capital calculation for operational risk is comparable to the calculations in non-life risk. On the basis of the loss data, a probability distribution is estimated. The economic capital is the difference between the average expected loss and the worst-case loss with a determined confidence interval (see Figure 5.2).

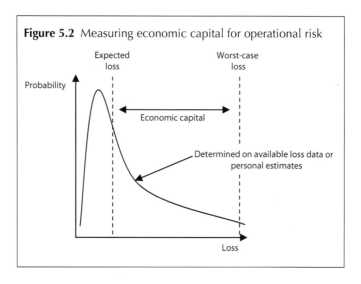

Figure 5.2 Measuring economic capital for operational risk

Compiling and analysing all incidents is not as simple as it seems. The actual administrative systems do not register the losses caused by operational risk separately. Therefore, specific software needs to be developed for operational loss registration. In general, the risk manager is somewhat apart from the business processes and has insufficient insight into all incidents.

The risk manager therefore has to trust the willingness of others to register and report operational losses, and must be aware that most line managers hesitate to report errors as these will be settled in their remuneration structure (ie, their bonus and potential for promotion). Therefore, establishing a "no-blame" culture is an important precondition for registering operational loss data successfully.

Scorecards and self-assessments

The scorecard method is based on subjective estimations of possible losses. Using this method, experts (for instance, line managers) are asked to assess the operational risks. Therefore, the term "self-assessment" also applies here. The scorecard is a structured questionnaire containing such questions as "how often could a crucial IT system break down?" and "how big would the damage be if a crucial IT system breaks down?" Within some insurers, experts can choose from high, middle or low categories. In others, the experts have to underpin their estimates with figures. In the possible loss estimate, the control instruments at the disposal of the respective expert are also explicitly taken into account. When an important IT system breaks down and the functions are immediately taken over by another system, the insurer is unlikely to suffer a great loss. Such control aspects are expressed in the scorecard method.

The results of the questionnaire are often categorised according to the event classification mentioned above. The risk manager can also estimate a probability distribution per category. As the probability distribution is based on an expert's personal estimates, this probability distribution indicates a kind of subjective probability function for operational risks.

The calculation of the economic capital is not really different from the calculations based on the loss data method (see Figure 5.2). The only difference is that the probability distributions are based on personal estimates instead of loss data. On the basis of the probability distribution functions, the risk manager can determine the (average) expected loss and the economic capital. The economic capital is the difference between the (average) expected loss and the worst-case loss (based on the chosen confidence level).

The scorecard method is often incorporated into primary business processes. For each activity within this business process, separate questionnaires are designed in order to chart the probability of losses and the potential loss amounts. As a scorecard is custom-made, each expert is given questions focusing on the type of activities in which they specialise. For instance, the questionnaire for an underwriting manager is not comparable with that for a policy administration employee.

The risk manager runs the risk that the expert may try to present the situation more positively than it actually is. This could have a negative influence on the economic capital calculations. In order to prevent this, the answers of the questionnaire are often validated by an independent entity – such as the audit department – but also the manager responsible for that particular expert.

The loss data and the scorecard method are often compared with each other. As both methods have pros and cons, the methods need to be applied in conjunction. Table 5.1 presents the differences in more detail.

Table 5.1 Differences between measurement methods for operational risk

Loss data	Scorecards
Objective, based on real suffered losses	Subjective, based on estimates of experts
Retrospective: historical incidents that quickly could lose their actual value through changes in the environment	Prospective: estimates are based on the actual situation and the future measures taken
Few data points as losses are normally less-extreme incidents	Abundant data available due to the great number of experts
Consistent method for each department and activity	Each department or activity receives a special questionnaire (consistency problems)
Consistent with other risk categories such as market and non-life risk	Subjective foundation, differs widely from other risk categories

Key risk indicators and key control indicators

The two methods mentioned above are often amended or validated by KRIs and KCIs. A KRI indicates the risk that the insurer is running, or the probability of an incident occurring and its corresponding impact. A KCI indicates to what extent the risks are controlled. If, for instance, an emergency power aggregate is automatically introduced when a power failure takes place, then business processes will suffer no resulting interference. In other cases, manual controls are in place – such as manual checks and reconciliations. In such a case, the risk is well controlled. As such, it is preferable to link a KRI to one or more KCIs.

Since operational risk is often related to the operational processes of the company, it is logical to document the KRIs/KCIs in the process descriptions. Most software for documenting processes support this. The business needs to provide evidence that a control is actually in place and functions accurately. Example evidence can be a report, a signature or proof that a check has been made.

Risk indicators are not based on past experience, but are an instrument for spotting future risks over time. Therefore, KRIs are often applied as a supplement to the statistics. Incidents which have not yet resulted in direct losses become visible – for instance, by keeping track of temporary system breakdowns and the duration of these breakdowns, how absence due to illness develops, how often and by whom restrictions are broken and how many complaints are reported.

The risk and control indicators are applied with three objectives:

❏ regular management information on risk and control indicators increases the transparency and awareness of risks in operational processes;
❏ the function of the indicators is to check to what extent the organisation has gaps in its control framework and how vulnerable it is to operational risks; and
❏ they are early warning signals, as they give more insight into the trends within the risk, making it possible for management to intervene at an early stage.

ECONOMIC CAPITAL FOR OPERATIONAL RISK: THE HEART OF THE PROBLEM

Measuring operational risk within the framework of economic capital takes some doing. The first measurement methods for operational risk in banking were based on the statistical methods applied for market and credit risk. However, it gradually became clear that operational risk was different from the other risk categories. An organisation can influence its operational risk to a large extent by taking control measures. In addition, the models based on data loss have a large number of disadvantages, as previously discussed.

Although many big international financial institutions have already taken huge steps in data gathering (both the loss data method and the scorecard method), some critical questions remain unanswered. Will reporting bad news be discouraged even more if capital requirements within the framework of economic capital are in place? Will financial institutions with well-charted risks be punished when they are open about their business? Could large incidents in the financial sector have been prevented by the current models for operational risk?

Good operational risk management is, in fact, the same as good management. Good management information is a precondition for this. The developments in the field of measuring operational risk can contribute only if some of the above-mentioned conceptual problems are resolved.

In Solvency II, only a very simple approach is used to calculate the capital requirement. It is simply a predetermined factor multiplied by technical provisions and premiums (see Chapter 8). This simple method does, of course, not reflect any risk-sensitivity in the calculation. However, it also shows that, in Solvency II, people recognised the difficulty of measuring operational risk in terms of capital.

WHAT IS BUSINESS RISK?

Apart from operational risk, insurers also suffer the consequences of other non-financial risks, namely business risk. For this risk category, the term strategic risk can also be used, but this book will use the term business risk. In fact, the discussion around business risk is still at a premature stage. Business risk is sometimes used as a "rubbish bin" – and is defined as "the risk that does not fall under the other risks". However, a positive definition of business risk is gradually being developed.

> Business risk is the risk of losses due to changes in the competitive environment or internal flexibility.

The concept of "competitive environment" comprises the totality of competitors, clients, possible new market players and the government. When changes take place in the competitive environment and the insurer cannot adapt itself quickly enough, it will end up in a situation of loss. Various waves of privatisation in the insurance industry makes this a topical subject. Privatisation provides opportunities to insurers, but also exposes them to new threats that did not exist during the time that the market was strictly controlled by the government.

Life insurance is influenced by the fiscal system, because private life insurance is seen as the so-called third pillar of the pension scheme.[2] To encourage individuals to build up capital, some countries have fiscal incentives to stimulate individuals to buy life insurance. While this is beneficial for insurance companies, it also makes them sensitive to changes in the fiscal system. The Dutch market provides a good example. Taking out annuities had been fiscally encouraged up until 2002. In December 2002, annuity sales hit an unprecedented peak as people wanted to benefit from the tax benefit for the last time. From January 2003, the annuity market collapsed dramatically as the new fiscal system came into force. Insurers became painfully aware that a certain tax rule had de facto provided them with a constant income stream. The new tax legislation had erased that almost completely.

This example points to the importance of business risk. It is clear that business risk is not a new risk. On the contrary, it has always been the essence of the day-to-day management of financial institutions. However, the privatisation of products and increasing internationalisation and competition has increased the importance of business risk. Therefore, business risk within the economic capital framework has gained an explicit place in most of the large financial institutions.

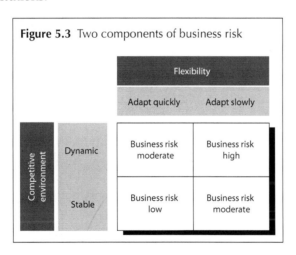

Figure 5.3 Two components of business risk

As mentioned, business risk consists of two components (see Figure 5.3). The competitive environment of the insurer is full of possible threats. Existing competitors or potential new market players are constantly after market share. In addition, the internet has become a new distribution channel for insurers, as a result of which other channels could be under pressure. The government plays also an important part in the competitive environment, as we have seen in the case of the Dutch fiscal regime. This holds for life as well as for non-life and health insurers, where some products are government-sponsored or made compulsory by law. In fact, the insurer has barely any influence over incidents in the competitive environment.

Can one observe passively how the demand for financial products decreases and makes way for new products? Fortunately not! As a last resort, the insurer can reduce costs when the demand for products decreases, in order to prevent losses. We call this cost flexibility. A large fixed cost is an indicator of a large business risk. The insurer can flexibly deploy employees and resources within the changing environment. The board of directors can also strategically apply organisational flexibility – for instance, by handling two distribution channels for the same product. Should clients avoid one channel for a particular reason, then the organisation has an alternative to fall back on.

CONTROLLING BUSINESS RISK

Through periodical strategic analysis of the competitive environment, insurers create an image of the current position in the market. Some have a permanent strategy department performing such analysis, while others put together varying teams to perform market analysis. A well-known instrument is SWOT analysis (strengths, weaknesses, opportunities and threats). For instance, SWOT analysis can identify extreme sensitivity to interest rate levels, equity prices or weather conditions. However, the SWOT analysis looks at these sensitivities in a different way than the traditional interest rate risk analysis or an ALM study. Within the framework of an ALM study, for example, the influence of interest rate fluctuations in a given balance-sheet position is observed. However, when interest rates are high, private clients might prefer to take out deposits with a bank rather than buying life insurance. This is only partially taken into consideration in the interest rate risk analysis, while business risk analysis does reveal such strategic sensitivities.

In addition, controllers often keep an eye on the cost structure: which costs are fixed and which are variable? Without explicitly asking the question, the idea behind it is, of course, how fast the costs can be reduced when turnover appears to be disappointing. Often the costs will respond slower to turnover decreases than is desired. On the one hand, this is due to fixed costs and contract terms but, on the other, the management often hesitates in cutting costs. Finally, cost cutbacks are carried out gradually and it may take some time before they are implemented and costs are reduced to the desired level. This implies that there is a time gap in implementing cost cuts that has to be covered as an element of business risk.

Lapse and expense risk
One element that is often specifically addressed is lapse and expense risk in life insurance, although it is also important in non-life insurance. This item will be discussed here rather than in Chapter 3 since lapse and expense risk relates more to client behaviour and the organisational cost structure than mortality rates. Lapse is the phenomenon of policyholders cancelling their insurance products. In the pricing strategy and embedded value calculations of life insurance products, an assumed lapse rate is taken into account. Lapse risk is the risk that this assumption differs from the reality and that the company has to face a loss. In the pricing strategy, an expected cost level (expenses) is also taken into account. In parallel, there is a risk that the real expenses will differ from the expectations, resulting in a loss – called expense risk. It is the view of this book that lapse risk and expense risk is an element of business risk, rather than an underwriting risk.

In risk models, lapse and expense risk are included in the embedded value models of life insurers. This is because these effects can determine future cash flows as much as mortality rates and premium levels. Both lapse rates and expense levels can be analysed in a statistical manner, generating statistical scenarios and assessing the impact of the scenarios on the fair value. Thus, lapse and expense risk is often addressed using statistical models. Solvency II also identifies these risks separately (see Chapter 8). While statistical models are widely available for market and underwriting risk variables, relevant data points are scarcer for lapse and expense risk. First, massive lapses normally occur due to a certain event, such as regulation changes or an event affecting the company. Historically, these events have occurred insufficiently for the statistical analysis to be relevant. Of course, extreme confidence levels can be extracted from the "normal" times, but fundamentally looking into what drives client behaviour is much more relevant. Second, expenses analysis on a statistical basis does not sufficiently take into account that expenses are both fixed and variable. Also, future costs may differ from past costs. Despite seemingly convincing plans for cost reduction by management's multi-year business forecasts, it appears that ensuring fundamental cost cutting is much more difficult than expected. At the same time, cost cutting in times of serious distress might be much more achievable than on a going-concern basis. These two reasons call for a fundamental analysis of lapse and expense risk rather than a simple statistical analysis. This does not imply that statistics are irrelevant at all – they are an input of the analysis rather than an output.

ECONOMIC CAPITAL FOR BUSINESS RISK

Measuring business risk is not that simple. The development of a good method is, however, not at the top of the priority list for most insurers. That is defendable, as Solvency II (see Chapter 8) is considered more important and business risk is not explicitly included in the Solvency II framework. A comparable movement also took place in the banking sector, where three different approaches for business risk can be identified: the analogue company approach, the volatility of income and the scenario method. These approaches are also applied among a few large insurers.

Analogue company approach

With this method, the activities of the insurer are compared with those of non-financial (analogue) companies. It can be said, for instance, that insurance partly involves providing financial advice and partly information processing. In the analogue company approach, the assumption is that the capital of advisory companies, for instance, is entirely meant to cover business risk, as these companies have no underwriting or investment risks. In principle, the economic capital for the benefit of the business risk for that particular part of the insurer should be equal to the capital of analogue companies. Alternatively, an adjustment could be applied to the analogue companies for the operational risk involved. In the analogue company approach, for each activity of the insurer a few comparable, analogue, non-financial companies are addressed. Naturally, in the application of this approach, there needs to be adjustments for the business volumes.

The analogue company approach was introduced in the mid 1990s as an initial rough approach. It was meant as a rule of thumb for determining economic capital for business risk. The hypothesis that the capital of analogue companies especially covers business risk implies that this capital is determined optimally. As a first estimate of the economic capital for business risk, this is a good hypothesis, but in the long run it is not sustainable. Often, the capital of analogue companies has developed as a result of past circumstances rather than on the basis of rational decisions. Another question is whether the analogue companies consider business risk in decisions regarding their capital structure. The average cost of capital (debt and equity), rather than business risk, will mostly feed into decision-making when establishing the capital amounts. A majority of insurers, however, still work with such a rough measure for business risk.

PANEL 5.1 EXAMPLE OF AN ANALOGUE COMPANY APPROACH

An insurer supposes that it is 40% comparable with financial service providers and 60% comparable with information-processing institutions. In order to compare the business risk of an insurer with the business risk of these two categories of analogue companies, this approach looks at the relationship between the capital of the analogue companies and their operational costs.

Using several information sources, the insurer knows that in an average service-providing company the relationship between the capital and the fixed operational expenses is approximately 45%. For an average information-processing institution, it is 70%.

For the insurer as a whole, the relationship between economic capital for business risk and fixed operational costs should be approximately 60% (40% of 45% for the service-providing part and 60% of 70% for the information-processing part). If the organisation spends €300 million on fixed operational costs, the economic capital for business risk is €180 million (60% of €300 million).

Volatility of income

This approach has a more statistical nature than the previous method. The turnover is divided into several categories and the volatility of the turnover is determined per category. Naturally, the volatility of the turnover of, for instance, the insurance industry is not only determined by the business risk, but also by all other risk categories. Therefore, attempts are made to "clean" the turnover for the income of each risk category. This is a complex exercise. Finally, the part of the turnover that is caused by the assumed business risks remains. On the basis of historical data, a statistical distribution can be estimated whereby corrections are made for the yearly growth of the turnover if necessary. On the basis of, for instance, an assumed normal probability distribution, the economic capital can be determined as the difference between the expected turnover and the worst case (eg, using a simplified method of a multiple of the standard deviation).

The advantage of this approach, compared to the analogue company approach, is its statistical foundation, which makes it consistent with the economic capital framework for the other risks. The method of cleaning income data from the remaining risk categories is, however, a difficult exercise. Organisations applying this approach have, in general, had much difficulty establishing a good method for this cleaning. Each cleaning method has it pros and cons and all methods could be questioned in some way. To this day, no universal system has been found. At least one large insurer applies this method to its business risk. It is, however, used more widely in banking.

A crucial point in the volatility approach is its statistical foundation. To what extent can statistical analyses for this risk category be trusted? Are changes in the competitive environment not, by definition, a reason to decide that the past is no longer a model for the future? The expectation is that institutions applying this method will improve it to such an extent that satisfactory answers will be found for these questions in the future.

Scenario analysis

A few financial institutions apply a form of scenario analysis to measure business risk. Within this framework, the scenarios should not be confused with the statistical scenarios applied, eg, for market risk. The basis for scenario analyses here is a thorough analysis of the income sources of a specific department or of the insurer as a whole. In applying scenario analyses for business risk, management will identify the most important threats in the competitive environment. This is comparable to self-assessment for operational risk. As the list of possible threats is, in principle, unlimited, the threats are often grouped into several scenarios. For each scenario, the possible impact is determined in terms of profit margin or volume decrease, increase in costs and the probability of this scenario taking place. Then, by scenario, the possible management actions are determined. The two previously mentioned forms of flexibility are important; cost flexibility and organisational flexibility. For that purpose, existing instruments for controlling business risk are used: cutbacks, deploying staff flexibly, outsourcing, etc. The capital (economic capital) ultimately required for business risk is determined on the basis of probability and impact of the scenario and the actions of the management.

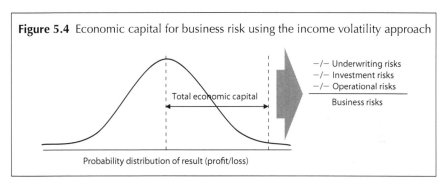

Figure 5.4 Economic capital for business risk using the income volatility approach

The most important disadvantage of the scenario approach is its subjective foundation. In the establishment of the scenarios, a judgement is expected from management on the most important risks. Criticism of this approach is therefore significantly similar to the criticism of the scorecard method for operational risk. However, the major advantage of the scenario method is that management can actually take actions on the basis of scenario analyses, because controlling and measuring business risk are integrated. This allows management to make better strategic decisions, in addition to determining the business risk economic capital.

CONCLUSION

This chapter has described the non-financial risks, namely operational and business risk. These two risk categories are less developed than the investment and underwriting risks. This can be seen especially in the measurement methods. This chapter also described the methods and instruments used to control the risks. As discussed, controlling risks is more important than the pure "measurement" in terms of economic capital. Also, the relation between the individual products is less obvious – which is why relating operational and business risks to pricing could be complex.

1   Chapter 9 will look at Basel II in more detail (as well as Basel III).
2   The first pillar is considered the state pension allowance. The second pillar is the company-defined pension scheme. The exact composition of these pillars differ by country.

6

The Global Financial Crisis

It is unclear when exactly the great financial crisis started. The most visible events were the collapse of the big global investment banks that had been Wall Street's cornerstone for many years. Bear Stearns, Lehman Brothers, Merrill Lynch, all were transformed in a matter of weeks during 2008. These collapses brought massive media attention, and uncovered a series of underlying phenomena that were already underway during the entire first decade of the 2000s. This chapter will describe how the financial crisis started (although it was initially called the subprime crisis, indicating that it only related to a specific financial market). However, as we all know, the effects spread and hit other markets as well. This happened in such a way that entire countries and their national economies struggled to survive. The chapter will look at the underlying causes and the implications for the insurance industry, as well as the lessons learned.

THE EARLY START OF THE CRISIS

In 2006, there were the first signs that specific groups of home-owners in the US could not pay their mortgage debts and were defaulting on their homes. It became clear during the early 2000s that mortgage providers had used aggressive sales techniques to sell mortgages that were hardly viable. Interest rates were low and housing prices were expected to continue increasing. This encouraged homeowners to buy houses, basically without any amortisation scheme on their mortgage. Due to fierce competition on the mortgage markets, mortgage providers competed for market share and offered low prices.

Special mortgage structures were designed, with so-called teaser rates. These 2/28 mortgages offered low interest rates in the first two years of the mortgage and higher rates thereafter. Other structures included so-called ninja loans (no income, no job or assets), where mortgages were granted to people that could not really afford them. Mortgage providers did not see the risk in such mortgages, since the house that serves as the collateral was assumed to compensate for the losses. It was generally believed that housing prices would always increase. This was also the reason why homeowners were willing to accept the mortgages and buy houses. However, as we have seen since, mortgages do bear risk.

Mortgages with higher risk are called subprime – or Alt-A, relating to the credit scoring system common in the US. Credit scores vary between 300 (lowest) and 850 (highest). Subprime mortgages have credit scores between 500 and 620, whereas Alt-A mortgages score above 620. In practice, many of the credit scoring applications included fraud in the documentation. All these were signs that mortgage providers tried to boost their sales volumes at any cost by widening the mortgage criteria. In 2006, about 20% of the newly issued US mortgages were subprime.

PANEL 6.1 SECURITATION, HOW DOES IT WORK?

Securitisation is a process in the financial markets that has existed for a quite a number of years, but which really took off in the 2000s. In fact, three well-known organisations have been practising the concept since the late 1960s in the US: the Federal National Mortgage Association (Fannie Mae), Government National Mortgage Association (Ginnie Mae) and the Federal Home Long Mortgage Corporation (Freddie Mac). These institutions were set up by the government with the objective to support home ownership by US citizens. They initially guaranteed the mortgages, but that later they could take over mortgage loans from banks and transfer the mortgages to the capital markets. In this way, banks could grant more mortgages to their clients. To begin with, only a limited range of mortgage types qualified for such a transfer, which is why the US mortgage market was transparent until the late 1990s and early 2000s.

By copying the process of Fannie Mae, Ginnie Mae and Freddie Mac, gradually more and more banks started to sell mortgages to the capital market via so-called securitisation. In itself, the process is very simple: a bank sells the mortgages to a specially set-up company (special purpose vehicle, SPV, or special purpose entity, SPE). The SPV finances itself mainly with bonds that are sold to investors. The mortgage continues to be serviced by the original bank, which receives a fee for this process. There is no impact for the client. In the US, roughly 75% of the mortgages are securitised, a number that is much lower in Europe.

Of course, the devil is in the detail. The SPV finances itself mainly with bonds and, of course, has to have some equity as well, which is kept by the originating bank. The bonds are organised in a certain hierarchy such that there are multiple tranches, with each tranche having a different risk profile for the investor. The highest tranche has a triple A rating and is relatively secure for interest and principal payments. When credit losses in the mortgage portfolio arise, they will first hit the equity of the SPV, then the lowest tranche, until – in the most extreme case – they hit the highest tranche. The highest tranches are good investments for risk-averse investors, but bear a lower yield. Lower tranches (called mezzanine tranches) are, of course, riskier, but have a higher yield. Often the originating bank keeps the capital on its own balance sheet as a signal to the market. The bonds are called mortgage-backed securities (MBSs) or collateralised mortgage obligations (CMOs), depending on the structure of the SPV. Initially, the higher tranches were roughly 70% of the SPVs balance, but later this changed as a result of the market need for higher yield.

The advantage of securitisation for the bank is simple: it frees up the balance sheet and allows the bank to grow. Securitisation allows the investor to invest specifically in a certain asset category not otherwise available in the market, such as mortgages.

Mortgages are generally long term, and many have a duration of around 30 years. The MBSs that the SPV issues can be more short term in order to generate a profitable mismatch within the SPV. Mostly they were two-years collateralised debt obligations (CDOs) or commercial paper with shorter terms. This creates a liquidity risk for the SPV, because it assumes that the short-term bonds can be easily refinanced whenever due. Under normal circumstances, that is likely to be valid but, as we will see in this chapter, it can have severe impact in non-normal circumstances.

As mentioned, securitisation started in the mortgage market. However, in the 2000s it expanded rapidly into other markets as well: banks started to securitise credit card loans, student loans, car loans, etc. The bonds in these SPVs were called CDOs.

There were even SPVs that consisted of other CDOs (CDO², or later CDO³). This caused the securitisation market to become extremely opaque. It became less and less clear which assets actually underpinned the CDOs. This holds especially for the subprime mortgages that were the basis for the CDOs causing the market to crash in 2007.

SPVs are not banks, so they do not come under banking regulations such as Basel II and Basel III (see Chapter 9). This is because there are no private depositors, just financial assets. Therefore, securitisation was also often used for so-called regulatory arbitrage.

Let me clarify this with an example. Assume that a certain bank has a mortgage portfolio of €100 million, backed up by €95 million deposits and €5 million equity. The solvency requirement of this is 4% (under Basel I, again see Chapter 9), hence €4 million. With €5 million available capital, there is a solvency requirement ratio of 125% (= 5/4*100%).

Table 6.1 Balance sheet of the bank before securitisation (€ millions)

Assets	Balance sheet bank	Liabilities
Mortgages	€100	Equity	€5
		Deposits	€95
	€100		€100

Now, assume that the bank wants to securitise 50% of the portfolio. The SPV is funded by 5% equity, 25% BBB tranche and 70% AAA tranche. In this way the solvency requirement of the bank is €2 million (4% over €50 million), with a small amount extra to cover for the equity part. However, that is negligible compared to the original solvency requirement. The SPV is funded with €2.5 million equity and €47.5 million issued bonds (= €35.0 + 12.5 million). These received funds are cash on the balance sheet of the bank, and this cash can be used for growth. Also, the solvency requirement ratio has increased up to 250% (= 5/2*100%).

Table 6.2 Balance sheet of the bank after securitisation (€ millions)

Assets	Balance sheet bank	Liabilities
Mortgages	€50	Equity	€5
Equity investment	€2.5	Deposits	€95
Cash	€47.5		
	€100		€100

Table 6.3 Balance sheet SPV (€ millions)

Assets	Balance sheet SPV		Liabilities
Mortgages	€50	Equity	€2.5
		AAA tranche	€35
		BBB tranche	€12.5
	€50		€50

Subprime and Alt-A mortgages were securitised significantly more often than 'normal' mortgages. Capital markets faced a low interest rate environment in the early 2000s, and the Federal Reserve had deliberately kept interest rates low in order to boost the economy (see Figure 6.1). For investors in search of higher yield on assets, the low interest rate forced them to look for alternatives beyond the regular bond markets. Subprime securitisations were an interesting option. Even more, this created a moral hazard for mortgage providers, because mortgage providers would not bear the higher risk of the mortgage.

Figure 6.1 shows the relation between housing prices and interest rates in the US. Interest rates are highlighted by the central banks' rates (The Fed), since this is an indicator of commercial banks' mortgage rates. Housing prices are reflected by the Case–Shiller index, an index composed by an agency that assembles sales prices of private homes per region. Figure 6.1 shows the composite US Case–Shiller index, and shows how interest rates increased in 2004 and 2005. This caused housing prices to decrease from 2006 onwards. There was a logical time delay in the decrease of the housing prices since interest rate on many mortgages were kept contractually low during the first two years using the above-mentioned teaser rates. Homeowners started becoming unable to pay their mortgage interest rates and started selling their houses. Due to normal supply and demand dynamics, housing prices decreased. Over time, the decrease in housing prices caused homeowners to default on mortgages rather than selling the house (see Figure 6.2). Whereas foreclosure rates of homes had been relatively stable between 2000 and 2005, they skyrocketed from 2006 onwards. This is how the housing prices kicked off a domino effect in subprime MBSs.

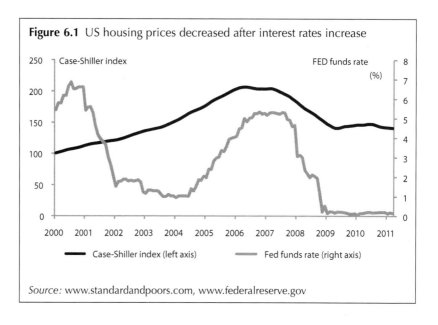

Figure 6.1 US housing prices decreased after interest rates increase

Source: www.standardandpoors.com, www.federalreserve.gov

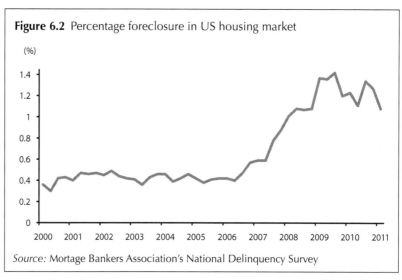

Figure 6.2 Percentage foreclosure in US housing market

Source: Mortage Bankers Association's National Delinquency Survey

The first signs of crisis were noticed in the capital markets when a number of hedge funds could no longer be sustained. Their obligations were taken onto the balance sheets of the originator because the hedge funds had problems renewing their short-term debts. The most obvious example is Bear Stearns, which had to support two hedge funds with US$3.2 billion in total, even without the contractual obligation to do so. Even though Bear Stearns finally took the hedge funds' obligation back on the balance sheet, JP Morgan had to rescue Bear Stearns by taking over the bank for a tiny price per share. The European markets were hit as well, with the first main sign being the default of the German mortgage bank IKB.

Investors started to get worried that subprime problems were in their specific MBS portfolios. Since the documentation of SPVs was not sufficiently detailed, the MBSs' originators were unable to explain to investors exactly what subprime risks were in the portfolio and what risks were not. As a result, many MBSs and related hedge funds dropped in value. As a result of these concerns, credit lines were either cut or prices increased. This was a classic example of a liquidity crunch: short-term credit was either unavailable or unaffordable.

At the same time, credit rating agencies also started to get involved. The credit ratings of SPVs (specifically MBSs) were generally high, since the risk was considered low due to the collateral in place for mortgage loans. However, in the early months of the crisis, ratings were adjusted downwards for many financial institutions, including hedge funds and SPVs. From the perspective of the rating agencies themselves, this was a logical conclusion. However, from the SPVs' perspective, this worsened the situation, because obtaining liquidity – or financing in general – grew even more difficult. At the same time, investors also faced additional problems, because the value of their investments decreased due to the downgrading activities of the rating agencies. Gradually the downgradings started to spread through the capital markets like an oil slick. All investors in bonds faced similar problems. The downgrading process was worsened by the fact that credit spreads exploded in the financial markets (see Figure 6.3). As was explained in Chapter 4, the credit spread is the additional interest rate that a bond investor wants over the risk-free interest rate as a compensation for the credit risk they run. When credit spreads increase, the value of bonds decrease. After relatively stable and low credit spreads, credit spreads multiplied by factors of between four and five during 2008. Add to that the downgrading by the rating agencies, and the reader will understand that bond portfolios decreased massively. That the widespread concerns in the capital markets also caused share prices to drop needs probably no explanation. And share prices did drop severely. Between October 2007 and November 2008, the S&P500 index lost roughly 50% in value. Other indexes dropped by a similar amount, and sometimes even worse. Central banks (such as the European Central Bank and the Federal Reserve) tried to provide liquidity to the market by lending enormous amounts of money to the financial system, but this did not seem to help.

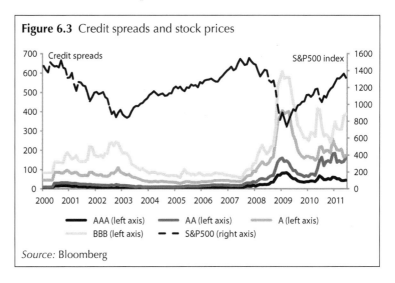

Figure 6.3 Credit spreads and stock prices

Source: Bloomberg

Practically every financial institution faced significant problems during the financial crisis. In the early phase of the crisis, three of the big five US investment banks failed (Lehman Brothers) or had to be rescued (Bear Stearns, Merrill Lynch). The three big mortgage associations (Fannie Mae, Freddie Mac, Ginnie Mae) were put into conservatorship by the US government for US$5.4 trillion. And not only the investment banks were hit: commercial banks also faced losses in their investment portfolios and had to cut their credit lines to customers. The losses faced by banks increased significantly over time, driving down stock values and hence banks' capital positions.

Banks in trouble were driven towards the minimum level of regulatory capital (Basel II, see Chapter 9). However, getting out of this situation was very difficult. On the one hand, banks could not easily de-risk their portfolios since there was hardly a market for assets. If assets could be sold at all, banks faced losses, which hit their capital levels even more. On the other hand, banks could also not increase their capital levels in order to build up more buffers. After all, capital markets hardly had appetite for new capital issues and every attempt would be placed far below par. Since this would then deteriorate the value of existing stockholders, the companies' appetite for this was understandably low. This meant that banks, and also some insurers, faced problems in their search for a solution. They were forced to rely on governments, as will be shown below.

The crisis was initially just seen as a banking issue. The bonus-driven culture within the banking industry had not helped the public image of investment bankers and CEOs. In the UK, the financial problems of Northern Rock caused the first classical bank run in the western world in the 21st Century, with lengthy queues at bank offices. In order to stabilise the economies, European finance ministers decided to enlarge their banking guarantee schemes (deposit insurance schemes), hoping that this would help create trust with customers. At the same time, finance ministers also developed new instruments to support individual banks in avoiding bankruptcy. In the US, the Troubled Asset Relief Program (TARP) was set up, which allowed the US government to buy or guarantee certain assets from banks, so they could return to good health. Qualifying assets are mainly mortgages or mortgage-related products, mostly illiquid and difficult-to-value products. In total, about US$300 billion of funds were made available. Another solution was to separate banks into healthy and bad parts, thereby isolating the bad loans and making them easier to handle. Other countries nationalised entire banks, such as Northern Rock in the UK and Fortis in the Benelux countries (although Fortis was a special case in many aspects). Other banks in the UK that received support were Bradford & Bingley, Lloyds TSB, HBOS and RBS. Commerzbank was also supported in Germany, and in the Netherlands, the government helped troubled financial institutions by buying specially issued capital against certain criteria. In Switzerland, the investment bank

UBS converted to a commercial bank in order to qualify for state support, and was rescued by the regulator for an initial amount of US$54 billion to isolate the troubled assets and rescue the healthy parts of the bank. This happened after many years of capital markets and mortgage-related investment banking activities.

All this caused problems for the real economy as well. Banks narrowed their credit criteria because they could not obtain sufficient funding, and also because the lower confidence in the economy deteriorated the creditworthiness of their client base. Non-financial companies suffered losses because of limited growth opportunities, again affecting other companies. As a consequence, companies decreased staff and limited their projects for investing in growth. This spread through the economy, with many multiple countries facing recession, higher unemployment and inflation (and even stagflation: the combination of stagnating economies and inflation). All these uncertainties created volatility for the financial markets, and had a negative impact on banks and insurance companies. During the years 2008–10, many non-financial companies faced financial difficulties, resulting in modest GDP outcomes and layoffs. The unemployment rate also increased significantly from 2007 onwards (see Figure 6.4). Within the Organsation for Economic Co-operation and Development (OECD) countries, unemployment increased by 146% between 2007 and 2008, and in the US it rose from 4.6% to 9.3%. Fortunately, not all countries were hit as hard by the crisis.

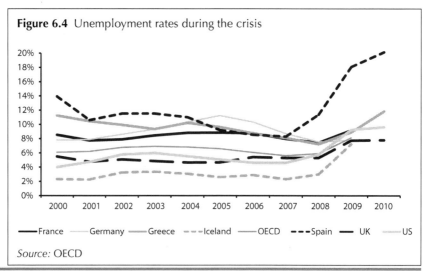

Figure 6.4 Unemployment rates during the crisis

Source: OECD

The economic crisis turned into a sovereign debt or country crisis when the concerns over creditworthiness of financial institutions and the economy as a whole spread turned into concerns over sovereign debts. During economic recessions, it is not unusual for a government to spend more money to keep the economy going. According to the Keynesian line of thought, many governments invested in all kinds of projects to revive their economies during the recession; the rescues of the various banks with financial problems also cost governments quite a lot of money. These actions had to be financed by government debt, which increased in almost all western countries. The key issue here is who finances that debt. Countries that financed the govern- ment deficit heavily with foreign funds were impacted by the hesita- tion of the capital markets to provide credit. During the first part of the 2000s, US Treasury bills were mainly bought by Chinese inves- tors. This was fortunately without major calls by the Chinese that potentially could have created a US default. Figure 6.5 shows that many countries faced a budget deficit in 2008, with Greece, Portugal, Ireland and Spain being the most remarkable cases. For these coun- tries, perception of risk in the capital markets increased significantly. During 2009 and 2010, credit spreads on some government bonds increased, especially that of Greece. Portugal, Ireland and Spain were later impacted in a similar way, earning them the sobriquet of PIGS countries (Portugal, Ireland, Greece, Spain). Italy is also a potential concern for analysts (then the abbreviation becomes PIIGS).

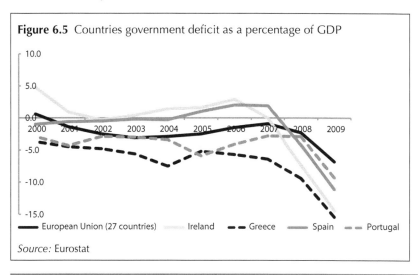

Figure 6.5 Countries government deficit as a percentage of GDP

Source: Eurostat

The credit spreads of government bonds increased, showing the capital markets' doubts about some countries' ability to repay debts and interest payments. After some months, this was also reflected in the credit ratings of the various countries. Traditionally governments are rated triple A since governments are considered to be risk-free. Table 6.4 indicates that a number of European countries have been downgraded by Standard & Poor's. Of course, this is a problem for the countries in question, and analysts suggest that the main solution could be to fundamentally restructure debt positions. Although this is similar to the situation of a company in distress, it will impact a nation and all its citizens and companies – rather than a selected number of employees and suppliers. In other words, many people have been impacted and will continue to face the consequences over the coming years.

Table 6.4 Sovereign ratings per country

Country	Long-term ratings (S&P)
Portugal	BBB–
Ireland	BBB+
Greece	CCC
Spain	AA
Germany	AAA
UK	AAA
Italy	A+
Iceland	BBB–
France	AAA
United States	AAA

The Greek government had issued government bonds in the late 20th Century to finance many social benefits. Initially, Greece benefited from the introduction of the euro, since it could borrow against relatively low interest rates. However, the financial crisis hit two important Greek industries: tourism and transport (shipping). Specially arranged financial transactions allowed the Greek government to report budget deficits within the boundaries of the EU monetary limits, while at the same time borrowing much more than actually reported. In 2009, it appeared that the budget deficit was not around the 6% mark, but actually about 12%. Despite these uncertainties around the Greek budget deficit, new government bond issues in January 2010 were subsequently oversubscribed. During Spring 2010 and 2011 however, the rating agencies downgraded the Greek government bonds to the junk status, in fear of a default of the Greek government. Despite interventions of the ECB, Greek government bonds continued to be traded with a credit spread of over 500bp compared to other government bonds (eg, Germany). In order to bail out Greece, a €100 billion loan was arranged between the Eurozone countries and the IMF. This loan was provided only after strong political concerns were expressed, especially from Germany. Conditional to this loan were strong budgetary measures by the Greek government, such as tax increases, pension cuts and wage decreases for the public sector. In Greece especially, measures were required to increase the percentage of collected tax revenues and to prevent tax evasion. Further restructuring was required when the rating agencies downgraded Greece again in 2011.

A fundamental issue is whether or not Greece restructures its government debts. Also, potentially Greek government-owned companies will need to be privatised, including a number of banks and insurers and some utility companies. As an aside, some academics remarked that Greece is in a liquidity crisis rather than a solvency crisis, since the government owns a number of valuable state companies that it could sell to free up funds. In any case, Greek government debt restructuring implies that either all investors will receive a part of the repayments, or some will get full repayment while others receive none. Another viable option is to lengthen the duration of the support, implying that Greece needs more time to restructure rather than improve liquidity. All these measures have put the Greek economy in a deep recession and are expected to keep it there for a few years to come.

Another special case of a country with financial problems is Iceland. Iceland is a relatively small country and economy, and has a population of only 300,000 and a GDP of €2.3 billion. Intending to generate more economic growth for the country, Iceland decided to privatise a number of key banks, including Kaupthing, Glitnir and Landsbanki. Since the Icelandic economy was relatively small, these banks expanded into Europe, and attracted savings from private consumers due to rates that were generally higher than regularly available in the savings market, but lower than the interbank rates that they would have paid for interbank lending. Then the central banks' interest rate in Iceland hit 18% in 2008. Jointly, the three banks had foreign deposits of around €14 billion, six times the GDP of Iceland at that time. Finally, the credit crisis hit the financial markets and the Icelandic banks, which were under relatively inexperienced financial supervision compared to the main European markets. Since the three banks had expanded into mainland Europe, European governments had to bail out the three banks' subsidiaries (IceSave was one of those often mentioned in headlines). These governments then demanded compensation from the Icelandic government. Since Iceland was unable to lend at this time, the IMF had to step in to provide a US$2.1 billion loan to Iceland, which basically hit the entire economy, because the exchange rate dropped in value – in turn, boosting the euro-denominated debt of both the public and companies. Because the Icelandic economy depends on imports, goods began to increase in price. As a result, the Icelandic economy ended up in a severe recession, which seemed to come to an end only in late 2010 after a number of severe measures such as allowing the failure of banks and a strong devaluation of the Icelandic krona.

Other countries also faced difficulties. Ireland was one of the strong economies in the eurozone during the early 2000s. The low corporate tax rate attracted many companies to settle in Ireland, creating a strong economy. Many of these companies were financial institutions. The credit crisis hit the economy hard, as the real estate bubble burst and financial institutions became impacted. Portugal and Spain faced high budget deficits as well, so the impact on the downgrades of their government bonds led the country into recession, and both countries faced property bubbles and high inflation rates. For both, fiscal changes were required to revert the situation.

AN INITIAL REFLECTION
I will now offer some preliminary conclusions on the causes of this chain of crises, despite the knowledge that scientists and policymak-

ers will continue to discuss the details over the coming decades. As we have seen, the subprime crisis turned into a liquidity crisis because investors grew reluctant to refinance SPVs/MBSs. In turn, this made banks reluctant to provide credit to the economy, lowering the general confidence in the economy. This caused an economic crisis (recessions and depressions in various countries). Government deficits were increased in order to weather the crises. After that, a sovereign crisis arose when some governments were downgraded as a risk of default. Figure 6.6 highlights this chain of events.

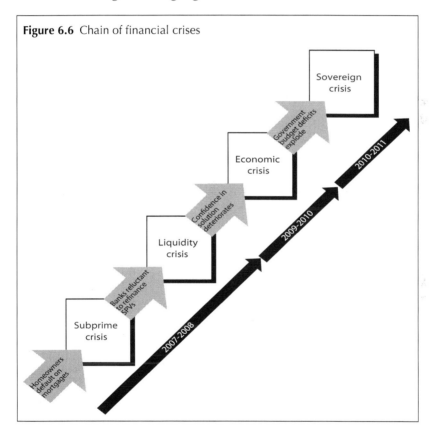

Figure 6.6 Chain of financial crises

First, the crisis was ignited by extremely complex products that investors generally did not properly understand. By the way, the notorious debacle at Barings in the early 1990s was also caused by an insufficient understanding of the complex derivatives portfolio of

Nick Leeson's Singaporean trading books. Investors in MBSs and SPVs had little specific knowledge of what products were underlying their investments, even though massive amounts of money were involved. This held especially for CDOs of CDOs (CDO^2 or CDO^3).

Underlying the boom and bust of the subprime market is the credit appetite of the US economy. In general, much of the US growth in the period 2000–07 seems to have been financed by Chinese funds. In the US, the high credit appetite caused many people to lend, even in situations when that was not realistic. For instance, individuals were used to too many credit card loans. This led to a relatively high lending ratio in the US. The US economy was stimulated by low interest rates, kept low by the Fed in order to further stimulate the economy (the so-called Greenspan put). There was a strong belief in the power of the capital markets – and the financial industry was widely deregulated. This led to the combination of large all-finance financial institutions, but also to powerful investment banks. In addition, deregulation caused a change in the function of banks. Traditionally, banks issued loans with the objective to keep them on the balance sheet. This is called the warehousing function of banks. After the wider take-up of securitisation, US banks got increasingly used to issuing loans and then selling them on the capital markets (originate and distribute function). This means that the real risk coming from private individuals is not within the bank any more, but spread throughout the capital markets. What remained within the balance sheet of the banks was a high liquidity risk.

Investors in this powerful capital market grew more and more powerful and urged companies to generate gradually higher returns. Against the background of low interest rates, financial institutions searched for alternative ways to generate higher yields. And, as we all know, there is no free lunch in the capital markets. In other words: higher yields imply higher risks. Innovative products were considered a good and relatively low-risk solution to the challenge of higher yields. The initial MBSs were indeed relatively low-risk, but the search for higher and higher returns developed into the subprime MBSs.

But then the interest rates increased, triggering the subprime crisis. The complexity of subprime products led to fear in the financial markets, spilling over into other parts of the capital markets due to the liquidity problems and the risk-aversion of investors. In this way, the subprime crisis turned into a liquidity crisis, causing banking problems and bail-outs by national governments. Remaining banks grew reluctant to lend to the real economy, and the financial markets basically came to a standstill. An economic crisis was the consequence. Again, national governments intervened to get their economies on their feet again, but that came at a cost of increased national debts. Some countries exceeded a limit of their national debt, leading to the trigger of the sovereign crisis in 2010.

WHAT WAS IMPACT ON INSURERS
The subprime crisis started in the banking industry, with its impact on mortgage loans and later on a wider range of issues. The impact for insurers has been much less debated in the media, but it has been significant. For instance, in the life industry capital levels decreased by 25% in 2008 compared with 2007. Let us now discuss six major ways in which insurers were impacted by the crisis.

First, insurers have been hit through their holding of MBSs and subprime securities. Compared to the total investment portfolio, these securities were relatively small and losses could have been absorbed relatively easy. However, we have seen that the chain of events (see Figure 6.6) has hit insurers like a brick.

Second, during the liquidity crunch stock markets went down. Insurers were not affected as much by the liquidity crunch as were the banks. After all, insurers do not create liquidity by issuing on-demand liabilities like banks do. Also, the funding of insurers is less short term compared to banks' commercial paper programmes, which need to be rolled over frequently. However, insurers were affected by the decreasing of the equity markets that accompanied the liquidity crunch. This impacted equity portfolios, which are larger in size, and hence losses were more significant. As indicated by Figure 6.3, the stock markets went down by roughly 50% in a short period of time. Many insurers faced significant losses and had to de-risk their asset portfolios. Although losses were severe in the insurance industry, generally insurers are not likely to have gone bankrupt due to this equity shock alone. In the pension industry, where equity holdings are higher than in insurance, the decrease in value of equities was much more severe. Many pension funds were kept under strong supervision by pension supervisors because they breached capital requirements. Of course, the current ageing problem only exacerbated the equity losses. For many pension funds, this was a harsh wake-up call.

Third, credit spreads widened, which caused losses in bond portfolios. The massive downgrades of bond portfolios only worsened the losses. As an illustration, let us make a simple calculation. An average AA-rated bond portfolio with a duration of five years decreased by 6.3% in value when credit spreads increased from 15bp to 140bp ($5 \times (0.15-1.40) = -6.3\%$). Now, assume that this bond portfolio was downgraded to BBB with a credit spread of 550bp. The loss in value now results in 26.8% ($5 \times (0.15-5.50) = -26.8\%$). This resulted in enormous losses. For instance, Aegon reported in a press release that the credit spread increases of Q3 2008 resulted in €2.5 billion losses of value in the bond portfolio. Write-offs of the bond portfolio were certainly more significant than just the write-offs of the subprime securities and, depending on the insurer, also higher than the equity losses. This is because bond portfolios are normally bigger than equity portfolios (see Figure 4.1).

Fourth, interest rates were generally low and central banks decreased interest rates in order to provide liquidity to the market and to revive the economy. This had a massive effect. Since most insurers have a mismatch in their portfolio, low interest rates normally result in a loss. In the life insurance industry, however, this problem got even worse due to options and guarantees. Guaranteed bonus rates in traditional life and with-profits products impacted the insurers profit significantly. The exact size of this problem is unclear, since public information is hardly available at this level of detail. However, from disclosed embedded value reports and risk reports, it is clear that insurers suffered significant losses. Generally, options and guarantees are a serious problem in traditional life portfolios. Even though they were not issued to the same extent as they once were in the late 1990s, the duration of the product is long Consequentially, the embedded options are still in place in many insurance products, and continue to cause problems.

Fifth, non-life insurers generally follow the insurance cycle. In recessions, claims are higher than during economic prosperity. This is because insurance clients face higher losses at the time that premiums are under even more commercial pressure than normally. Most countries faced a decrease in demand for insurance products, both in the life and the non-life sectors. A number of life companies also faced higher lapses during the severe economic recession because clients needed the cash value of their insurance product. This all resulted in deteriorating income streams for insurance companies.

Sixth, risk averse as insurers generally are, they traditionally invest in government bonds to match long-term liabilities. Moreover, government bonds are the only possibility to invest in assets with longer durations, since corporate bonds with long durations are scarce. In search of higher yields, insurance companies invested in the government bonds that had been downgraded as well. There are also the losses that insurers in particular countries faced. Hence, losses also arose as a consequence of the country crisis.

Almost all insurance companies faced lower profits as a result of the crisis. Figure 6.7 presents an illustration of some leading insurers in the market. It takes the year 2005 as a starting point and plots the profit developments from there. We can see that all insurance companies faced lower profitability, although not all were loss making. Also, it is interesting to see that the decrease in profits did not happen at the same time for each insurer. Apparently, some insurers managed to postpone the impact of the crisis better than others, or were impacted by other phases of the crisis.

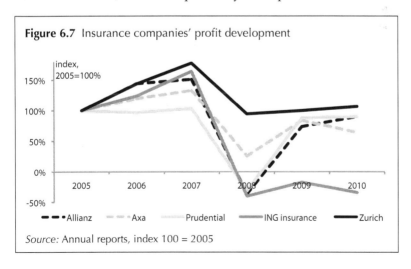

Figure 6.7 Insurance companies' profit development

Source: Annual reports, index 100 = 2005

Most insurers had already faced market value losses during the 2002–03 crisis, and had lengthened the duration of their asset portfolio to decrease the mismatch. The supply and rise of long-term bonds is clearly a result of insurers' demands to decrease the mismatch. Also, insurers had partially hedged their equity risks using options and other structured products. Initially, it seemed that this would be sufficient to weather the latest crisis. Soon, however, it became clear that this was being too optimistic. The crisis turned out to be worse than expected, even though risk models potentially had already predicted losses of this kind. For instance, one insurer commented that the losses in 2008–09 were reflected in the risk models as a 1-in-20 years' loss. In other words, existing capital on the balance sheet would be sufficient to withstand the market circumstances. Although many insurers faced difficulties, there have not been many waves of insurance failures. The insurance industry seemed to withstand the financial crisis relatively well.

It may be clear that virtually all insurers faced financial distress during the various phases of the crisis. Panel 6.2 highlights a special case, AIG. AIG played a special role during the boom of the securitisation markets; unfortunately, however, what went up, also came down. AIG also had a central role in the parliamentary debates in the US that analysed the causes and consequences of the crisis. However, AIG was not alone, as can be seen from Figure 6.7.

As a consequence of the financial crisis, insurers have started to de-risk their activities, mostly by rebalancing their asset portfolios. This is because underwriting activities can be changed less easy than investment portfolios. The de-risking process came at a time of low markets. As a result, financial losses materialised into the profit and loss (P&L) statements. The de-risking could be done in multiple ways, such as hedging equity risk with options, decreasing durations with swaps and swaptions, and simply selling assets such as corporate bonds. However, it should be noted that there were hardly liquid markets during certain periods. For instance, when the credit markets started to be concerned about the sovereign debt risk of Greece, Greek government bonds could hardly be traded. Potential buyers remained silent due to the risk of a debt restructuring, potentially resulting in concrete losses for Greek government bondholders.

In Europe, the Solvency II debate was already ongoing during start of the crisis. The debates got more intense and there is a strong belief that supervision would help to prevent future crises, or at least lessen the impact. However, the Solvency II framework is built upon the principle of supervision of a single legal entity. In the banking industry, additional focus was created to monitor the stability of the financial system as a whole. However, insurance companies are much less intertwined than banks and, as a result, the failure of one insurer is less likely to have severe impact on other insurers. The insurance industry supervisors have not set up a new entity to monitor the stability of the system, but added this item to the agenda of the existing supervisory bodies. In Europe, the European Insurance and Occupational Pensions Authority (EIOPA) have adopted this as one of the central themes, in addition to the existing Solvency II agenda. However, significant changes to the Solvency II proposals were not deemed necessary. However, the financial crisis reconfirmed the need for a strong risk-based supervisory framework. Chapter 8 will discuss Solvency II in more detail.

PANEL 6.2 CASESTUDY AIG

American International Group was founded in the early 1900s and grew into a global financial conglomerate that was active in over 130 countries. During the period 2005–08, it was one of the top-20 public-rated companies in the world. AIGs business used to be focused on traditional insurance, both life and non-life. In 1987, it set up a special unit that began trading actively on the capital markets, serving clients with a wide range of financial transactions. From 1998, the company also started selling credit insurance and credit default swaps in the capital markets to financial institutions, often SPVs. During the early 2000s, most of counterparties in these transactions were rated triple A. AIG also engaged in securities lending transactions and invested widely in securitisation transactions. In total, it was providing almost US$500 billion of credit protection to financial institutions across the globe. Roughly 15% of these credit instruments related to subprime products. AIGs subprime exposure exploded in the period 2005–07, even though they were mainly triple A-rated.

But then the subprime crisis started, and suddenly AIG found itself in severe circumstances. Due to the losses in the real estate market, the wide downgradings of the SPVs and other financial transactions, AIG was forced to report significant losses, even though traditional underwriting results were healthy at that time. The market value losses decreased

---

AIGs capital base. As a result, AIG was downgraded from AA– to A by the main rating agencies. Due to the downgrade, AIG was contractually forced to deposit more collateral with counterparties in the credit default swap agreements. However, AIG did not have adequate liquidity available at that time since liquidity markets had dried up due to the same subprime crisis. In September 2008, the Fed provided AIG with a two-year secured loan of US$85 billion in exchange for a 79.9% equity stake through preferred stock. The rate on this loan was Libor plus 850bp, with an extreme credit spread being built in. Later, additional capital of US$40 billion was made available. In total, this made the US government a 90% shareholder. AIG had effectively been nationalised, and its stock dropped to US$1.25 from a US$70 peak a year earlier (see Figure 6.8).

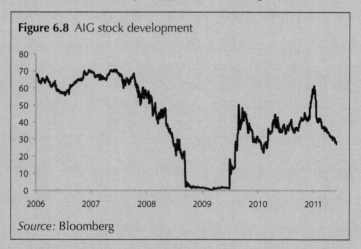

Figure 6.8 AIG stock development

Source: Bloomberg

Massive amounts of US taxpayer's money was used to keep AIG alive, which resulted in fierce political debates in the country. What made it worse is that the company had not been able to cancel expensive off-sites and business trips that were already planned. Also, millions of executive bonuses were planned for 2008. Unfortunately for AIG, this attracted a lot of attention in the media – a key operational risk needing to be managed to limit reputational damage. It was clear that AIG was rescued because it was considered to be too big to fail. In other words: letting AIG go bust would incur more costs to the taxpayer.

The loss over the year 2008 (US$99.3 billion) was classified as the largest corporate loss in history at that time. In order to be able to repay the US government's support, AIG has been selling its assets or companies since December 2008. Also, the financial portfolio is being de-risked, with counterparties being reduced by 75% and the number of transactions by almost 90%. This frees up capital and liquidity so that AIG can restore the situation.

In the early 2000s, AIG was the leading example of how to be a "new" and "modern" insurance company. However, nowadays, AIG is considered an expensive example of overly bonus-driven management. As an example, during the testimony in the US Senate, Fed chairman Ben Bernanke stated that "AIG exploited a huge gap in the regulatory system," ... and "to nobody's surprise, made irresponsible bets and took huge losses".

While the truth is always somewhere in the middle, one key lesson learnt from the AIG experience is that risk management needs to be taken seriously. It seems that top management had no fundamental understanding of the credit default swap business. For example, credit risk was inadequately captured in AIG's Value-at-Risk (VaR) calculations. At the same time, there was doubt whether adequate VaR calculations would solve the problem in itself. Management often takes the risk calculations for granted, since the underlying assumptions are considered too harsh. The general line of thought seems to be "Economic capital is a good risk measure, but such a catastrophic event will never happen in practice, will it...?" At the same time, we need to be aware that some key assumptions drive the calculations and, hence, creative minds are required to see the real risks beyond the calculations. In other words: could there be a black swan? (This refers to the great book by Nassim Taleb, *The Black Swan*, which describes how to identify unimaginable risks.)

Another lesson learnt is that liquidity risk is for real, and that it can severely harm your business model when an entire market is out of liquidity. This, of course, is simpler to identify in hindsight than in advance. However, it is obvious that the high leverage ratio of AIG depended on liquidity and, in their case, there was not only the traditional financial leverage, but also intensive credit leverage. The value of credit default swaps is extremely sensitive to small changes in credit default rates, much more so than traditional bonds. This was worsened by the fact that management seemed to not fully understand the business model of CDSs.

While recognising the importance of all corporate governance discussions that have taken place, it would be unfair to blame the entire crisis only on the simple greed of top managers. In hindsight, such conclusions could be drawn rather too quickly. It is fair to say that, in general, top managers' bonuses were significant and – during the early 2000s – stretched far beyond the imagination of ordinary citizens around the world. However, the capitalist market economy is based upon reward for performance. Top management bonuses were driven by performance, and also shareholders drove companies to increase performance. One way to increase performance was to take higher risk, eg, by increasing the company's financial leverage. Leverage was high and had increased over the last few years; at the same time, the financial industry that considered the higher leverage to be "normal", is now arguing with each other over the high leverage numbers. Chapter 11 will discuss corporate governance and bonuses in more detail.

SOME LESSONS LEARNED

With the financial markets having all but stabilised, there seems to be less turmoil than in 2008. This implies that the time might be right for addressing some of the lessons learned, while others will become clearer in years to come. Before we examine some of these lessons, it is worth mentioning risk awareness. Because of the crisis, people have become more aware of the risk of securitisations, for instance. This has made market participants risk averse. As a consequence, the same crisis is unlikely to ever re-occur. However, it is still crucial to imagine the improbable and be able to identify potential risks – and act accordingly to prevent future crises arising.

Analysts and practitioners had warned against the risks of the credit bubble, the subprime characteristics and the risk of liquidity. However, they were not really taken seriously, allowing the crisis to occur. The lesson here is that risk managers should be taken seriously within the industry. Risk management is a serious profession and has a legitimate purpose. This was not only a wake-up call for managers, but also to risk managers themselves on how to communicate their messages effectively, despite the fact that many may find the message unpleasant.

Of course, the financial markets have experienced bubbles since their inception. Crises have also happened ever since bubbles started bursting. Identifying bubbles in the market has proven key, and supervisors should take this into consideration and act accordingly in their supervisory practices. The second pillar in Solvency II (see Chapter 8) could be the appropriate way to address this. Insurers themselves could also take action on how to limit the dependence on bubbles. Scenario analysis and stress testing is a way to do this, including quantitative and model-based stress-testing (a type of scenario analysis is described at the end of Chapter 5).

Risk models are based on the efficient market hypothesis, which works on the assumption that financial market participants act rationally and that the financial markets themselves are always deep and liquid. Both assumptions were proven false by the crisis. However, it is good to use the regular economic capital outcomes based on these assumptions, as they provide us with a common language to measure risks in normal circumstances, although additional stress-testing is required to provide insight and understanding of times of crisis. Here, a calamity action plan could be a more appropriate outcome than a higher economic capital number.

Traditionally, banking supervision was focused on individual banks. The problem of the Icelandic banks shows that a wider viewpoint is required. This holds for the banking as well as insurance industry, and is of growing importance due to the increasing complexity of capital markets. Since the crisis, insurance supervisors have included financial market stability in their practices in addition to solo-level supervision in order to highlight the vulnerability of the industry to general market circumstances as a whole – and to provide insight into the joint effect of multiple companies facing the same financial distress.

In addition, insurance supervisors have become aware that some financial institutions (both banks and insurers) are too big to fail – this is an academic theme, the TBTF principle. Therefore, one key company could be a catalyst in a country, both positively and negatively. This urges boards and supervisors to consider appropriate measures to implement triggers that could limit the impact of a company crisis on the total economy. For instance, supervisors could potentially limit a company from pursuing further growth until required measures that reduce the dependency on a specific country are in place.

Liquidity risk is a real issue. Until now insurers have considered liquidity risk less important than banks; however, the crisis showed that liquidity can cause enormous problems. Although it cannot be expressed in an economic capital number, it needs specific attention by insurance companies (see Chapter 4). Despite the fact that insurers do not create liquidity as banks do, liquidity risk is significant for insurance companies, not least because market liquidity creates substantial risks when an insurance company wishes to change its asset allocation.

CONCLUSION
This chapter discussed the main developments that contributed to the financial crisis – or actually the chain of a number of crises. What started as financial problems in a relatively modest financial market evolved into one of the largest financial debacles in history, even bringing sovereigns into difficulties. Credit markets have proven to

be of key importance for insurance firms during times when insurers were in search of higher yields on their asset portfolios. Credit risks manifested themselves strongly and in an unexpected way. Although an exactly identical crisis is unlikely to re-occur, insurers should be aware of the underlying risks of asset bubbles and interconnected markets. To that end, this chapter discussed the key lessons learned so far. We can be sure that more will be said and learned about these developments, but at least risk managers can make a start implementing the most important actions.

7

Insurance Regulation and Supervision

Insurance firms in many countries were previously heavily regulated, for instance through prescribed methods to calculate premiums and technical provisions. The objective was to safeguard adequate, but not too excessive, insurance premiums. The first insurance regulations date back to the 1860s in the US, followed by the UK in 1870. Supervision basically aimed to ensure that insurers followed the rules, ie, were compliance-oriented. Gradual deregulation over time, combined with the more risk-based focus of the 1990s, has led to new regimes as will be seen in this chapter.

This chapter describes the regulatory framework that has been in force in Europe since the 1970s. This framework has become outdated for a number of reasons. This chapter will show how this has led to new approaches in countries such as the UK, Switzerland and the Netherlands. Ultimately, Solvency II will redesign the European framework for insurance supervision, as discussed in the next chapter.

HISTORICAL BACKGROUND AND THE CURRENT FRAMEWORK
As discussed in Chapter 2, the objective of insurance supervision is to safeguard the stakes of the policyholders. After all, it is more effective and efficient if one delegated, well-equipped agency monitors the behaviour and financial soundness of the insurance company.

There are basically four classes of supervisory systems. The so-called disclosure system requires companies to publish all relevant information in order for individual policyholders to assess the soundness of companies themselves. It will be seen in Chapter 8 that the Solvency II framework includes parts of this philosophy but aims mostly at the market discipline coming from investors rather than policyholders. The so-called normative system includes general requirements on how insurance companies should run their business. Within the boundaries, insurance companies are free to act as they wish. Supervision is ex post and there is no monitoring of individual products. The so-called material system includes more restrictive requirements on individual product conditions and pricing strategies. Here, supervision is more preventive and also more costly. An extreme form of material supervision is basically the state-owned insurance company, which is the last form. Traditionally, most EU member states apply a mix of normative and material supervision to insurance companies. Over time, however, the focus has shifted from material towards normative rules.

The European insurance regulations in place at the time of writing date back to the 1970s. Since then, they have been adjusted to support the objective of a single European market of the European Union, or its predecessor the European Economic Community. These updates focused in particular on the licensing procedure and the rules for providing services in multiple member states. A major milestone in European insurance regulation was the first generation of Insurance Directives. The non-life directive was adopted in 1973 and the life directive in 1979. These directives regulated the process of insurance licensing such that the requirements for a licence were consistent throughout Europe. They also set out financial requirements for technical provisions and capital, and included asset restrictions. In the context of European integration, it was important that insurance companies were allowed to open subsidiaries in all member states based on consistent licensing principles. The second-generation directives were adopted in 1988 and 1990 for non-life and life insurance, respectively. They further opened up the European market for large risks. For these risks, insurance companies were allowed to provide services throughout Europe without having a licensed subsidiary in a member state. However, certain notification requirements remained in place. The third generation directives of 1992 really paved the way for a European market by applying the single-licence principle. This principle allowed companies to operate throughout Europe with only one licence.

The third generation directives also generally described coordination between supervisors. An important step in European harmonisation is that throughout Europe all supervisors apply normative supervision, ie, that there is no ex ante requirement for insurance supervisors to approve insurance companies' product conditions and rates. As we will see below, the directives have been updated in 2002 by adjusting a number of thresholds in the calculations that assess the financial soundness of the insurance company.

In the regulatory framework, an insurance regulator or supervisor has the following tools.

❏ Licensing insurance firms: every insurance firm needs a licence in order to do business. Supervisors that provide the licence ensure that companies fulfil the necessary criteria on a permanent basis. General criteria to obtain a licence include articles of association, sufficiently sound management, minimum corporate governance arrangements, legal form of the company and adequate financial resources.

❏ Limiting business activities: a regulator could limit business activities, for instance the type of insurance contracts that a company may sell. Indeed, it is generally applied that non-life insurers are not allowed to write life insurance and vice versa.

❏ Requiring minimum financial resources: most regulations prescribe that insurers have adequate financial resources to cover future liabilities towards policyholders. This supervisory tool will be discussed in depth throughout this chapter.

❏ Day-to-day supervision and reporting: normally, insurance companies have to report the statutory accounts to the supervisor, eg, on an annual basis. These statutory accounts provide the basis for general reviews by the supervisor or even to execute on-site investigations. In addition, there is both on-site and off-site supervision in order to identify issues and potential risks.

Although the European insurance directives have been updated several times, the structure of the prudential rules has remained the same since the first generation directives. Thus, the prudential supervision aims to address the financial soundness of insurance companies, based on three components:

❏ an insurance firm should have adequate technical provisions;
❏ investments are subject to asset limits in order to avoid risk concentrations; and
❏ the equity capital is subject to a certain minimum.

The rules for technical provisions should ensure that adequate funds are available to policyholders when the liabilities are due. Traditionally, insurers have estimated the expected value of future liabilities conservatively, for example by setting prudent parameters and discount rates in the calculations. This is often different from a best estimate, which is based on expected values (ie, the statistical average of all outcomes). The legal texts of the EU regulations are stated at a relatively high level: "The home member state shall require every assurance undertaking to establish sufficient technical provisions. ... A prudent technical provision is not a best-estimate technical provision".[1] Furthermore, the directives provide general guidelines for the discount rates and other technical elements.

The general wording of the legal text means that further guidance is required to apply the rules at the national level. Over time, differences have arisen in the interpretation of the legal texts. This has resulted in differences in the methods used to determine technical provisions. For instance, discounting technical provisions in non-life insurance business is generally not applied but allowed in some countries. It is even prohibited in Germany, whereas it is allowed in the UK under certain circumstances. Also in non-life, the methods underlying the loss triangle differ throughout Europe. Both in non-life and life technical provisions, the level of prudence required is not set out clearly. This has also resulted in interpretational differences across Europe.

Traditionally, assets have been valued on a historic cost-basis (also called accrual accounting). The "real" value of assets could change over time without the cost value reflecting this change. This clearly distorts the presentation of the financial soundness of the company. It also resulted in significant problems for insurance companies during the capital market crashes in the early 2000s, when asset values declined far below their cost values. Since then, the international preference for valuing financial assets has shifted towards market value. Because the majority of insurance assets are traded on the capital markets, market values of assets are generally available. For other assets, models are used to extrapolate the value. In discussing fair value later in this chapter we will show how fair value can also be used to value the technical provisions.

In order to ensure that liabilities can also be paid to policyholders when due, assets should be invested in a conservative manner. In other words, risk concentrations and too risky assets should be avoided. Under the Solvency I regime, investment risk and, in particular, the concentration of investment portfolios is addressed by setting asset limits. There are limits that apply to the total portfolio and limits that set maximum concentrations to investments to one single counterparty (see Table 7.1).

Table 7.1 Portfolio limits

Asset category	Concentration limit (%)
Any one piece of land or building	10
Total shares and negotiable instruments of one company	5
Total unlisted shares	10
Total unsecured loans	5
Any one unsecured loan, other than to financial institutions	1
Cash	3

In addition, there is a solvency requirement for insurance firms. Rather than a proactive buffer to absorb risks, the solvency requirement has become de facto, the last resort for policyholders. After all, the focus is on the technical provisions. Risks have been addressed by setting out technical provisions in a prudent manner and also by limiting the investments. The solvency requirements are relatively straightforward and are set out as a percentage of technical provisions (for life) and premiums (for non-life). Table 6.2 sets out the minimum capital requirements. While the structure of the capital requirements dates back to the 1970s, the thresholds were adapted in 2002 in order to take into account inflation effects, etc. In addition to the capital requirements laid out in Table 7.2, insurance companies need to set up a minimum guarantee fund as a bare minimum level of capital. This is only a couple of million euros, depending on the type of insurance company. This is relevant only for very small companies, since medium-sized and larger companies all have capital requirements in excess of that.

Table 7.2 Minimum capital requirements (Solvency I)

Life insurance	Non-life insurance
The sum of:	The maximum of:
❏ 4% of technical provisions	❏ 18% of premiums under €50 million and 16% of premiums above €50 million
❏ 1% of technical provisions of unit-linked products	❏ 26% of average claims up to a limit of 35 million and 23% of average claims above that limit
❏ 0.1–0.3% of risk capital, depending on the remaining term	

The structure of the European solvency requirements dates back to the 1970s. They were partly based on the earlier findings of the Dutch Professor Campagne, who studied the probability distributions of the profit of a series of companies over time. His findings showed that life insurance companies would need an amount of capital of approximately 4% of technical provisions to be able to survive with a 95% confidence level. His analysis included the variability of investment income and mortality assumptions, Campagne presented his results in the late 1950s. This 4% formed the basis for the life directives set in the late 1970s, as will be seen later in this section. Apparently, Professor Campagne had applied the VaR measure *avant la lettre*.

This structure of capital requirements is extremely simple and they are easy to calculate. However, the simplicity also has disadvantages, even worse, the structure includes some inverse incentives. Risk-reducing measures, such as increasing non-life premiums, directly result in rising capital requirements. The same holds for adding layers of prudence in the life technical provisions.

In addition, market risks are not explicitly addressed in the capital requirements. This could provide incentives for companies to invest more in high-risk assets or even speculate with risky derivatives positions. There is a potential extra reward without a direct capital charge. Perhaps, traditionally, one could have assumed that the risk of an average investment portfolio could be covered implicitly by the crude calculations of Table 7.2. However, this is not valid for the complexity of modern investment strategies. Therefore, there is a need to incorporate the market risks in the capital requirements as well.

The capital requirements are not risk sensitive because risk-reducing effects do not result in reductions in the requirements and because certain risks are not addressed explicitly. In other words, there is no relation between the risk profile of the insurance firm and the capital requirements, even though equity capital serves as a buffer for risks.

This has resulted in companies holding much higher capital than they are strictly required to. Table 7.3 shows that insurance firms operate with capital buffers high above the minimum. However, we should be careful in drawing strong conclusions from this table about the underlying risk profile of these insurance firms and their true solvency position. After all, the principles of determining the technical provisions (ie, the implicit levels of prudence) and the risks involved in the asset portfolio are likely to differ from one company to another. Table 7.3 mainly shows that companies have historically maintained their solvency position well above the minimum requirements.

Table 7.3 Capital positions of some large European firms

		2005 (%)	2010 (%)
Aegon	The Netherlands	272	198
Ageas	Belgium	234	234
Allianz	Germany	307	173
Aviva	UK	280	160
AXA	France	216	182
Eureko	The Netherlands	259	220
ING Insurance	The Netherlands	259	250
Munich Re	Germany	326	260
Standard Life	UK	244	205
Swiss Re	Switzerland	329	>200

As a consequence of the drawbacks in the Solvency I regime, some countries have developed alternative frameworks. The most well-known alternatives, ie, ICAS, FTK and SST will be discussed in more detail later in this chapter. Other examples include the traffic-light regime in some Scandinavian countries. Australia and Canada have also updated their supervisory regulations. Table 7.4 provides an overview of "new" regimes and distinguishes static/ accounting-based regulatory models from dynamic/ cash flow-based models. The conclusion from this table is that since 2005 more and more regulators have gradually improved their frameworks towards fair value and risk models that are aligned with the economic capital models that were described in the preceding chapters. In addition to these regulatory frameworks, companies have implemented economic capital frameworks as discussed in previous chapters.

Table 7.4 Classification of solvency models

Static/accounting-based models		Dynamic/cashflow-based models	
Simple-factor-based	Risk-factor-based	Scenario-based	Principles-based
❏ Solvency I (2002 but structure 1970s) ❏ Australia (1973)	❏ NAIC (1993/1994) ❏ Basel II (for banks) ❏ ICAS (non-life and non-profit life) ❏ FKT (underwriting risks) ❏ Canada (life, P&C) ❏ Singapore (non-life, some life risks) ❏ Australia (non-life)	❏ ICAS (with profit life) ❏ SST (investment risks) ❏ FTK (investments risks) ❏ NAIC (ALM risk) ❏ Canada (segregated life funds) ❏ Australia (life) ❏ Canada (non-life liability risk)	❏ ICAS (with profits life) ❏ SST (additional scenarios, non-life)

PANEL 7.1 THE FAILURE OF EQUITABLE LIFE

Equitable Life was founded in the 18th Century as a mutual society. Since the 1950s, Equitable Life had sold annuity products with a guaranteed rate, so-called Guaranteed Annuity Options (GAO). During the 1970s, additional bonus payments were added to the contract provisions in addition to the guaranteed rates. For most of the time, the bonus payments exceeded the guaranteed rates. This was partially caused by increasing interest rates. Additionally, guaranteed rates increased as well, as a response to competitive forces and a continuous need for growth during the 1990s.

Towards the end of 1993, interest rates started to fall. At the same time, increased life expectancy caused technical provisions to rise as well. These two developments resulted in inadequacies in the technical provisions, even more because assets and liability were not properly matched. Recognising the general challenges faced by life insurance companies, the supervisor took measures for other insurance firms with similar problems. However, Equitable Life did not take sufficient action. Instead, it grew significantly by selling new policies. Ultimately, Equitable Life cut the bonus payments in order to meet the guaranteed rates. A court decision ruled that cutting bonuses was against the policyholder agreement. This caused Equitable Life problems that ultimately led to the supervisor having to close the company to new business.

This important failure created financial problems for many policyholders. Even more, it led to a debate about the role of financial supervisors within the UK and up to the European Parliament.

DETERMINING THE FAIR VALUE

Fair value, or market value or market-consistent value, is becoming more and more the standard measure by which to value financial instruments such as stocks and bonds as well as insurance liabilities (technical provisions). Traditionally, such instruments were valued at the price at which they were acquired: the historic cost value. Financial instruments are most often bought to sell again in the long run (obviously with the objective of gaining a reward). At the moment of sale of the financial instrument, the company suddenly realises a profit that has actually grown over time. By using the market value (ie, the current price that the company would realise should it sell the instrument now), the profit gradually accumulates because market values steadily increase. When an instrument is suddenly sold, there is no exorbitant profit because it has already been realised gradually over time.

Fair value is a leading principle for the valuation of financial instruments. We see this not only in supervision, but also in the accounting principles such as IAS/IFRS.[2] The International Accounting Standards Board (IASB) defines fair value as "the amount for which an asset could be exchanged or a liability be settled between knowledgeable, willing parties in an arms-length transaction". Briefly put, fair value is the price for which an instrument would be traded between well-informed parties. But, how is the fair value determined?

Most investments of insurers, such as equities and bonds, are traded on international capital markets. The fair value is almost visible because it is the most recent exchange rate on the stock-exchange listings. The fair value of stocks can even change per minute. Real-estate properties are also revalued from time to time. This produces the fair value. Other financial instruments are not frequently traded at liquid markets, but bear resemblance to instruments that are traded. In these cases, the fair value is determined by taking the traded instrument and adjusting the potential value. This is the case, for instance, with variable-rate mortgages that resemble variable-rate bonds. For again other instruments, models must be used to determine the fair value.

Insurance contracts are of the third category: they are not traded on a liquid, secondary market. Thus, models are required to determine the fair value. Most obviously, net present value techniques are used to discount the expected future cash flows (incoming and outgoing flows), taking into account the time value of money. The expected cash flows are discounted by a risk-free interest rate curve, for instance derived from swap rates (see Panel 2.3).

However, the insurance cash flows are exposed to risk and are thus uncertain. The fair value is broken down into two parts: the best estimate and the market-value margin (MVM). The best-estimate value reflects the expected value and is based on long-term average claim patterns (in non-life) and mortality rates (in life). The MVM separately takes into account that realised cash flows can differ from expectations.

Hedgeable and non-hedgeable risks should be separately addressed. Hedgeable risks can be offset by financial-market instruments such as derivatives (swaps, options, etc). Life insurance contracts in particular include guarantees that can be hedged by options. The value of the hedgeable risk is derived from the price of the hedge transaction on the financial markets. Non-hedgeable risks include underwriting risks and should be separately valued.

By determining the net present value of the contracts, one should take into account the expected value of the non-hedgeable risks. This refers to the long-term average claim rate or mortality rate. In fact, that is the result of the expected value of the future claim pattern without any prudence. The best estimate is therefore the net present value discounted by a risk-free discount rate.

However, should an insurance firm "sell" the insurance liabilities to a well-informed counterparty, then the price would most likely not equal the best-estimate value. Note that the seller pays the buyer, because it concerns a liability, ie, a future obligation to compensate policyholders. The buyer wishes to receive an amount on top of the best estimate to be compensated for the non-hedgeable risks. Assume that a buyer can choose between buying two identically priced portfolios: A and B. They have an equal best-estimate value, but portfolio A has higher risks. A rational buyer would have a preference for portfolio B unless the price of portfolio A increases.[3] The higher price reflects the compensation for the risks borne on top of the best estimate: this compensation is the MVM. The higher the risk profile, the higher the MVM.

It may seem that there are two buffers to absorb risks and in a sense that is true. Most obviously, the solvency requirement is the main buffer to absorb risks. At the same time, the fair value also includes an element that absorbs risks. While the MVM is available to absorb risks, it actually belongs to technical provisions. After all, it is likely to be transferred when liabilities are transferred as well.

At this moment, there are two methods to determine the MVM. The first method is the percentile approach, also called the quantile approach (see Figure 7.1). It was developed by the Australian supervisor. In a probability distribution, the best estimate refers to the expected value. For a symmetrical probability distribution (eg, normal distribution), this is the 50% confidence level. The total fair value is then derived at a certain probability distribution, for instance 75%. This means that the fair value is sufficient in 75% (= 50 + 25%) of the cases to cover the insurance liability. The MVM is the percentile on top of the best estimate, in our example 25%. The choice for a certain higher percentile is relatively arbitrary. In the Solvency II initial discussions multiple confidence levels were investigated, 60%, 75% and 90%.

The Australian supervisor uses a 25% MVM such that the total fair value refers to the 75th percentile. The major disadvantage of the percentile approach is that it is extremely difficult to derive the "correct" percentile. There is a possibility to analyse situations where portfolios were transferred from one insurer to another. However, in practice these portfolio transfers are not traded in a liquid, secondary market, so these prices cannot be considered to result in the fair value.

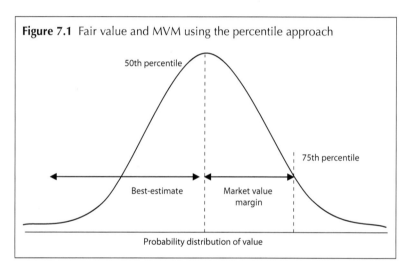

Figure 7.1 Fair value and MVM using the percentile approach

The second method for determining the MVM is the so-called cost of capital approach (CoC), which is now considered the standard method in the insurance industry. This method has been developed by the insurance industry itself and was first incorporated into a supervisory framework by Switzerland (Swiss Solvency Test, SST, see below). It has been further taken up by the insurance industry in the context of Solvency II (parties that worked on it are amongst others the European Insurance Federation CEA and the Chief Risk Officer (CRO) forum). When an insurance portfolio is transferred, the buyer will be compensated for the expected value of the cash flows, ie, the best estimate. In addition, the buyer must set a certain amount of capital aside to absorb risks, for instance the solvency requirement. This involves capital costs. The buyer wants to be compensated for this as well. This compensation for the cost of capital is the MVM.

The MVM is determined by calculating the solvency requirement and multiplying this by a certain cost of capital, eg, 6%. This refers to the cost of capital of a certain (initially unknown) buyer rather than the cost of capital of the seller. The Swiss framework sets the cost of capital at 6%. One should refine this calculation by taking into account that not only are the current requirements relevant, but also all future capital requirements. After all, insurance liabilities involve a long time horizon. Therefore, a simple methodology is developed to derive the capital requirements for all future years during the run-off of a portfolio and to determine the net present value. See Panel 7.2 for an example.

The cost of capital is a well-known parameter in various corporate-finance theories such as the capital asset pricing model (CAPM). It is assumed that the cost of equity capital comprises two elements: the risk-free interest rate and a risk margin. The risk-free rate is a compensation for the time value of money (ie, inflation effects). The interest rate that is used on the interbank swap markets can serve as a good proxy. This risk-free rate is used to discount future cash flows. The risk margin reflects the fact that market participants most often require an additional reward for risky investments. In valuing cash flows of investments, market participants use as a discount rate the sum of the risk-free rate plus the risk margin. This addresses both the time value of money and the risk effects at once. However, by discounting future cash flows of insurance liabilities, one already incorporates the time value of money separately. Therefore, the cost of capital methodology only should take into account this risk margin for the market-value margin. An example: if the risk-free rate is 5% and the total cost of capital is 11%, then the risk margin is 6%. The 5% rate should be used in the discounting process and the 6% rate should be used to determine the MVM.

At the time of writing the current accounting principles are not yet based on fair value for insurance liabilities. However, IAS39 and

IFRS4 set out the directions for future developments. We will discuss below in a separate section how IFRS4 phase II sets out a full fair value-based accounting framework for insurance companies.

PANEL 7.2 MARKET VALUE MARGIN USING THE COST OF CAPITAL APPROACH

Assume a certain portfolio for which we would like to calculate the fair value. The net present value of an insurance portfolio is €96.7 million, consisting of a series of cash flows of €20 million in the first year. The run-off is ten years and the run-off pattern is proportionally decreased over time. This portfolio has a solvency requirement of €15 million in the first year. Table 7.5 shows that the solvency requirement decreases with the insurance liabilities over time. Instead of decreasing the solvency requirement proportionally to insurance liabilities, one could also choose risk drivers such as capital at risk.

Table 7.5 Fair value and MVM using the cost of capital approach (€ millions)

Year	1	2	3	4	5
Risk-free rate	3.00%	3.00%	3.20%	3.20%	3.40%
Discount rate	0.971	0.943	0.910	0.882	0.846
Provision	€ 20.0	€ 18.0	€ 16.0	€ 14.0	€ 12.0
Run-off	100%	90%	80%	70%	60%
Present value	€ 19.4	€ 17.0	€ 14.6	€ 12.3	€ 10.2
NPV (provision)	€ 96.7 = Best estimate				
Solvency requirement	15	13.5	12	10.5	9
Run-off	1	0.9	0.8	0.7	0.6
Present value	€ 14.6	€ 12.7	€ 10.9	€ 9.3	€ 7.6
NPV (solvency)	€ 72.6				
Cost of capital	6%				
MVM	€ 4.4 = Market value margin				
Fair value	€ 101.1 = total fair value				

Table 7.5 (continued)

Year	6	7	8	9	10
Risk-free rate	3.40%	3.50%	3.50%	3.70%	3.70%
Discount rate	0.818	0.786	0.759	0.721	0.695
Provision	€ 10.0	€ 8.0	€ 6.0	€ 4.0	€ 2.0
Run-off	50%	40%	30%	20%	10%
Present value	€ 8.2	€ 6.3	€ 4.6	€ 2.9	€ 1.4
NPV (provision)					
Solvency requirement	7.5	6	4.5	3	1.5
Run-off	0.5	0.4	0.3	0.2	0.1
Present value	€ 6.1	€ 4.7	€ 3.4	€ 2.2	€ 1.0
NPV (solvency)					
Cost of capital					
MVM					
Fair value					

The net present value of the solvency requirement, using the risk-free rate, is €72.6 million. Multiplying this by 6% results in the cost of capital: €4.4 million. The total fair value is €101.1 million (= 96.7 + 4.4).

FAIR VALUE IN ACCOUNTING

The accounting framework for insurance companies in Europe is laid down in the International Financial Reporting Standards (IFRS), a body of accounting principles developed by the International Accounting Standards Board (IASB). Previously the IASB issued International Accounting Standards (IAS), but since the early 2000s these have been gradually renamed into IFRS. For insurance companies, IAS39 is also an important principle because it regulates the valuation principles for assets and financial products. In 2004, the IASB published IFRS4 "Insurance Contracts" detailing the definition of an insurance contract. However, IFRS4 was considered an interim solution until the final details on fair value of an insurance contract were clarified. In 2007, the IASB issued a preliminary view paper and in 2010 it issued an official exposure draft, open for comments from the industry. The final proposals will be published in 2011, probably to be implemented by insurance companies by 2015 – although the official implementation date is not yet fixed.

The accounting body in the US, the Financial Accounting Setting Board (FASB), worked together with the IASB in order to also incorporate a fair value measure in the US Generally Accepted Accounting Principle (US GAAP).

We will see in the remainder of this section that some differences exist between IFRS4 and Solvency II. However, both projects have taken an enormous step forward in aligning the frameworks and using fair value as the basis for the valuation of technical provisions.

Let us firstly identify the differences in objective and focus between IFRS and Solvency II. Solvency II is a supervisory framework aimed at protecting policyholders. The IFRS is a general accounting framework aimed at providing information to all economic decision-makers. This could include policyholders, but also investors. Another difference between the frameworks is that Solvency II focuses on the balance sheet, in order to maintain an adequate capital buffer for policyholder protection. IFRS, on the other hand, does not only focus on the balance sheet, but also aims to reflect the changes between reporting periods by means of a P&L statement. Revenues and expenses need also to be presented adequately and consistently. In fact, there is no P&L statement in Solvency II. It can also be said that IFRS is a transaction-based framework because it focuses on the insurance contract as a legal transaction. In Solvency II it is clear what falls under the scope, since the first part of the Solvency II Directive explicitly explains that entities with an insurance licence are within its scope. IFRS4 explains that insurance contracts are contacts that transfer a significant insurance risk, irrespective of the legal form. It may be that licensed entities do not fall under the IFRS4 definition and that IFRS4 qualifying contracts are sold by a non-licensed entity. In the calculations details, this could well result in complexities and differences. An example is a single premium unit-linked product that falls under IAS39 rather than IFRS4. However, it would fall under Solvency II if it was sold by a licensed insurer. Without going into the details of the accounting principles, the reader will understand that this could potentially create complexity.

IFRS4 Phase II will require companies to value the insurance liabilities to be based on fair value. For most of the assets, insurers already use fair value as required by IAS39. A full fair value system would at least remove the difference in valuation basis between assets and liabilities. It might however make an insurance companies' balance sheet more difficult to understand. This is similar to the challenge of Solvency II. IASB has agreed to use a prospective valuation method for insurance liabilities, to be based on the current estimate of the present value of all expected future cash flows arising from the insurance contract. However, there are at the moment still two options on how to calculate that value: the exit value and fulfilment value. The principle of exit value is the value that a company would need in order to sell an insurance liability to a third party. It could be based on three building blocks: (1) estimates of future cash flows; (2) time effect of money, or discounting; and (3) market value margin to take into account risks in the cash flows. These elements are similar to what we discussed so far in this book. The fulfilment value might take into account more company-specific elements in the determination of the market value margin. The market value margin under Solvency II is clearly prescribed including the accompanying spreadsheets of the various Quantitative Impact Studies QISs. A CoC of 6% is to be used. The market value margin in IFRS4 could potentially be higher or lower than this, having a clear impact on the value.

IFRS4 also discusses a potential service margin that might be needed to honour future policyholder liabilities in addition to bearing the insurance risk. Examples are costs incurred. This service margin does not exist in Solvency II. Also, IFRS4 aims to prevent an upfront profit at the moment that the insurance product is sold (so-called profit at inception). Accounting principles are normally based on the principle that profits are only recognised when they are really certain. At the sale of an insurance product, it is likely that a profit will be made, but not sufficiently certain (inverse production cycle). Hence, IFRS4 includes an additional margin in the technical provisions to prevent occurrence of profits at inception. Another area where potential differences might arise is for profit-sharing businesses. We will see in Chapter 8 that determining the loss-absorbing capacity of profit sharing can be difficult to calculate. The IASB has not yet reached a final agreement on profit sharing. This is especially relevant when potential future management actions could be taken into account when determining the value of profit-sharing liabilities.

Although the focus of the current section has been on the differences in the details of the calculations, we would like to emphasise that the two frameworks are aligned to a large extent. The underlying principle of both frameworks is to determine insurance liabilities based on fair value. This is an enormous step forward compared to the traditional situation where supervisory and accounting frameworks were hardly aligned, but were both very opaque. The convergence towards fair value will contribute to greater transparency in the insurance industry.

NAIC FRAMEWORK IN THE US

The National Association of Insurance Commissioners (NAIC) is the US federal advisory body of insurance regulators. It was established in the 1870s in order to arrange supervision of multi-state insurance companies. The first major step in that process was the development of uniform financial reporting by insurance companies. Gradually, it expanded its role towards other areas, such as insurance regulation in general.

During the 1980s and early 1990s, there was an increase in insurance company failures in the US. The losses were partially absorbed by guarantee schemes. Based on work done by the actuarial society, the NAIC implemented the so-called risk-based capital (RBC) requirements for life (1993) and non-life (1994) insurance companies. Because the structure of the RBC requirements was far from optimal, it was intensively questioned by the industry. The RBC framework is not as advanced as the frameworks described below (cf, ICAS, SST, FTK). However, the RBC requirements helped to identify weak insurers and thus allowed for early intervention. Most predominantly, they were an important step forward at that time.

The RBC requirements that were proposed in the 1990s were factor-based formulas, with separate factors for life, non-life and health insurance firms (Table 7.6). The RBC framework includes capital requirements for market risk, credit risk, underwriting risk and business risk. For each of the RBC classes, the risk elements are aggregated using a square-root formula. This implies full diversification between the risk types. While this might not be fully consistent with the true underlying risk profile, it is good that at least diversification is recognised. In all three classes, the affiliate investment risk is kept out of the diversification.

Table 7.6 NAIC RBC structure

Life RBC	Non-life RBC	Health RBC
C0 Affiliate investments and (non-derivative) off-balance-sheet risk	R0 Affiliate investments (non-derivative) off-balance-sheet risk	H0 Affiliate investments and (non-derivative) off-balance sheet risk
C1 Market risk (equity risk and fixed-income risk) and reinsurance credit risk	R1 Market risk (fixed-income risk)	H1 Market risk
C2 Underwriting risk	R2 Market risk (equity risk)	H2 Insurance risk
C3 Market risk (interest rate risk) and health risk	R3 Credit risk including one half reinsurance credit risk	H3 Credit risk (reinsurance, health providers, other receivables)
C4 Business risk, guarantee fund assessment and administrative expenses risk	R4 Reserve risk, including one half reinsurance credit risk, growth risk	H4 Business risk (health and administrative expenses risk, guarantee fund assessment, excessive growth)
R5 Premium risk, growth risk		

In non-life, the reserve-risk component (R4) dominates the RBC outcome for most business lines, whereas market risk (C1 and C3) is predominant for the life RBC. The initial RBC formulas were all based on simple formulas. An example of the factor-based approach is set out in Table 7.7. The market-risk RBC charge is calculated by multiplying the value by the factor set out in the table. It is based on the book value or the fair value of the assets, depending on the accounting policy. The structure of the other RBC components is similar to this. The life RBC formulas include some additional subcomponents within the categories C1 and C3 that reflect specificities of the life business. Additionally, innovations of the RBC formulas introduce scenarios for interest rate risk (C3). In the non-life RBC formula, the underwriting risk is separated between premium risk and reserve risk (R4 and R5).

In addition to the RBC formulae, there is a so-called ladder of intervention in the US system that provides an additional safety buffer for firms whose capital position is below a certain percentage of the RBC. The first action level is triggered when a company falls below 200% of the RBC. At this action level, the company needs to submit a plan to the supervisor that identifies potential additional risks and contains proposals for corrective actions that it will take.

More severe actions are triggered as a company's capital falls further, down to 70% of the RBC. This is the level where the supervisor takes control over the insurance firm. This means that the supervisor has the power to close the firm to new business and to de-risk the portfolio.

Table 7.7 NAIC market risk factors for life and non-life

NAIC market-risk factors (C1/R1)	Life (%)	Non-life (%)
US Government bonds	0.0	0.0
Cash	0.3	0.3
Bonds (AAA to A rating)	0.3	0.3
Bonds (BBB rating)	1.0	1.0
Bonds (BB rating)	4.0	2.0
Bonds (B rating)	9.0	4.5
Bonds (CCC rating)	20.0	10.0
Bonds (near default)	30.0	30.0
Residential mortgages	0.5	5.0
Commercial mortgages	3.0	5.0
Common stock	30.0	15.0
Preferred stock	2.0	2.0

ICA REGULATIONS IN THE UK

The UK insurance industry is the largest insurance market in Europe and the third largest in the world after the US and Japan and very competitive. The UK's insurance regulator is the Financial Services Authority (FSA). To improve the UK supervisory system, the FSA proposed a new framework in the early 2000s that came into force in 2005. This new framework is officially referred to as "individual capital assessment" (ICA), but "individual capital adequacy standards" (ICAS) is also used. With the ICA framework, the FSA clearly aims for more focus on fair value and a risk-based approach. This creates incentives for insurance firms to develop risk management frameworks, which should lead to better business decisions. The importance of ICA also explicitly places responsibility on the management of the company to develop a view of the capital position in relation to the risk profile of the firm. Ultimately, this should be beneficial to policyholder protection while simultaneously stimulating market efficiency.

Because the technical work required for ICA could be significant for companies, ICA is only mandatory for life companies with a significant size and for non-life companies that are regulated under the EU directives. This means that, for instance, small non-life mutuals are excluded, as are life firms with profit-sharing technical provisions below £500 million.

The ICA framework consists of two pillars (which should not be confused with the three-pillar approach in Solvency II that will be discussed in the next chapter). Pillar I contains the strict capital requirements and includes a so-called twin-peak approach where the old and new methodologies are combined. Under Pillar I, firms must hold the higher of:

❏ the Solvency I technical provisions and minimum capital requirements (statutory peak); and
❏ the so-called enhanced capital requirement (ECR) – a realistic value of the technical provisions and a kind of fair-value capital requirement (realistic peak).

Pillar II includes the ICA where insurance companies are requested to provide their own views on the capital position in relation to the risk profile of the firm. The types of risks to be included in the analysis are provided. However, no methodology or formulas are prescribed by the supervisor. The objective is to make the management consider the necessary tools and analysis required to come to an opinion on the individual capital adequacy of the firm.

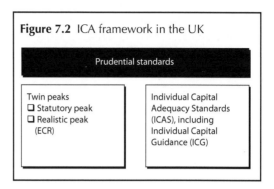

Figure 7.2 ICA framework in the UK

The Pillar I requirements for non-life business are based on the existing Solvency I rules and the enhanced capital requirement (ECR). The non-life capital requirements include market risks and non-life underwriting risks and are based on factors. For instance, they include a percentage of technical provisions and a percentage of premiums. With the exception of information on derivatives contracts, most of the information required to calculate a non-life ECR would already be available for most firms.

Pillar I is especially complex for profit-sharing life-insurance businesses. The Solvency I rules for the valuation of the technical provisions for such businesses do not separately take profit sharing into account. Therefore, the ECR for profit-sharing life businesses was considered much more complex than the traditional Solvency I approach. For instance, the realistic (fair) valuation of the profit-sharing technical provisions might not always be straightforward. The capital requirement in the realistic valuation is called risk capital margin (RCM). It is calculated by applying stress tests for market risk, credit risk and life underwriting risks (persistency or longevity risk). This requires companies to have at minimum risk-based cash flow models available with which they can test scenarios. The scenarios required to calculate the RCM are prescribed by the supervisor.

Pillar II includes the ICAS, ie, it is based on companies' own internal estimates of their risk profile and their capital adequacy. It is mandatory for all life and non-life insurance companies in the UK. It is the objective of the supervisor that companies do a self-assessment of the capital required by the firm, taking into account the risk profile. The relevant risks that should be addressed are market risk, credit risk, underwriting risk, operational risk and liquidity risk. This may include high-impact, low-frequency events and the quality of risk systems and controls that may exist. The capital calculated should be calibrated to a 99.5% for a one-year time horizon – or the equivalent for a longer time horizon.

In reviewing the material provided by the firms, the supervisor has the power to request an add-on on top of the internal estimate, this is called individual capital guidance (ICG). In most cases during the initial years, the FSA indeed applied these powers to firms and requested them to keep higher capital levels, up to 10% additional capital. A key element is that the entire capital analysis of the company is confidential and is not normally disclosed to the market. Thus the supervisor encourages companies to include all information that is necessary to make a sensible assessment of the capital position and the risks involved.

Basically, ICAS requires insurance firms to develop internal economic capital models for internal purposes. However, the complexity and granularity in the models could differ significantly from smaller to larger companies. Larger companies are likely to have built risk models and cash flow projection models as described in preceding chapters, whereas smaller firms might adopt simpler approaches. This is also clearly in the level of detail reported to the supervisor, which, according to the FSA, could vary between four-page documents and 800-page reports.

One overarching consequence is that companies in the UK have improved their risk management practices. Many companies have made efforts to value their business using market-consistent techniques. This includes the valuation of implicit options and guarantees. For some companies, the outcomes led them to cut down implicit options, whereas others started to adjust the way in which these options are incorporated in the premiums. There has also been a move away from with-profit business and an increase in unit-linked products. Parts of this shift may also have been caused by the greater transparency and flexibility of unit-linked products. It is not only ICA that has triggered these developments. The financial market crashes in the early 2000s probably helped to create awareness that options and guarantees were not "for free". The losses in the financial crisis (see Chapter 6) indicate that this effect had not fully materialised yet.

Outcomes of the ICA process indicate that, for non-life insurers, about 68% of the capital requirements is allocated to underwriting risk, whereas for life insurers this was about 26%. Market risk in life insurance amounted to 48%. One of FSAs conclusions was that life insurers have increased the level of capital since the introduction of ICA by roughly 30%. Since one of the reasons for introducing ICA was to increase resilience, the FSA considers this a positive effect of ICA.

FTK IN THE NETHERLANDS

The Dutch insurance market is quite mature and concentrated. Approximately 300 companies operate in the Dutch market, but the main market share is dominated by the top 10 firms. Non-life premiums have increased drastically, partly due to privatisation of some insurance categories.

In the Netherlands, the Dutch insurance supervisor used to be the Pension and Insurance Chamber (PVK), which merged in 2004 with its banking counterpart, De Nederlandsche Bank (DNB). Since 1994, the PVK had issued the actuarial principles for life insurance that laid out the interpretation of the European directives to determine the technical provisions. The process of updating these actuarial principles ultimately resulted in the Financial Assessment Framework (FTK) in the Netherlands. In cooperation with the industry, a number of white papers were developed until a formal consultation process started in autumn 2004. The consultative paper triggered many responses and the basic response from the industry was positive. However, a logical debate about the details started as well. At that time, it became clear that Solvency II was gaining pace. Therefore, it was decided in 2005 not to further implement the FTK into formal national law but to use the principles for the supervisory toolkit of the DNB for insurance supervision. A review of pension law had already been planned and, as a result, the FTK principles were turned into regulation for pension funds as of 2007. In addition, the Dutch Ministry of Finance also streamlined the various laws on prudential and market conduct supervision for financial institutions into one Law for Financial Supervision (WFT). However, this does not include FTK aspects of fair value and risk-based supervision.

The FTK, like ICA, relies heavily on fair value, on both the asset side and the liability side of the balance sheet. As there was no alternative to determine the fair value for insurance liabilities, the FTK prescribes the percentile approach to value technical provisions. The best estimate and the market-value margin should be determined per homogeneous risk classes. The percentile to determine the market-value margin is set at 75%. As an alternative, the FTK includes an extensive set of tables to derive the market-value margin as well. This mainly targets companies that use the standardised approach of the FTK (see below). In the tables for life insurance and pension funds, underwriting trend risk and underwriting volatility risk are separately addressed in determining the charges to derive the market-value margin. For non-life insurance, the approach is similar and distinguishes between underwriting premium risk and underwriting reserve risk.

Obviously, risk-based supervision plays an important role in the FTK as well. There are two important elements: the solvency test and the continuity analysis. The solvency test aims to derive a minimum capital requirement based on the risks that the company runs over the short term (one-year perspective). It is based on a 99.5% VaR. The continuity analysis, however, addresses a much longer time horizon and is more qualitatively oriented. Furthermore, there is not necessarily a direct relation between the outcomes of the continuity analysis and the minimum capital position.

The FTK includes three approaches to determine the solvency test: the simplified, the standardised and the internal model approaches. The simplified approach may only be used by small insurance companies that have a simple product portfolio. The standardised method should be available for all insurance companies, whereas larger firms are likely to be using the internal model approach.

In general, the solvency test requires the fair value of insurance liabilities to be adequately covered by assets and, in addition, the equity capital position is subject to minimum capital requirements (based on 99.5% VaR). In the standardised approach, capital requirements for market and credit risk are determined by scenarios, whereas the underwriting risks are addressed through factor-based approaches (see Table 7.8). Aggregation in the standardised approach takes into account full diversification between the risk components, except for interest rate and the sum of equity and real-estate risk. Here a correlation factor reflects a limited amount of diversification.

Table 7.8 Scenarios in FTK's standardised approach

Risk	Scenario[4]
Interest rate risk	Table including prescribed upward and downward shift of the interest rate curves
Inflation risk	Increase/decrease by factor 1.5
Equity risk	40% decrease, 45% for private equity and emerging markets
Real-estate risk	20% decrease of prices
Commodity risk	40% decrease of prices
Currency risk	25% drop related to euro rate
Credit risk	60% increase of credit spreads
Underwriting risks	Tables setting out risk charges

The internal model approach allows insurance firms to use internal risk models to determine the capital requirements based on a 99.5% VaR and a one-year time horizon. Pension funds are required to use a 97.5% VaR. The FTK framework does not prescribe a certain structure for the risk models. However, some guidance is provided in terms of a risk classification that is similar to the one presented in Chapter 2. In addition, there are requirements for the quality of the model (ie, it should at least produce statistically sensible projections of the firm's capital positions under various scenarios). The outcomes of the risk model should also be embedded in the management processes (ie, through reporting and monitoring of the risk profile, and clear governance policies).

As stated, the second important element in the FTK is the continuity analysis, which is based on a multiyear perspective. The minimum time horizon is three years for non-life insurers, five years for life insurers and 15 years for pension funds. It differs from the solvency test because: (1) the time horizon is longer; (2) intended management actions can be taken into account; and (3) new business may be addressed.

The objective of the FTK's continuity analysis is comparable to the FSA's ICAS requirements: to emphasise the responsibility of the board of directors (or equivalent) of the insurance company to form an opinion about the risk profile. Unlike the FSA's ICAS, the continuity analysis does not imply a clear and direct link between the outcome of the analysis and the capital position of the company. The time horizon is also different because the FTK continuity analysis refers to a multi-year perspective. However, the risk-based nature of the continuity analysis implies a focus on the available capital of the firm because capital is a buffer to absorb risks. Table 7.9 provides an overview of the elements of the continuity analysis. It is not necessary to perform continuity analysis annually, except for firms under stress conditions.

As stated, the FTK has not been incorporated into the legal basis for insurance firms. However, for pension funds the legal character of the FTK has resulted in many firms improving their understanding of the risk profiles and increasing their risk management activities. For example, many pension funds decided to decrease their mismatch profile by buying hedges on the capital markets. To a certain extent, the same is true for insurance firms that are increasingly improving their risk management processes, including risk measurement frameworks. Obviously, this is not entirely due to the FTK. Moreover, the FTK reinforces a development that was already taking place in the Netherlands.

Table 7.9 Elements of FTKs continuity analysis

Element of continuity analysis	Character	Objective
A Objectives, strategies and strategic instruments	Prospective, qualitative	Underpinning the business projections
B Economic assumptions and expectations	Prospective, quantitative	Underpinning the business projections
C Future prognoses based on own expectations (base scenario)	Prospective, quantitative	View on future developments
D Sensitivity analysis	Prospective, quantitative	View on sensitivities of outcomes for the various economic assumptions
E Stress-testing	Prospective, quantitative	Provides management actions an business outcomes under adverse circumstances
F Analysis of differences between prognoses and reality	Retrospective	Reality check of management intentions

Source: DNB

SWISS SOLVENCY TEST IN SWITZERLAND

Historically, the Swiss financial sector has been very healthy. The Swiss insurance market is a relatively small but advanced market. The Swiss insurance supervisor took up the challenge of redesigning the supervisory system in Autumn 2002, right at the time that a draft Insurance Supervision Act was submitted to the Swiss Federal Council. This led to the first proposals for the SST in 2003 and refinements followed afterwards. The SST came legally into force in 2011 after a series of tests between 2005 and 2010. Under the SST, insurers have to calculate the minimum statutory capital (comparable to Solvency I, based on traditional standards) and a target capital (based on market-consistent valuation). The target capital is compared to the so-called risk-bearing capital, which refers to the amount of capital that is available to absorb risks. In this sense, SST resembles the twins-peak approach in Pillar I of ICA.

The target capital is the market-consistent capital requirement. To determine this, the SST requires insurers to calculate the market-consistent value of the balance sheets, including the fair value of technical provisions based on the cost of capital approach. Importantly, the value of guarantees and embedded options should be valued as well. While this is easily said, the efforts to value these options can be significant due to the underlying stochastic simulations. The target capital includes two elements: a standard or internal model-based calculation based on tail-VaR[5] and a set of prescribed scenarios.

Companies can choose between using a standardised approach or an internal model to determine the first element of the target capital. Both the standardised approach and internal model are based on tail-VaR, calibrated to 99% and a one-year time horizon. Reinsurers are not allowed to use the standardised approach. The SST requires them to develop internal models that best fit the specificities and complexities of the reinsurance business. Companies' internal models must be well-designed and based on all relevant and up-to-date information. They must also be properly embedded in the risk management organisation, including validation and stress-testing.

The standardised approach comprises capital charges for market risks, life underwriting risk, non-life underwriting risk, health underwriting risk and credit risk. Operational risk is covered by a qualitative self-assessment questionnaire that is required to be filled out at least on a three-yearly basis. Other risks such as liquidity and concentration risks should be qualitatively addressed. All capital charges in the standardised approach result in a probability distribution, except for credit risk. Here, the SST follows Basel II in order to prevent banks and insurers "gaming the system". In contrast with ICA in the UK, the non-life underwriting risk module in the standardised approach is more complex than the life underwriting risk module. The non-life risk is separated into reserve risk and premium risk, as discussed in Chapter 3. For premium risk, companies have to estimate separate probability distributions for frequency and severity of the losses based on prescribed assumptions. Catastrophic losses are estimated separately from high-frequency, low-impact losses. Then, reserve risk is calculated as the volatility in the loss triangles. Finally, these two elements are aggregated by taking diversification into account. Rather than using correlation matrices to aggregate outcomes of the probability distribution, the SST uses a technique called convolution, which basically aggregates entire probability distributions.

In addition to the outcomes of the standardised approach or internal model, the SST requires companies to evaluate a series of predetermined scenarios. These include large (man-made and natural) catastrophes, pandemic events, financial market turbulence (both hypothetical and historic scenarios), severe weather events, etc. In total 10 scenarios are to be evaluated. The company must explain to the supervisor the reasoning of the extent to which each of the scenarios is relevant. In addition to prescribed scenarios, companies must evaluate company specific scenarios. The outcomes of the scenarios are aggregated to the outcomes of the standardised approach/internal models by taking diversification into account.

Finally, the company needs to provide the supervisor with a detailed risk report, including valuation methodologies and assumptions, a market-consistent presentation of the balance sheet, risk exposures, measurement and composition of the available risk-bearing capital, risk mitigation strategies, etc.

Figure 7.3 SST in Switzerland

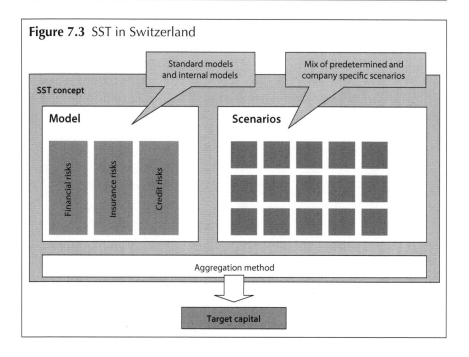

After a preliminary field test in 2005, SST has been in place transitionally since 2006, although the supervisor encouraged as many insurers to participate as possible. This indeed happened, until finally the SST entered into formal regulation in 2011. A conclusion from the SST reports has been that non-life insurers have much more excess capital over the requirements than life insurers. Generally, the impact of the first element (standard/internal model calculations) creates much higher requirements than the additional scenarios that SST prescribes. Also, the Swiss supervisor concludes that diversification is about 30% of the total capital requirement, although diversification in non-life insurance seems slightly higher than for life insurance.

All in all, the SST has encouraged companies to develop risk management models and improve risk management standards. The underlying theme of the SST is similar to that of ICA and the FTK: better measurement of the risk profile by using modern, state-of-the-art risk management techniques. The next chapter will discuss Solvency II, developing a risk-based framework for Europe.

CONCLUSIONS

Chapter 2 discussed the main reasons for insurance supervision. It is the delegated monitoring function on behalf of policyholders and economic stability. This chapter provided an overview of the European system in place at the time of writing and highlighted why this system is no longer satisfactory. Thus, a number of countries have updated their national regimes. It is extremely relevant for this book, since they served as an example for Solvency II, described in the next chapter. What they share in common is that they are based on fair value and capital requirements founded on modern quantitative techniques. Also, they allow the use of companies' internal risk models.

The frameworks of ICA, FTK and SST are not identical. The UK regime includes an internal capital assessment: an equivalent of internal economic capital outcomes. The FTK includes, in addition to a one-year view, a long-term perspective via continuity analysis. SST combines factor-based approaches with additional scenario analysis in capital assessments.

While the exact tools and methods may differ, the described frameworks share the objective of risk-based supervision based on state-of-the-art risk management and fair valuation techniques. These aspects are also incorporated in the Solvency II framework, as will be seen in the next chapter.

Finally, we have briefly touched upon the new accounting framework for insurers, IFRS4 Phase II. Although the accounting objective differs from supervision, both frameworks are based on fair value. This holds for the supervisory frameworks discussed in this chapter as well as Solvency II.

---

1   Source: EU Life Directive (Directive 2002/83/EC), November 5, 2002, art. 20.
2   IAS is International Accounting Standards, IFRS is International Financial Reporting Standards. IFRS is the new name for IAS.
3   Please note that the reference here is to selling a liability. Hence, the price increases with the risk profile. Selling an asset with higher risk would result in lowering the price.
4   For pension funds there are other scenarios.
5   The Concept of tail-VaR and how it differs from VaR is explained in Chapter 2, pages 26–29.

8

Solvency II

As discussed in the previous chapter, the Solvency I regulations do not adequately take risks into account. Furthermore, the framework contains inverse incentives for companies. As indicated, this also triggered a number of countries to develop their own frameworks, resulting in a patchwork of regulations for insurance firms throughout Europe. The Solvency II project of the European Commission aims to revise the supervisory rules to overcome these issues. Solvency II started in 2002 with the decision to implement Solvency I, which updated a number of thresholds dating back to the 1970s but kept the structure of the supervision rules basically unchanged.

SOLVENCY II – THE PROCESS AND STAKEHOLDERS

With the introduction of Solvency I, the European Parliament articulated the key principles for Solvency II such as the three-pillar structure, risk-based supervision, increasing reliance on fair value and options for companies to use standard approaches and internal models to determine the requirements. These principles will be discussed in more depth in the next section. The objective of the new Solvency II structure is to bring the supervision to an up-to-date standard. Additionally, it is viewed as an opportunity to combine a number of other insurance directives into one in order to decrease the overall number of insurance-related directives. In this so-called "recasting" exercise, the meaning of the regulations is unlikely to change, with the obvious exception of the new elements of supervision described below.

Solvency II is the first European insurance regulation whose decision making process follows the so-called Lamfalussy process. This approach to regulation prescribes the roles of various players during the design phase of the regulation. It aims to ensure that all these stakeholders are adequately covered in the various phases. The Lamfalussy process contains four levels, set out in Table 8.1.

Table 8.1 The Lamfalussy approach to Solvency II

	What is it?	What does it include?	Who develops?	Who decides?
Level 1	Solvency II Directive	Overall framework principles	European Commission	European Parliament European Council
Level 2	Implementing measures	Detailed implementation measures	European Commission	European Commission, but with consent of EIOPC and European Parliament
Level 3	Supervisory standards	Guidelines to apply in day-to-day supervision	EIOPA	EIOPA
Level 4	Evaluation	Monitoring compliance and enforcement	European Commission	European Commission

Source: CEA

The European Commission prepares a draft Solvency II Framework Directive, which is approved by both the European Parliament and the European Council in a process called "co-decision". This is called the level 1 regulation. The Directive is, however, relatively high level and it requires interpretation. This interpretation is laid out in so-called "implementing measures" (Level 2) that are decided upon with the agreement of the European Insurance and Occupational Pensions Committee (EIOPC). The EIOPC consists of representatives from the national Ministries of Finance. In addition, the European Parliament has a formal say in this decision.

National insurance supervisors are responsible for the actual execution of day-to-day supervision of the insurance companies. To that end, they will interpret the EIOPC's implementing measures in a certain way, in what is called Level 3 legislation. The interpretations are decided upon by the European Insurance and Occupational Pensions Authority (EIOPA). EIOPA was established in 2009, in response of to the financial crisis by the European Commission (see Chapter 6). Before that, the work of EIOPA was done by the Committee of European Insurance and Occupational Pensions Supervisors (CEIOPS). In practice, EIOPA replace CEIOPS, with the members being practically identical. However, EIOPA has received more powers to help withstand future potential crises. Furthermore, the organisation acts as a permanent authority in joint co-operation with its banking and securities equivalents. The fact that supervisors jointly (rather than individually) determine the interpretations and supervisory standards ensures a harmonised application of Solvency II throughout Europe.

The European Commission monitors, and ultimately enforces, compliance with the regulations in all member states of the European Union. In the Level 4 of the Lamfalussy structure, the European Commission monitors compliance of the framework throughout Europe. In order for an official directive to be approved, many legal steps have to be completed. If all the elements of Solvency II were forced to follow those steps, then updating Solvency II would prove very inefficient. Therefore, only the high-level principles are laid out in the Solvency II Framework Directive. Details are put in Level 2 and 3, and can be updated more efficiently without having to complete all these steps. The ultimate objective of this four-level structure is to ensure harmonised application of the Solvency II Framework Directive throughout Europe. The advantage of this approach is that once the directive is agreed upon, it can be updated relatively quickly for new innovations. All in all, many stakeholders are involved, let alone when the industry participants are taken into account (see Panel 8.1).

The Lamfalussy process structures the elements required for implementing the Solvency II framework. However, the parties mentioned above also have a role during the design phase of the Solvency II Framework Directive, during which the European Commission has asked CEIOPS (EIOPA) for technical advice in a number of areas through the so-called Calls for Advice in 2004 and 2005.

PANEL 8.1 KEY PLAYERS IN THE SOLVENCY II DEBATE

Solvency II is an important project for the European insurance industry and many stakeholders are involved. The European Commission is the body that drafts the regulation in the form of a Solvency II Framework Directive. This document is approved within the European Parliament and the European Council. The national Ministries of Finance are involved through the EIOPC during the phase when the European Commission prepares the texts of the Solvency II Framework Directive, and then EIOPC approves the implementing measures.

The national supervisors are brought together in the EIOPA, formerly called CEIOPS. They assist the European Commission in the design of the Solvency II Framework by providing answers to the Calls for Advice. The QISs are organised by EIOPA/CEIOPS in order to test the framework in practice during the design phase of Solvency II. After that, the supervisors are obviously the stakeholders that have a role in the operational supervision of the insurance industry. To that end CEIOPS develops supervisory standards.

The European Insurance Federation (CEA) is the European insurance and reinsurance association and hence represents the entire (re)insurance industry. Its members are the national insurance associations, whose members are insurance companies. In addition, other associations represent specific groups of insurance companies, for instance mutual insurers or certain specialised insurers.

A number of large insurance firms have come together in the Chief Financial Officer (CFO) Forum and Chief Risk Officer (CRO) Forum. Although the two forums are not identical, many of the large European insurers are represented in both the CFO Forum and the CRO Forum. The CRO Forum in particular is active in the Solvency II debate, for instance in the discussion about internal models and diversification effects. The CFO Forum is more active on the accounting principles (eg, IFRS 4). The industry players most often liaise together via the CEA and their joint influence is tangible. Mutual insurers are unified in Association of Mutual Insurers and Insurance Cooperatives in Europe (AMICE), the federation for mutual insurers.

The actuarial profession is involved through the Groupe Consultatif (Actuariel Européen), which is the overarching European body of national actuarial organisations. The global actuarial body, the International Actuarial Association (IAA), has also contributed to the Solvency II debate through its key paper, "A global framework for insurer solvency assessment", which set the direction for a number of issues such as risk classification.

The International Association of Insurance Supervisors (IAIS) is the global platform for insurance supervisors, the global equivalent of EIOPA/CEIOPS. It has members from most countries, so it has a strong global presence.

One focus of the IAIS is convergence in supervisory principles and practices. IAIS liaises for instance with the Basel Committee on Banking Supervision (see Chapter 9).

In 2004 and 2005, the European Commission launched three waves of Calls for Advice to CEIOPS. In total, there were 24 Calls for Advice. In responding to these Calls for Advice, CEIOPS consulted the industry. The consultations were, in principle, open to everyone. Initially, mainly the CEA and a few large companies responded. Over time, the participation of the industry increased, indicating that awareness had risen. The main industry body to gather industry views, opinions and preferences has been CEA, in addition to the CRO Forum. Also technical issues are discussed in-depth in these bodies. This has contributed to aligning views and building consensus in order to maximise its impact on the drafted Solvency II Directive (and the answers to the Calls for Advice that fed into the Solvency II Directive). This approach appears to have been effective, because over time many suggestions made by the industry were incorporated into the Solvency II proposals, such as the use of the cost of capital approach to determine the market value margin.

In addition to the waves of Calls for Advice, CEIOPS/EIOPA also issues separate consultation papers. The first set of separate consultative papers (CPs) was issued by CEIOPS during autumn 2006, which dealt with a number of technical aspects of the Solvency II framework. Other CPs since then have focused on a wide range of technical areas, such as internal models, risk governance, group supervision, calibration of standard formula and risk-free interest rates. The CPs mostly address Pillar I items such as valuation principles for the technical provisions based on fair value and the cost of capital approach, and the principles to determine the capital requirements. CPs triggered numerous responses from the insurance industry, which highlights its increasing awareness and involvement. In total, CEIOPS and EIOPA have issued almost 90 consultative papers (see Appendix to this chapter).

In November 2005, CEIOPS launched the first Quantitative Impact Study (QIS1). Insurers were asked to voluntarily analyse the proposals quantitatively by filling out predefined spreadsheets. QIS1 focused on the methods for determining the fair value of technical provisions, especially the percentile approach. In total, 272 insurance companies participated. The general conclusion is that QIS1 confirmed that a high level of implicit prudence is incorporated in the technical provisions based on traditional methodologies. QIS1 also highlighted that the advanced companies that participated were able to perform the required calculations. However, during the QIS1 exercise the industry and other stakeholders increasingly commented on the percentile approach for the technical provisions. An alternative was being implemented in the SST (cf Chapter 7) at that time: the cost of capital approach.

In May 2006, CEIOPS published QIS2 in which companies were asked to analyse the technical provisions and the structure of the standard approach to determine the capital requirements. In total, 514 companies participated. In addition to the percentile approach, the cost of capital approach was allowed for in the calculation of the fair value of technical provisions. The standard approach to determine the capital requirements was based on factors and also included a number of options. While the data requirements could be significant, the calculation of the capital requirements was relatively simple for most of the components as it required multiplication of certain variables with prescribed factors. However, there was much debate about the level of certain factors (ie, the calibration of the requirements). The structure of QIS2 was also criticised. The capital requirements for each risk type were calculated in separate modules, which simplified calculations, then aggregation was performed by partly allowing for diversification effects.

QIS3 was launched in April 2007. Here, the focus was on the calibration of the formulas. Again, companies were asked to fill in predefined spreadsheets in order to calculate the fair value of technical provisions and the capital requirements. In QIS3, CEIOPS adopted the cost of capital approach as the only method for the valuation of the technical provisions. Special attention was paid to companies that provided information on their internal models. That allowed supervisors to fine-tune the factors in the standard approach and compare the outcomes with those of internal models.

QIS4 was held between April and July 2008. QIS4 tested the entire

Solvency II framework, in a similar way of QIS3. For the first time, simplifications of the formulas were allowed in the spreadsheets as well as undertaking specific parameters in the standard formula for those areas where companies felt that they could better specify the parameters than the QIS4 documents. While the approach for the minimum capital requirement (MCR) was still unclear, one single MCR method based on simple factors was tested in QIS4. This was received relatively positively by the industry, although concerns remained about the level of the MCR. QIS4 also tested the impact of Solvency II on groups, with 111 groups participating. The diversification effects for groups can be significant, and increasingly significant depending on the size of the group. Also, recognition of the ability to transfer own funds between entities within the group was considered an area for further work.

QIS5 took place between September and December 2010. At the time of writing, it is foreseen that QIS5 is the last planned QIS. The participation rate of QIS5 was very high, with the participation of almost 70% of insurance companies that will fall under the Solvency II regime. The calculations of QIS5 were based on year-end 2009 financial data – that is, the year after the first impact from the financial crisis. Between 2007 and 2009, EIOPA reports that capital has decreased by roughly 17%. Consistent with expectations of Solvency II, QIS5 resulted in lower technical provisions and higher capital levels, but also higher capital requirements. Overall, the majority of the market still have capital levels over the regulatory minimum, but the excess over the minimum level is expected to decrease. QIS5 reports that there is about 12% lower excess than under the Solvency I regime. EIOPA reports that 15% of the participants would not meet the regulatory minimum of QIS5. While this can be considered relatively high, it should be noted that the formulas are not yet final and hence changes can be expected in the final Solvency II framework.

The objective of the QISs has been for the supervisors to test the framework. However, they also proved beneficial for insurance companies, which is probably also why insurers have increasingly participated in it. The advantage for an insurance company is that it could familiarise themselves with the structure and methodology well in advance of the formal deadline of Solvency II – in other words, it allowed them to test their readiness for the new regulations. It is fair to say that no European insurer was ready during the initial QISs, and even during QIS5 data issues remained to be solved. Apart from the technical issues, timing is also an important element. The initial QISs required significantly more time for most insurers than the later QISs. Therefore, insurers gained experience with the QISs and were able to speed up the process of the calculations. In addition to this, the QISs created awareness for the most important risk types that insurers face. Many insurers better understood the proportions of the total risk profile only after performing a QIS. For companies running internal an economic capital model, this probably did not produce any big news, but QISs have created a few new surprises for those companies without such models.

However, some key issues do remain, even though QIS5 was the last planned QIS organised by EIOPA. For non-life insurers, the calibration of the non-life formulas seems to be relatively high, especially when back-tested with internal model outcomes. Group diversification and recognition of the ability to transfer the groups' own funds also remain issues that require further work. All in all, the Solvency II framework is considered to be highly complex by many stakeholders in the debate, even though simplifications are allowed in some areas of the standard formula. We will discuss this in more detail for the rest of this chapter.

Table 8.2 Quantitative Impact Studies (QISs) to test Solvency II

	Timing	Participation	Main topics
QIS1	Nov–Dec 2005	312	Level of prudence in technical provisions
QIS2	May–Jul 2006	514	Practicability of modular approach for SCR, two methodologies for insurance liabilities (CoC)
QIS3	Apr–Jul 2007	1027	Entire framework
QIS4	Apr–Jul 2008	1412	Entire framework
QIS5	Sep–Dec 2010	2520	Entire framework

In Summer 2007, the European Commission presented the final Solvency II Framework Directive. Some components will be further dealt with via implementing measures or even Level 3 guidelines. The publication of the Solvency II Framework Directive formed the start of the decision-making process in the European Parliament and the European Council. The formal approval of the Solvency II Directive took place in 2010. After this formal approval, member states of the European Union need to implement Solvency II at a national level, although technically the directive itself is already legally binding for insurance companies. In parallel, insurance companies can prepare by gathering historical datasets and building the systems and risk models required to do the calculations, if they have not already done so. Moreover, time is required to prepare supervisory reports and to implement other required risk processes. In 2011, the European Commission prepared the so-called Omnibus 2 Directive[1] to amend the Solvency II Directive and to move the implementation date to January 2013. This means that from that date onwards, Solvency II will be in force for all European insurance companies. Also, the Omnibus 2 Directive arranges the formal launch of EIOPA as a replacement of CEIOPS.

Transitional measures laid out in the Omnibus 2 Directive will apply to ensure a smooth transition from the old Solvency I regime and the new Solvency II system. Under the transitional measures, some of the specific elements can be phased in over a certain period, varying between three and 10 years, depending on the exact element. This allows a gradual phase-in of Solvency II without too much disruption, in order to avoid destabilising the insurance or capital markets. Allowing transitional elements is at the discretion of the supervisors. At the same time, parallel runs should not be overly burdensome in terms of costs for insurance firms.

As indicated, the Solvency II Directive that has been adopted by the European Parliament and European Council is relatively high-level. So-called implementing measures are required to provide the technical details. EIOPA have developed a number of these implementing measures to be issued to European Commission by the end of 2011. Basically, they entail all the details of the Solvency II framework, similarly to the technical guidance of the QISs. As QIS5 was the last exercise, one would expect that the implementing measures will be broadly in line with the QIS5 guidance.

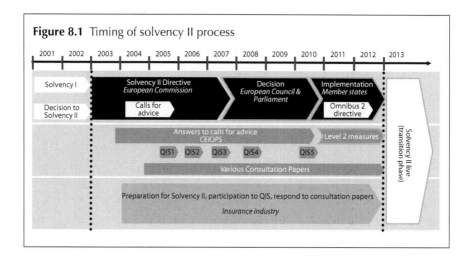

Figure 8.1 Timing of solvency II process

THE STRUCTURE OF SOLVENCY II

The Solvency II framework is based on three mutually reinforcing pillars. A similar structure was designed during the creation of Basel II, in order to amend plain capital requirements by other supervisory instruments. Basel II can be considered the equivalent of Solvency II in the banking industry. Chapter 9 will highlight Basel II (and Basel III), including the similarities and differences with Solvency II. The three pillars of Solvency II are as follows.

Pillar I: financial requirements

This lays out the valuation of the technical provisions and capital requirements. In addition, it describes the criteria for eligible capital to cover the capital requirements. As will be seen, Pillar I forms the foundation of the Solvency II framework, comprising both quantitative and qualitative elements.

Pillar II: supervisory review process

The insurance supervisor should have a complete and comprehensive overview of all risk and the risk management techniques that companies use internally. Pillar II sets out the criteria for a constructive dialogue between supervisors and the supervised companies to ensure that all material risks are adequately addressed. The underlying principle of Pillar II is that the company itself is responsible for risk management and ensuring adequate capital levels to withstand all material risks. We will see that the so-called Own Risk and Solvency Assessment (ORSA) is a key element of Pillar II.

Pillar III: disclosure and market discipline

This entails supervisory reporting as well as public disclosure. By publishing risk management information, all market participants such as investors (and potentially policyholders) could gain insight into the risk profile of an insurance company. This could act as another incentive for companies to adopt good risk management practices. The supervisory reporting allows the supervisor to form an in-depth opinion of the insurance company.

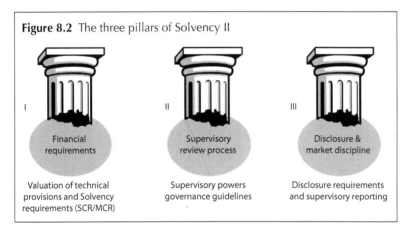

Figure 8.2 The three pillars of Solvency II

I — Financial requirements
Valuation of technical provisions and Solvency requirements (SCR/MCR)

II — Supervisory review process
Supervisory powers governance guidelines

III — Disclosure & market discipline
Disclosure requirements and supervisory reporting

In theory, if capital markets were complete and efficient, then all relevant market information would be incorporated into the risk premium of capital instruments (equity and debt capital) of the company. As a consequence, investors and other stakeholders would reward companies with a low risk profile and punish companies with higher risks. The risk management would be reflected in the credit spreads of debt capital and equity rates. The credit spread of a debt instrument is the difference between the interest rate of this instrument and the rate of comparable government bonds bearing no credit risks. Because markets are not theoretically perfect, one could question whether all market participants adequately assess all information. Additionally, there are other reasons why the credit spread could not be a perfect measure of the total risk profile of the insurance company.

Therefore, Pillar II of the Solvency II framework provides insurance supervisors with the possibility to assess the overall risk profile of a company, including all aspects of the risk profile: risk measurement, risk governance, risk management, etc. The supervisor can look behind the scenes. This ensures adequate risk management and financial stability.

Depending on the operation of this supervisory review process, Pillar I could be considered the foundation of the two other pillars. For instance, it includes minimum capital requirements as the bottom line for each insurance company. Additionally, Pillar I addresses the principles for the valuation of technical provisions and the eligible elements of capital.

Fair value is the leading principle for the technical provisions under Solvency II. The cost of capital approach is adopted. This means that companies need to assess the best-estimate value of their insurance liabilities, including the value of the hedgeable risks and the value of embedded options and guarantees. For unhedgeable risks, the cost of capital approach is used to determine the market value margin. The discount rate for calculating the fair value is the risk-free rate. In practice, EIOPA have chosen to use a swap rate to discount future cash flows. The rest of the fair value balance sheet is derived from the IFRS balance sheet that European companies will need to publish for accounting purposes. Most of the balance-sheet items can either be completely copies from the IFRS balance sheet, or will need to be adjusted using relatively simple methods.

PANEL 8.2: ILLIQUIDITY PREMIUMS

In the preceding chapters (cf Chapters 2 and 7) we have highlighted that the fair value of technical provisions is the net present value of future cash flows, discounting by a risk-free interest rate. Separately a market value margin is added to reflect the non-hedgeable risks in the cash flows. Since the financial crisis, insurers have become aware that illiquid assets and liabilities have a lower value than liquid ones. In order to reflect this in the technical provisions, a discount needed to

---

be made for illiquid liabilities. Please note that insurance liabilities are normally extremely illiquid especially when they are long-term such as life insurance liabilities.

In order to reflect this in the value of the technical provisions, it is proposed to include a illiquidity premium in the discount rate (confusingly, this is sometimes also referred to as liquidity premium, but it still refers to a higher discount rate for illiquid liabilities rather than a lower discount rate for liquid liabilities). In theory there should be a continuous change in the discount rate over the remaining lifetime of the liability. Solvency II opts for a pragmatic solution, by suggesting three alternative choices for the illiquidity premium. In each of these alternatives, the discount rate is increased by a certain factor: 0%, 50%, 75% and 100%. This increases the discount rate and hence, decreases the value of the liabilities. Normally one could say, the more risky a liability, the higher the illiquidity premium. The QIS5 technical specifications include criteria on when and how insurers are allowed to use an illiquidity premium and for which cash flows.

Both the supervisors and the industry have worked hard to determine the exact value of the illiquidity premium, like a 2010 CEIOPS report and work of the CRO Forum. It is fair to say that the Solvency II approach is a practical solution that has the buy-in of both insurers and the supervisors.

Pillar I includes two capital requirements: SCR and MCR.

Solvency Capital Requirement (SCR)
This is the target level of capital under normal circumstances. The calculation principles for the SCR are based on a VaR measure. Should available capital levels drop below the SCR, the company should at minimum deliver a restoration plan to the supervisor. This might require the supervisor to take corrective measures.

Minimum Capital Requirement (MCR)
This indicates an absolute minimum level of capital. If the available capital drops below this level, supervisors are likely to interfere forcefully. Potential actions include forced liquidation of the portfolio, run-off and closing down to new business and transfer of the portfolio to another party.

Obviously, SCR and MCR are interrelated. In normal circumstances, a company is likely to steer its business using the SCR as an important target. In stressful circumstances, the available capital drops below the SCR. The deeper the available capital is below SCR, the more urgent the situation and thus the more forcefully the supervisor is likely to act. This is called a "ladder of intervention", whereby supervisory actions are related to the urgency and severity of the financial problems. An insurer whose capital level dropped to 50% of its SCR is obviously in more serious problems than its competitor with 90% of the SCR available.

SCR

There are two ways to calculate the SCR: the standardised approach and the internal models approach. Advanced insurance companies are likely to use internal models because they already have them in place. The internal models need to be calibrated to 99.5% VaR with a one-year time horizon, although alternative calibrations are also allowed as long as they provide equivalent protection (for instance a 99% VaR with a multi-year time horizon). The risk models should at least cover the risk types addressed in Chapter 2. To ensure internal risk models have high quality standards, they should satisfy a number of basic criteria (see Table 8.3). These ensure that the models are based on appropriate methodologies, assumptions and data.

The use test (see Table 8.3) is key in this respect, since it requires companies using an internal model to really use the outcomes of the model for business decisions. If the company apparently does not trust the outcomes, why should the supervisor? This means that the model outcomes should be used in a wide variety of decision-making processes, such as investment and reinsurance strategies, pricing processes and strategy development, but also for performance evaluation (see Chapter 10).

In any case, companies that use internal models still need to provide standard model outcomes to the supervisors, including evidence that the internal model better captures the risk than the standard model.

Table 8.3 Requirements for internal models

Requirement	Comments
Statistical quality standards	Are the data and methodology of the internal model based on adequate actuarial and statistical techniques?
Calibration standards	Is the internal model consistent with a fair and unbiased 99.5% VaR measure?
Use test	Are outcomes of the internal model genuinely used within the insurance company for risk management and other decisions? Does the management of the insurance company continuously aim to improve the internal model in order for it to better reflect the risk profile?
Profit and loss attribution	Can the insurance company explain outcomes of the internal model and relate them to the profit and loss sources of business units?
Valuation standards	Is the internal model adequately internally reviewed using independent validation, taking into account various probability distributions and potential new data?
Documentation standards	Does the documentation of the internal model explain the theory, assumptions and empirical basis adequately? Does the documentation highlight potential circumstances when the model does not work effectively?

Companies that do not have internal models available will use the standardised approach. Companies that have internal models only for certain risk types or some business lines are allowed to use the partial internal models approach, in which internal models are combined with a standardised approach.

Although the standardised approach does not make reference to a certain risk measure in itself, it is calibrated to a one-year VaR with a 99.5% confidence level. This way the standardised approach targets an outcome that is assumed to be equivalent to a triple B-rated company.

In the standardised approach, the SCR contains a module for each risk type, based on factors and scenarios (see Figure 8.3). For some risk types, the sub-types are combined (eg, premium and reserve risk in non-life). For health underwriting, companies can choose whether the product portfolio better fits a non-life or a life methodology, depending on the nature of the products. In Europe, there is a wide variety of health products that differ with respect to levels of protection, duration of the protection and the support of the national government. For both approaches, capital calculations are available. In practice, allocation of products to the two sub-modules of health has not proven to be too straightforward. In each of the standard approach modules, the capital requirement is calculated by separate formulas or scenarios. For instance, the QIS5 capital requirement for equity risk is determined by a 30% decrease in global stock markets (40% of other equity markets, including emerging markets and non-listed equities, 22% for strategic participations). A separate risk module exists for intangible asset risks, relating to the item on the economic balance sheet of intangible assets. These assets are also subject to risks, ie, market risk (prices in the market) or operational risk (that could change the value of intangible assets). In the aggregation of the risks, there is no diversification effect for intangible asset risk.

The QIS5 capital requirement for non-life underwriting risk (premium and reserve risk combined) is determined by a function of the standard deviation multiplied by premium or reserves. Default standard deviations are provided by the QIS5 documentation for those companies that are unable to determine those themselves. Companies are allowed to use either the provided parameters by QIS5 or determine their own parameters, so-called undertaking specific parameters (USPs). However, before being allowed to use USPs, insurers must document why the USP would be better at capturing the risk than the provided default parameters. Over time, the risk modules in the QISs have changed – as has the extent of the shocks in the calculations. For instance, the equity risk shock in the market risk module has changed over time, until it is now 30% for global equity markets, although this was different for most of the QISs.

In many of the risk modules, insurers can make simplifications as and when necessary, such as for life catastrophe risk. Rather than running an entire scenario of mortality, insurers may also apply a simple percentage to the capital at risk in that particular life portfolio.

Figure 8.3 Modular approach of the SCR, based on QIS5

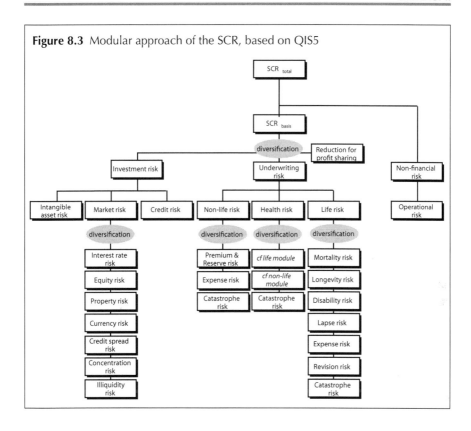

For each of the SCR modules, the basic principle is that a company must calculate the decrease in net asset value under a prescribed shock. The total SCR consists of the sum of the modules for each risk type. This takes into account diversification effects as shown in Figure 8.3. There is a separate adjustment for concentration risk in the market risk module.

In addition to capital, some liabilities have the economic ability to absorb risks. In particular, technical provisions for "with-profit businesses" include a component for expected profit sharing. Normally, the company provides these additional benefits to policyholders. In times of crisis, the company has the possibility of limiting these payments because they are discretionary. Therefore, on top of technical provisions based on a guaranteed rate, profit-sharing contracts have technical provisions with risk-absorbing characteristics. One could say that these technical provisions should not be nominated as liabilities but as available capital. However, that is incorrect, because the company expects to pay these benefits to policyholders under normal circumstances. Expected payments should be recognised in technical provisions. In extremely adverse situations, the company has the ability to use the profit-sharing element to absorb risks. However, there is a difference between conditional and unconditional profit sharing. For some products, management has historically also decided to provide profit sharing in adverse circumstances. In fact, this is unconditional profit sharing albeit in an implicit manner. Unconditional profit sharing will need to be granted irrespective of the circumstances and hence does not have the economic ability to absorb risks.

The risk-absorbing nature of future profit sharing has been the topic of intense debate. While the concept is agreed upon, it is by no means simple to translate it into methods of calculating the risk-absorbing component of technical provisions in life insurance. This is because there are many forms of profit sharing. Various approaches were tested from QIS2 onwards, and refinements have been made since. In QIS5, companies must calculate the loss in value with and without profit sharing separately. In the aggregation of most of the risk types, companies can take into account the risk-absorbing nature of profit sharing business (see Table 8.4). As a result, the total SCR decreases.

Table 8.4 Calculation methods for the SCR (QIS5)

Risk type	Sub-risk	Methodology for standard formula SCR (QIS5)
Intangible asset risk		80% of the value of this item on the economic balance sheet
Market risk	Interest rate risk	Maximum of upward and downward interest rate shocks (non-parallel)
	Equity risk	30% decrease in global equity markets, 40% in other markets
	Property risk	25% decrease in real estate value

Table 8.4 (*continued*)

	Currency risk	Maximum loss under a 25% upward and downward shock
	Credit spread risk	Market value times duration times shock factor, depending on the rating (adjusted approach for structured credits and derivatives)
	Illiquidity risk	65% decrease in illiquidity premium
	Concentration	Adjustment to address concentration in the asset portfolio
	Aggregation	Correlation matrix and taking into account risk-absorbing nature of profit sharing
Credit risk	Default risk	Different approach for rated and unrated counterparties in the underwriting process; calculation based on shocks in LGD and PD
Life risk	Mortality risk	15% increase in mortality tables
	Longevity risk	20% decrease in mortality tables
	Disability risk	35% increase in disability rates in next year, 25% thereafter; permanent 20% decrease of morbidity rates
	Lapse risk	Maximum of 50% increase and decrease of lapse rates and a mass lapse shock of 30% (retail), 70% (non-retail)

Table 8.4 (*continued*)

	Expense risk	10% increase in future expenses and annual 1% increase in inflation rates
	Revision risk	3% increase in annual annuity payments
	Catastrophe risk	0.15% increase of mortality in next year
	Aggregation	Correlation matrix and taking into account risk-absorbing nature of profit sharing
Non-life risk	Premium and reserve risk	Premium times factor plus reserves times factor, different factors per line of business
	Lapse risk	Maximum of 50% increase and decrease of lapse rates and a mass lapse shock of 30%
	Catastrophe risk	Impact of a series of prescribed scenarios
	Aggregation	Correlation matrix and taking into account risk-absorbing nature of profit sharing
Health risk		Choice of following the life or non-life calculation methods, depending on the product; some factors change in health risk module
Operational risk		Factor times premium or reserve plus 25% of expenses related to unit-linked products; operational risk charge is at least 30% of the basic SCR (diversified sum of the above)

Operational risk has not yet been fully elaborated. In the banking industry, the development of a capital requirement for operational risk has resulted in many debates, Chapter 5 indicated the background and reasons for this. Until now, the insurance industry did not put much pressure and effort in the development of operational risk measurement.

The insurance industry has put development for operational risk models on hold for the Solvency II debates. The SCR for operational risk has been based on relatively simple factors in QIS5: the maximum of two approaches. The first is a factor times premium income, while the second is a factor times technical provisions. The operational risk charge has a cap at 30% of the basic SCR (that is, SCR of all other risk types). However, we can expect similar developments to those in the banking industry concerning operational risk measurement. In banking, the difficulty of operational risk measurement has been the reason to include qualitative requirements for operational risk in the Basel II framework (see Chapter 9). Solvency II includes parts of those qualitative requirements in Pillar II via the ORSA.

In addition, operational risk is aggregated after the diversification charge. In this way, it is made clear that operational risk is different from the other risk types. After all, as was shown in Chapter 5, it is less logical for operational risk capital to be calculated using straight scenarios compared to the other risk types. Also, this representation shows that companies have generally better ways of quantifying other risk types than operational risk. At the same time, diversification effects for operational risk should not be overlooked. A simple way to resolve this is to adjust the parameters in the operational risk charge as explained above.

Business risk is even more in the infancy stage, with no capital charge at all in Solvency II, except for lapse and expense risk (see Table 8.4).

MCR

As indicated, the MCR constitutes a minimum level of capital that would trigger ultimate supervisory intervention. It is clear that insurance supervisors only take severe actions when the situation threatens the stakes of the policyholders. First of all, the MCR has an absolute floor, a minimum amount expressed in euros. This depends on the type of insurance company: €2.2 million for non-life insurers, €3.2 million for life insurers and reinsurers, except for captives – where the amount is €1 million. Next to this absolute minimum amount, the MCR is determined by a set of formulas as percentages of premium and technical provisions. In addition, it is a maximum 45% of the SCR and minimum 25% of the SCR. Although the set of formulas are relatively simple in nature, the MCR calculation still requires quite some effort. However, all elements of the MCR calculation are also requirements for the SCR calculation. Table 8.5 explains the calculation methods for the MCR.

Previously there has been an intensive debate to relate the MCR directly to the SCR. In the QIS5 framework, this is done using the 45%-25% setting the boundaries of the MCR. The advantage to link the MCR to the SCR is that the ladder of intervention can easily be linked to the SCR. A disadvantage arises when the SCR is calculated using internal models. In this way the entity-specific nature of internal models is used to trigger ultimate supervisory intervention. In some cases, legal court cases could be required to trigger supervisory intervention based upon the MCR.

Table 8.5 Calculation methods for the MCR (QIS5)

Risk	Sub-risk	Methodology for MCR
Life risk		Factor times provisions or capital at risk, per line of business
Non-life risk		Factor times premiums and provisions, per line of business
	Bounds	The MCR is between 25% and 45% of the SCR
	Absolute floor	€2.2 million for non-life and €3.2 million for reinsurance and life companies

Available capital

So far, this section has addressed the capital requirements of Pillar I. We will now discuss how these are to be covered by available capital. Solvency II will include three so-called tiers of eligible capital to reflect the differences in capital quality. These tiers depend on the permanence of the various capital instruments and their ability to absorb risks. A similar (but not completely identical) structure of three tiers exists in banking regulation. Criteria to classify capital instruments in the various tiers.

❏ Subordination: do other (re)payments rank higher in the case of wind-down?
❏ Loss-absorbency: can this capital item be used to absorb losses?
❏ Permanence: is this capital instrument callable on demand or is it permanently available to absorb losses?
❏ Perpetuality: is the instrument (long-) dated relative to the duration of obligations?
❏ Service costs: is the instrument free from mandatory charges (such as interest payments) or are there incentives to repay the sum?

Tier 1 is of the highest quality as it is permanently available to the company and is fully capable of absorbing risks. It includes mainly equity capital, retained earnings, hybrid capital instruments, some elements of subordinated capital, and members' capital (especially relevant for mutual insurers). Tier 2 capital is of lesser quality because it is less able to absorb losses than Tier 1 capital. This is because it is either not permanent or because it is subordinated debt. The fact that it is subordinated to policyholders implies that it may still be available to absorb losses. Tier 3 capital is capital that may only provide loss absorption under certain circumstances. Table 8.6 highlights the main components of eligible capital.

A special form of Tier 1 capital is expected profit in future premiums (EPIFP) that arises when an insurance contract incurs future premium payments with a profit margin that could be used to absorb future losses. In life insurance this is not unusual, but it also exists in non-life. This special Tier 1 item can only be used under certain criteria.

Table 8.6 Eligible elements of capital to cover MCR and SCR

Tier 1	Tier 2	Tier 3
Paid up capital	Other capital amounts meeting the criteria, original maturity at least five years	Deferred tax assets
Initial fund or members funds	Letters of credits or guarantees	Other capital instruments meeting the criteria, original maturity at least three years
Share premium account	Legally binding commitments from other (re)insurers	
Reserves (mainly retained earnings)	Mutual insurers' members calls	
Expected profit in future premiums (see page 191)		
Subordinated liabilities that meet the criteria, original maturity at least 10 years		
At least 50% covering SCR	Used to cover SCR	Maximum 15% covering SCR
At least 80% covering MCR	Maximum 20% covering MCR	Not eligible to cover MCR

Pillar II

Pillar II provides the supervisor with additional powers on top of the financial requirements. The supervisors ensure that they have a comprehensive overview of the risks, in addition to the "bare" measurement of the risks in Pillar I. If a supervisor considers the total risk profile to be unacceptable because some risks are not sufficiently covered in Pillar I (for instance, because they are difficult to measure), the supervisor can request the company to hold more capital. This is called a capital add-on. In order to ensure a level playing field, supervisors should use this power with care. To that end, supervisors have agreed that capital add-ons will be neither routinely nor commonly applied.

The core of Pillar II is, however, a constructive dialogue between the supervisor and the supervised company. The insurer is expected to have in place a proper risk framework, including a risk governance system and an ORSA.

The risk governance system ensures that it is clear who in the company is responsible for what decisions and what risks. Also, a number of key functions in an insurance company are clearly laid out in the Solvency II framework: internal audit, risk management, actuarial and compliance. These key functions should be clearly allocated to persons or departments within the company in order to ensure that the relevant tasks can be performed. The risk framework should be effective in the sense that it is embedded in the companies' management routines, eg, linked to decision-making processes. The risk framework should ensure that risks are properly identified, measured, monitored and reported, as well as being managed by the company.

The ORSA is the key element to undertake all this and to show it to the supervisor. Until late 2010, the requirements of the ORSA remained relatively high level, although it was considered to be the most important element of Pillar II. It seemed that the industry as well as the supervisors had no clear idea on how to address the ORSA and translate it into a number of clear deliverables. Little has been published in the sense of working papers or consultations to clarify the ORSA requirements. A Dutch working group published an ORSA paper in 2011 that has been the starting point for a Dutch ORSA pilot within the industry, jointly with the Dutch insurance supervisor, for developing an ORSA approach. It should be clear that ORSA is a process that is effectively run by the company and delivers an ORSA report to the supervisor. It is crucial that insurers have sufficient freedom to manage the risk in a way that fits with their own companies. In other words, supervisors could expect certain content, but not the exact presentation of the risk management framework. After all, the ORSA is insurers' "own" risk and solvency assessment.

Part of the ORSA report is:

❑ a description of the company and its risk profile (risk identification and measurement);
❑ the strategy of the company and its risk appetite (deriving boundaries for the risk profile);
❑ an assessment of risks in comparison to capital levels and contingencies; and
❑ forward-looking scenarios and stress tests.

Ultimately, the ORSA report contains many parts that stem from Pillar I elements, such as the outcomes of the SCR and a sensitivity analysis of the SCR to a wide range of factors. Some even say that Pillar I is the basis of the Solvency II framework, but the ORSA is the heart. The ORSA shows how risk management and capital management are related to the insurer's business strategy. Potentially, companies will be able to use information for the ORSA that already exists in other reports or documents. For example, the business strategy is normally laid out in a multi-year strategy document. Some elements of the ORSA report, such as organisation and risk governance, may even remain static over a certain period. Other elements may be more dynamic and change every year, such as the risk profile in terms of SCR and the outcomes of the forward-looking scenarios and stress tests.

Forward-looking scenarios and stress tests are an important element in the ORSA. There are various categories of scenarios. Some scenarios are more likely to be quantitative, such as analysing the potential impact of another financial crisis. Other scenarios are more qualitative, such as changing client demands. In any case, scenarios should have a qualitative narrative, explaining what the scenario is and what the analysis aims to identify. For each scenario, it is interesting to identify the trigger: what causes the scenario to happen? Also, scenario should be really forward-looking, in other words, looking beyond the current year, depending on the strategic planning horizon. Typical planning horizons are three or five years.

In all scenarios and stress tests, it is key to identify what is the impact of certain (chain of) events on capital levels, taking into account the actions that need to be taken. It is not unlikely that certain pre-defined levels of losses would ex ante trigger management intervention. Potential actions could be to cut the loss by terminating or transferring parts of the business.

Two stress tests are especially interesting. First, the worst-case scenario: what measures would need to be taken if a 99.5% event would hit the company? In other words, the current SCR is entirely absorbed. For extremely over-capitalised companies, sometimes nothing can endanger the policyholder protection. For others, there might be a cut-off point that forces the company to close itself to new business. Second, a reserve stress test: what event in the company, economy, financial market or otherwise could trigger a 99.5% event? For example, would a stock market crash linked with a natural disaster turn into a 99.5% event? Or is it more likely that policy-holder behaviour linked with general economic situations will be a 99.5% event. Irrespective of the exact outcomes, this process forces the company to think along the lines of its main weaknesses. This differs from company to company.

Finally, the ORSA will include a risk appetite statement of the company. What will this statement look like? Traditionally, insurers are likely to have an implicit view on risk appetite. However, making them explicit mostly identifies differences in opinion between important stakeholders (eg, CEO and CFO). Also, it forces the company to express the risk appetite as concretely as possible so that it can serve as a code of conduct for the business. Under Solvency II insurers are expected to have an explicit view on:

❏ the sorts of risks it would want to assume;
❏ what sort of products relate to these preferred risks;
❏ the maximum risk exposure, expressed per risk category or as a total – this could be expressed in an economic capital outcome; and
❏ the way in which risks relate to capital.

Advanced companies will use their internal economic capital models and outputs, while others may have other methods for assessing their capital adequacy. Ultimately, in Pillar II, the supervisor ensures that risk management and the risk profile of the company are continuously on the agenda of its board of directors. This explicitly emphasises the responsibility of the board of directors for risk management.

The ORSA explicitly brings together all the relevant people in risk management, ie the risk management, actuarial, financial, compliance and internal audit functions. This is important because it has traditionally not been simple to produce a comprehensive risk overview from these various functions. Of course, the core functions such as sales, underwriting and claims management will also need to be involved.

There is a clear link between ORSA and the use test of internal models. In the ORSA, insurers are expected to highlight how they use the outcome of the risk models (either standard or internal models) to determine the appropriate level of capital and other important business decisions. As indicated earlier in this chapter, this is also the key principle of the use test. Of course, the use test is officially only valid when an insurer uses an internal model. Practically, insurers without internal models can be expected to use the outcome of the standard model – for instance, for pricing, investment decisions and reinsurance strategies. A last element of the ORSA is to ensure that the decision makers within the company sufficiently understand the risk profile. This includes the outcomes of the models, but also the sensitivities of the parameters and potential weaknesses of the models.

The ladder of intervention is an important element of Pillars I and II. It explicitly outlines the options for insurance companies and supervisors in addressing circumstances where an insurer's capital position falls below certain threshold values of the SCR. A first step when a company's capital falls below the SCR is to put together a restoration plan that sets out how the company intends to reverse the situation. Companies are expected to have contingency plans in place that describe what to do in case available capital drops below the SCR. In effect, this is in anticipation of the supervisory ladder of intervention. Based on the ladder of intervention, companies will thus know in advance what can be expected should risks turn into severe losses. At present, the differences between countries are major, and not all supervisors have similar powers. Therefore, formulating Pillar II and the ladder of intervention will contribute to the harmonisation of supervisory rules, which is ultimately good for both companies and policyholders.

Pillar III

Pillar III includes two types of required reports: the reports to the supervisor (Regular Supervisory Reporting, RSR[2]) and the information to be disclosed publicly to various stakeholders (Solvency and Financial Condition report, SFCR). The SFCR will be publicly disclosed while the RSR will only be sent to the supervisor. In practice, the SFCR will be a part of the RSR. Let us first focus on the publicly disclosed report, SFCR. Solvency II increases market discipline for insurance companies. At present, insurance companies have a separate accounting system from other financial institutions. In addition, rules to determine the technical provisions differ enormously from one country to another. Clearly, this is not very transparent for market participants.

By requiring companies to publish information related to risk management, Solvency II allows outside stakeholders to make a founded assessment of the risk profile of a company. Supervisors will review the SFCR in order to ensure that the report satisfies the Solvency II requirements. There are no detailed prescriptions as yet, but it can be expected that the requirements will cover the list below. These requirements are aligned with the basic principles of IFRS, especially IFRS 7, which addresses disclosure of risk information. It can be expected that Solvency II and IFRS will be largely aligned in the area of disclosure.

The RSR and SFCR are likely to follow a similar structure, but disclosed information will logically be less detailed than information only intended for the supervisor. The required information to be reported is:

❏ business overview and performance;
❏ description of risk governance structure;
❏ valuation basis and risk measurement methodologies;
❏ risk management, including for each risk type a composition of the portfolio and the risk exposure, which might include sensitivity analysis; and
❏ capital management, capital structure in relation to internal and external requirements.

One of the key pieces of information that insurance companies already publish is the coverage ratio: the fraction of available to required capital. In practice, insurance companies hold a multiple of the required capital (cf Table 7.3). As it has already been concluded that the Solvency I requirements are insensitive to risk, this particular ratio is an inadequate reflection of the risk profile. As soon as Solvency II is implemented, the capital requirements will be based on risks and hence the coverage ratio will be a real risk measure. Also, the published economic balance sheet and capital requirements will be a better reflection of the underlying situation of the company than it currently is. Even more, outcomes of different companies will be increasingly be comparable, which increases transparency.

The Regular Supervisory Report (RSR) is an extensive report describing the insurance company's financial situation to a high level of detail. For instance, the report describes the technical provisions per product group and the SCR per risk module (see Figure 8.3). Also the economic balance sheet is to be provided in detail, as is the risk organisation and strategy. Since all this information is to be audited, everything should be well documented and verifiable, which should be done at the level of the legal entity. All this requires that systems produce the information in a clear manner and information flows can be traced back from the report to the source systems. The RSR is in principle an annual report, but parts will need to be submitted to the regulator on a quarterly basis as well.

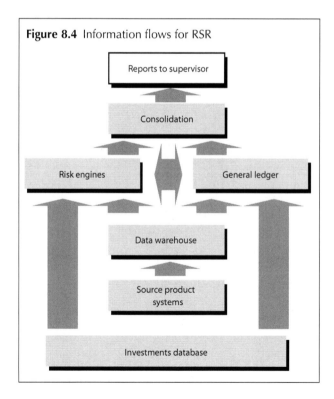

Figure 8.4 Information flows for RSR

Information required for the RSR is extracted from the source system and the investments database and fed into the general ledger system for accounting purposes and into the risk engines where the risk models are run. Most of the important information that flows into the risk engines is based on the cash flows of assets and liabilities. Also, for the asset portfolios, information on ratings and duration is required. The cash flow analysis is used to build an economic balance sheet in the general ledger, which then feeds into the risk engine. Information flows between general ledger and risk engines in both ways to prepare the required information for the consolidation the reports to the supervisor. The general ledger provides the economic balance sheet as a basis and the risk engines produce the information on the SCR and its components. Figure 8.4 provides an overview of this process.

In 2010, EIOPA shared its views on what the reports should look like and distributed over 50 reporting templates. Based on this, companies are now upgrading their systems to produce this information and the relating audit trails in such a way that this backtracking can indeed take place.

GROUP SUPERVISION

Insurance supervision has traditionally focused on the level of the legal entity; the so-called "solo level of supervision". In the past, life and non-life insurance companies were strictly separated in order to avoid the long-term nature of life insurance being affected by high-severity events in the non-life insurance business. As a result, there are still separate licensing procedures for life and non-life insurance.

Nowadays, however, companies may operate in various groups consisting of legal entities, combining life and non-life insurance and operating across borders. This has been incorporated in the European supervisory framework by designing the solo-plus regime. Group supervision exists on top of solo supervision and focuses on avoiding multiple gearing[3] and looking at specific characteristics of the group and intra-group transactions.

Companies' internal-management principles are mainly based on consolidated principles and accounts, most often organised in business units. The structure for legal entities and organisational business units is often not identical. One organisational business unit could operate through multiple legal entities and vice versa.

For instance, a large multinational such as Aegon or Axa consist of many business units and even more legal entities. Although the legal entities within an insurance company belong to one overarching group, the supervisory framework is still based on solo-level supervision. This requires companies to organise a supervisory reporting structure according to legal entities, in parallel to their internal management reporting. This problem is exacerbated for companies that operate internationally because they have to deal with multiple supervisors as well.

Moreover, risk models are most likely to be developed according to product classes and risk types rather than to the legal entity they are booked in. Furthermore, companies are starting to manage their business based on diversification effects, for example diversification between life mortality risk and non-life premium risk and the geographical diversification.

This poses challenges for regulators, supervisors and companies on how to incorporate group effects into the Solvency II framework. Completely consolidated supervision will only resolve this issue when sufficient legal safeguards are implemented that require a group to continue to support legal entities within the group even in adverse circumstances. This is especially true for internationally operating companies. At the same time, aggregated supervision requires close cooperation between the various supervisors who are responsible for supervising the legal entities within the group. In addition to this cooperation, a clear separation of responsibilities is made between supervising the technical provisions and the capital requirements. Local supervisors supervise the adequacy of the technical provisions with support from the group supervisor, whereas this is the other way around for capital requirements. Still, a solo-level entity needs to comply with the solo-level SCR at all times.

Internal model application is an interesting area where supervisors will need to co-operate. Internal models are typically applied throughout multiple entities within an insurance group. The approval of internal models requires the buy-in and understanding of all local supervisors of the group. It is not unlikely that the supervisors' viewpoints will differ during the process of internal model approval. After the implementation date of Solvency II, it will become clearer how this will be resolved.

IMPACT OF SOLVENCY II

At the time of writing, Solvency II is not yet fully known and the plans not sufficiently concrete for all consequences to be completely clear. However, one theme is certain: Solvency II will enhance risk awareness in the insurance industry, both for companies and supervisors. This will result in more efficient capital allocation, which means that capital is allocated to the areas where risks are. This is beneficial for the stability of the industry.

Because Solvency II links the solvency requirements to the risk profile, risks are likely to have a clearer price. For insurance firms, this is an incentive to manage the risk profile and actively steer their business based upon the risks. Advanced insurance companies will use the economic capital methodologies, whereas less advanced companies will use rules of thumb or other simpler methods.

Steering the business based on risks has real impact. Expensive (in terms of solvency) mismatch positions are likely to be decreased unless the rewards are significant. There is already an ongoing trend in the market to reduce mismatches by buying financial instruments. The financial crisis has resulted in de-risking strategies for virtually all insurance companies. Investment banks offer plain vanilla products or complex structures that fit the exact risk profile of the insurer. Pricing of insurance products might also be adjusted to the risk profile. Products with a high (low) risk profile might be increased (decreased). One area where Solvency II is likely to have an impact on is embedded options and guarantees: previously some of these embedded options may have been "hidden" and Solvency II will make them more visible. A trend is already ongoing for insurers to decrease the amount and level of these embedded options. Solvency II will only speed up this trend.

Some risks may be transferred by using reinsurance or alternative risk transfer (ART, see Chapter 3). These consequences can be largely without any consequences for policyholders because the measures are often taken at the portfolio level. In any case risk and reward are balanced, potentially by using RAROC and value (see Chapter 10) as a steering instrument. However, while the financial (and risk) viewpoint is an important driver for pricing decisions, it may not be the only one. There will always be strategic reasons for setting a non-optimal price and even allow single product lines to destroy economic value. While the exact consequences of Solvency II are not fully clear, it can be expected that changes will occur gradually rather than abruptly.

Solvency II will result in more model-based management processes within insurance companies. Advanced insurers are already using economic capital methodologies and Solvency II is an incentive for them to improve their models and continue along their chosen paths. This means more usage of more risk models, which have pros and cons. Models provide quantitative solutions for a problem, potentially based on clear economic reasoning. However, models will always remain a simplified version of reality. A human interpretation of the output is extremely important, especially to assess special cases. This is not to say that models are generally useless, because outcomes are always valuable. Model outcomes should, however, never be the only element that drives a decision.

Making wider use of market-consistent techniques (as Solvency II does) could pave the way for further innovations in underwriting risks. ART techniques are alternatives to reinsurance, whereby parts of the risk profile are transferred to international capital markets. Examples of ART techniques are cat bonds, weather derivatives and securitisations.[4] Until now, ART techniques have not been widely used, partly because there was no agreed method for a fair-value measure. If the insurance industry adopts the Solvency II definition of fair value, this could pave the way for ART techniques. However, other problems might still need to be resolved. For example, arbitrage has been one reason to use ART as well, but Solvency II is likely to decrease arbitrage opportunities because it better aligns supervision with the true underlying risks.

Solvency II will lead to harmonised supervisory practices in the insurance industry. This is because it will make all kinds of national interpretations and additional regulations redundant. Large international players will welcome these developments, especially as they experience the difficulties in coping with all kinds of differing supervisory regimes. Supervisory harmonisation could also lead to convergence in reporting and valuation standards, which will increase transparency within the insurance industry and enhance comparability between insurers. Investors, clients and other stakeholders will benefit from a more transparent European market. At the same time, harmonised application of supervision also paves the way for harmonised products. Hence Europe-wide product offerings will be possible for insurance companies. This provides enormous opportunities for companies to compete on a Europe-wide scale.

Most insurance markets in the various European countries are relatively concentrated: a small number of insurers have the majority of the market share. All these large parties will be using internal models to determine the capital requirements. Building and maintaining the risk models is, however, complex. Smaller insurance firms might not have the resources or technical capabilities to do so. This does not mean that their processes are of inherently less quality. However, smaller insurers with risks not fully captured in the standardised models might face a higher capital requirement, which is more expensive in terms of capital costs. Charging policyholders for this might be dangerous for long-term viability. However, not taking into account the risk in pricing strategies implies eating into their own capital, which could make them vulnerable to market shocks. Both developments are counter to the European Commission's objectives for Solvency II.

How exactly small- and medium-sized insurance companies will cope with these challenges is an important theme in the Solvency II debate. On the one hand, it cannot be true that Solvency II will drive smaller firms out of the market. On the other hand, it cannot also be true that smaller insurers provide fundamentally lower protection to policyholders than larger firms do. The same risk should imply the same capital requirements, irrespective of a firm's size or legal form. At the same time Solvency II will also allow smaller undertakings to benefit more from reinsurance as reinsurance and other risk mitigation instruments are better recognised under Solvency II. This is a commercial benefit as it decreases capital requirements and hence capital costs.

Reality is that smaller companies are normally less complex than larger ones. As a result, expenses for complying with Solvency II are lower than for large companies. At the same time, boards of smaller companies are likely to have a better overview of the key risks as a direct consequence of their simpler structure. This is a competitive advantage for smaller companies.

Procyclicality is another important theme within the financial industry. Assume that a market crisis results in an enormous shock in equity prices. The investment portfolios of all insurance companies will drop in value. Insurers with solvency problems might be forced to sell their equity portfolios in order to take their loss and reduce their risks in order to avoid further problems. The sudden supply in the equity market (without additional demand) could result in further drops in equity prices. This could cause the market to collapse entirely. In fact, the solvency requirement for equities would reinforce the economic crisis and this is undesirable in the context of financial stability. In the banking sector, this problem has been widely discussed. To resolve the issue, banks are requested to hold more capital on top of the minimum. The Solvency II structure of SCR and MCR, including the ladder of intervention for cases where the available capital drops below SCR, could resolve the risk of procyclicality for the insurance industry too.

There are, however, nuances in the above reasoning. In the Solvency I regime, without advanced capital requirements for market risk, procyclicality already exists, especially in the non-life industry. The non-life underwriting cycle refers to the effect that non-life claims are high during adverse economic times while claims are low during periods of boom. Insurance firms are used to setting premium rates by looking "through the cycle" in order to avoid procyclicality. Traditionally, firms were already used to anti-cyclical strategies.

SUMMARY AND CONCLUSIONS

This chapter discussed the revolution of Solvency II in insurance regulation. The previous chapter had already shown that the Solvency I framework has become outdated for a number of reasons. Solvency II aligns regulation with companies' internal risk management activities. It is likely that this will bring benefits for companies as well as policyholders. The central aspects of Solvency II are risk-based supervision and a focus on fair value.

While Pillar I elements of Solvency II may continue be the focus for many insurance companies, the ORSA turns out to be the part that binds all other elements together. The main outcomes of the calculations are to be included in the ORSA and assessed by the management of the insurance company. And the responsibility of risk management rests with management, which is especially emphasised in Pillar II.

Solvency II is not officially finalised and adjustments will continue to arise, coming from the regulators (European Commission, EIOPC) and the supervisors (EIOPA). However, most companies will need to speed up their implementation projects in order to be ready by 2013, even despite the transitional measures. For instance the application processes for internal models are time-consuming especially when not all source systems are fully Solvency II proof.

The Solvency II framework should be considered an enormous innovation in the insurance industry, both for companies and supervisors. For instance fair value is something that insurers were only becoming used to during the late 2000s. The same holds for risk models.

1   The Omnibus 1 Directive is used to update a number of banking legislations.
2   This is also called the Report to the Supervisor (RTS) or the Solvency Report to the Supervisor (SRS).
3   This is the use of the same capital to cover various capital requirements.
4   It is beyond the scope of this book to discuss this here in detail. The central idea is that the risk is packaged in separate, tradable pieces and then sold to investors (see Chapter 3).

APPENDIX

This appendix identifies all Consultative Papers that the joint European supervisors (in CEIOPS and EIOPS) have issued since 2004.

Table 8.A

CP 83	Draft Report on Variable Annuities	November 2010
CP 82	The methodology for equivalence assessments by CEIOPS under Solvency II	September 2010
CP 81	CEIOPS advice to the European Commission – equivalence assessment to be undertaken in relation to articles 172, 227 and 260 of the Solvency II Directive	July 2010
CP 80	CEIOPS Level 3 Guidance on Solvency II: pre-application process for internal models	January 2010

Table 8.A (*continued*)

	Call for Evidence on cross sectoral internal governance issues	
CP 79	Level 2 Advice on Simplifications for Captives	November 2009
CP 78	Level 2 Implementing Measures on Technical criteria for assessing 3rd country equivalence in relation to art. 172, 227 and 260	November 2009
CP 77	Level 2 Advice on Simplification for SCR	November 2009
CP 76	Level 2 Advice on Simplifications for Technical Provisions	November 2009
CP 75	Level 2 Advice on Undertaking Specific Parameters for SCR	November 2009
CP 74	Level 2 Advice on Correlation parameters	November 2009
CP 73	Level 2 Advice on Calibration of the MCR	November 2009
CP 72	Level 2 Advice on Calibration of the health-underwriting risk	November 2009
CP 71	Level 2 Advice on Calibration of the non-life underwriting risk	November 2009
CP 70	Level 2 Advice on Calibration of the market risk sub-module	November 2009
CP 69	Level 2 Advice on Design of the Equity risk sub-module	November 2009
CP 68	Level 2 Advice on Treatment of ring fenced Funds	November 2009
CP 67	Level 2 Advice on Treatment of Participations	November 2009
CP 66	Level 2 Advice on Group Solvency for Groups with centralised risk - management	November 2009
CP 65	Level 2 Advice on Partial Internal Models	November 2009
CP 64	Level 2 Advice on Extension of Recovery Period	November 2009
CP 63	Level 2 Advice on Repackaged loans investments	November 2009
CP 62	Level 2 Advice on Cooperation and Colleges of Supervisors	July 2009
CP 61	Level 2 Advice on Intra-group Transactions and Risk Concentration	July 2009

Table 8.A (*continued*)

CP 60	Level 2 Advice on Group Solvency Assessment	July 2009
CP 59	Level 2 Advice on Renumeration Issues	July 2009
CP 58	Level 2 Advice on Supervisory Reporting and Disclosure	July 2009
CP 57	Level 2 Advice on Capital add-on	July 2009
CP 56	Level 2 Advice on Tests and Standards for Internal Model Approval	July 2009
CP 55	Level 2 Advice on MCR calculation	July 2009
CP 54	Level 2 Advice on SCR Standard Formula - Loss Absorbing Capacity of Technical Provisions	July 2009
CP 53	Level 2 Advice on SCR Standard Formula - Operational Risk	July 2009
CP 52	Level 2 Advice on SCR Standard Formula - Reinsurance Mitigation	July 2009
CP 51	Level 2 Advice on SCR Standard Formula - Counterparty Default Risk	July 2009
CP 50	Level 2 Advice on SCR Standard Formula - Health Underwriting Risk	July 2009
CP 49	Level 2 Advice on SCR Standard Formula - Life Underwriting Risk	July 2009
CP 48	Level 2 Advice on SCR Standard Formula - Non-life Underwriting Risk	July 2009
CP 47	Level 2 Advice on SCR Standard Formula - Market Risk	July 2009
CP 46	Level 2 Advice on Own Funds - Classification and Eligibility	July 2009
CP 45	Level 2 Advice on Technical Provisions - Simplifications	July 2009
CP 44	Level 2 Advice on Technical Provisions - Counterparty Default Adjustment	July 2009
CP 43	Level 2 Advice on Technical Provisions - Standards for Data Quality	July 2009
CP 42	Level 2 Advice on Risk Margin	July 2009
CP 41	Level 2 Advice on Technical Provisions - Calculation as a whole	July 2009

Table 8.A (*continued*)

CP 40	Level 2 Advice on Technical Provisions - Risk Free Interest Rate	July 2009
CP 39	Level 2 Advice on Technical Provisions - Best Estimate	July 2009
	Review of the Financial Conglomerates Directive	May 2009
CP 38	Budapest Protocol	April 2009
CP 37	Level 2 Advice on the Procedure to be followed for the approval of an Internal Model	March 2009
CP 36	Level 2 Advice on Special Purpose Vehicles	March 2009
CP 35	Level 2 Advice on Valuation of Assets and "other Liabilities"	March 2009
CP 34	Level 2 Advice on Transparency and Accountability	March 2009
CP 33	Level 2 Advice on System of Governance	March 2009
CP 32	Level 2 Advice on Technical Provisions - Assumptions about future management actions	March 2009
CP 31	Level 2 Advice on SCR Standard Formula - Allowance of financial mitigation techniques	March 2009
CP 30	Level 2 Advice on Technical Provisions - Treatement of Future Premiums	March 2009
CP 29	Level 2 Advice on Own Funds - Criteria for supervisory approval of ancillary own funds	March 2009
CP 28	Level 2 Advice on SCR Standard Formula - Counterparty default risk	March 2009
CP 27	Level 2 Advice on Technical Provisions – Segmentation	March 2009
CP 26	Draft Level 2 Advice on Technical Provisions - Methods and statistical techniques for calculating the best estimate	March 2009
CP 25	Draft Advice on Aspects on the Framework Directive Proposal related to Insurance Groups	February 2008

Table 8.A (*continued*)

CP 24	Draft Advice on the Principle of Proportionality in the Solvency II Framework Directive Proposal	February 2008
CP 23	Final Report on Proxies	December 2007
CP 22	General Protocol on Collaboration	November 2007
CP 21	Establishment of a Mediation Mechanism between Insurance and Pensions Supervisors	July 2007
CP 20	Advice to the European Commission in the Framework of the Solvency II Project on Pillar I Issues - Further Advice	November 2006
CP 19	Advice to the European Commission in the Framework of the Solvency II Project on Safety Measures (Limits on Assets)	November 2006
CP 18	Advice to the European Commission in the Framework of the Solvency II project on Supervisory powers – further advice	November 2006
CP 17	Advice to the European Commission in the Framework of the Solvency II project on Pillar II capital add-ons for solo and group undertakings	November 2006
CP 16	Advice to the European Commission in the Framework of the Solvency II project on Pillar II issues relevant for reinsurance	November 2006
CP 15	Advice to the European Commission on Supervisory Reporting and Public Disclosure in the Framework of the Solvency II project	November 2006
CP 14	Advice on sub-group supervision, diversification effects, cooperation with third countries and issues related to the MCR and the SCR in a group context	July 2007
CP 13	Advice on insurance undertakings' Internal risk and capital requirements, supervisors' evaluation procedures and harmonised supervisors' powers and tools	July 2007
CP 12	Treatment of "Deeply Subordinated Debt"	December 2005
CP 11	Recommendation on Independence and Accountability	December 2005
CP 10	Developing CEIOPS' Medium-Work Programme	December 2005

Table 8.A (*continued*)

CP 09	Answers on the Third Wave of Calls for Advice in the Framework of the Solvency II Project	December 2005
CP 08	Insurance Mediation Protocol	June 2005
CP 07	Answers to the Second Wave of Calls for Advice in the Framework of the Solvency II Project	July 2005
CP 06	Recommendation on the Possible Need for Amendments to the Insurance Groups Directive	March 2005
CP 05	Occupational Pensions Protocol (in two rounds)	February 2005
CP 04	Answers to the First Wave of Calls for Advice in the Framework of the Solvency II Project	February 2005
CP 03	Implications of IAS/IFRS Introduction for the Prudential Supervision of Insurance Undertakings	November 2004
CP 02	Guidelines for Co-ordination Committees	March 2004
CP 01	Public Statement of Consultation Practices	July 2004

9

Banking Supervision: Basel I, II and III

This chapter will discuss banking supervision, as well as evaluating the differences and similarities between banking and insurance supervision. Banks and insurance firms jointly comprise the financial industry. Banking regulation is relevant background for the Solvency II debate, because much of the Solvency II framework is built upon experiences in the banking industry. After describing the historic origins of Basel II, this chapter will elaborate further upon its technical specifications, before examining the impact of Basel II on the banking industry and the economic system. The financial crisis (as described in Chapter 6) led to revisions of the banking supervisory framework and was amended by Basel III. At the time of writing, Basel III is not yet in place, but the lines of thought are clear. Finally, the chapter will compare the banking and insurance supervision frameworks.

BACKGROUND OF BANKING RISKS

First, let us look at the characteristics of a typical bank in order to better understand the historical background of banking. Banks typically issue long-term assets, such as mortgages and corporate loans. Their liabilities are short term, such as retail savings (the client can call these savings on demand) and six-months commercial paper obtained from the capital markets. Investment banking includes active trading on the capital markets and underwriting support for wholesale clients issuing capital markets instruments, including stocks and bonds. During the early 2000s, investment banks also focused on structuring activities: securitisations and other alternative assets. The activities of investment banks require a certain scale so that they can absorb temporary trading losses and underwriting capacity. The main risks in banking are traditionally credit risk deriving from the loan portfolio and interest rate risk from the mismatch between assets and liabilities. Market risk in the trading portfolio was traditionally considered relatively low compared to traditional credit risk, since it was assumed that the financial market would always be able to absorb additional supply of securities. In other words, it was generally assumed that whenever an investment bank wanted to cut losses by selling a position to minimise market risks, buyers could always be found at the spot rate.

However, the financial crisis of 2007–08 showed how dangerous this assumption was. This leads us to the fourth important banking risk (in addition to credit, market and interest rate risk): liquidity risk. Banks create liquidity. Liquid instruments (savings, short-term deposits) form the liabilities of the bank. However, during normal and stable periods, a core part of these liquid instruments are unlikely to be called. These liabilities are used to issue bonds that create liquidity: clients can use that money to spend. An example: assume a bank has €100 savings, callable on demand, and from a widely diversified group of people. The bank can easily use these savings to issue a €80 loan in cash. The €100 savings are considered liquidity in the economy, because the funds are callable on demand, and hence count towards the liquidity definition of monetary economics. However, the €80 loan also counts as liquidity in that same definition. This is an important function of a bank in an economy, but it also creates risk. This is liquidity risk (see Chapter 4).

FROM STABLE ENVIRONMENTS TO INTERNATIONAL SETTINGS

This section will discuss Basel II. Ever since the financial crisis of the Great Depression of the 1930s, banks have been heavily regulated – for instance, via deposit guarantee schemes and prescribed client rates. Also, the banking industry was highly segmented by law: investment banks, commercial banks, savings banks, mortgage banks, etc, all faced separate regulation and it was forbidden for these activities to be performed by the same bank. Traditionally, it was also prohibited for banking and insurance activities to be combined within the same institution, which is nowadays permitted. From the 1970s, all these regulations were gradually removed while, at the same time, several events caused more volatility in the financial markets – for instance, the collapse of the Bretton Woods system that regulated currency rates and kept interest rate volatility low. As a result, banks faced new risks during a period of gradual internationalisation and deregulation. This led to financial debacles in the 1980s, such as the savings and loans crisis in the US.

A group of 11 banking supervisors, the Basel Committee on Banking Supervision,[1] took up the challenge of designing a set of principles that increased the strength of the banking system and which could be applied in multiple jurisdictions. The latter was necessary to avoid unfair competition. These principles were issued in 1988 via the so-called Basel I proposals: "International Convergence of Capital Measurement and Capital Standards". The proposals were made by the Basel Committee, but in practice were implemented into law in many jurisdictions across the globe. For instance, it was implemented in Europe by the Capital Adequacy Directive (in force since 1990), and in the US by the Federal Deposit Insurance Corporation Improvement Act (in force since 1992).

The 1988 proposals set out requirements for credit risk: each bank was required to hold at least 8% of the lending portfolio as capital. They also included rules to assess the quality of capital according to the capability of absorbing losses (Tiers 1 and 2). Tier 1 consists of issued stocks and retained earnings, but also certain subordinated debt to a maximum of 50% of total Tier 1 capital, and certain qualifying hybrid capital structures. Tier 2 consists of, among others, long-term unsecured subordinated debt and certain provisions. The capital requirements were slightly risk sensitive because government bonds were not charged at all, residential mortgage loans received a 50% weighting and loans to banks were weighted at 20%. All other credits were weighted at 100%, and hence resulted in an 8% capital charge. Although it was recognised that banks were exposed to interest rate risks in the banking book[2] as well, a pragmatic approach was taken not to develop capital requirements for this complex risk type. It was also recognised that the risk weighting was relatively crude: no distinction was made in the 100%-risk weighting category. This meant that loans to a well-run company in a safe environment would bear the same capital requirement as a loan to a risky, small IT start-up. Both the industry and supervisors realised the shortcomings but recognised that the 1988 rules were a step forward.

While these requirements were risk sensitive to some extent, they resulted in increasing average levels of capital throughout the banking industry (see Figure 9.1). At the same time, banks started to increase their off-balance-sheet trading positions in order to take risk (and earn the related reward) without having to set aside capital: regulatory arbitrage. Examples include the increased number of swap transactions as well as, more obviously, securitisation transactions.

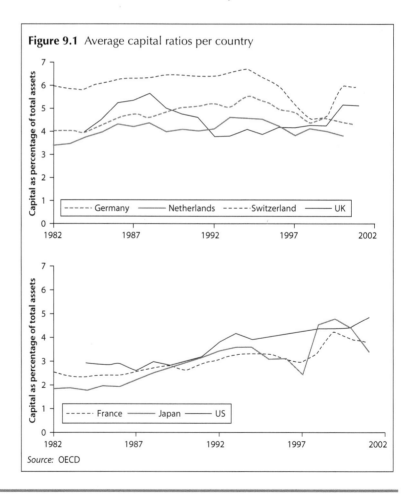

Figure 9.1 Average capital ratios per country

Source: OECD

In 1996, the Basel Committee amended its proposals by drafting a set of requirements to cover market risks in the trading book. In a revolutionary move, banks were allowed to use internal risk models to determine the capital requirements for market risks. During the early 1990s, banks had started to develop VaR models for their internal trading positions.

The rise of capital arbitrage and the relatively minor risk sensitivity gave rise to the initiative of revising the 1988 proposals. During the 1990s, banks had also upgraded their internal risk measurement systems (Bankers Trust's risk-adjusted return on capital, RAROC, methodology had become famous). Basel II began in 1999 via an initial consultative paper of the Basel Committee. This eventually led to the publication of "International Convergence of Capital Measurement and Capital Standards: A Revised Framework" in 2004, which is known as Basel II. The Basel Committee on Banking Supervision proposed that Basel II should come into effect in 2007. In Europe, it was implemented into law via the Capital Requirements Directive of 2007.

Basel II included four revolutionary elements.

❏ It is a comprehensive framework that includes other supervisory elements, in addition to the capital requirements in Pillar I. Other pillars are "Supervisory Review" (Pillar II) and "Market Discipline" (Pillar III). These three pillars of the Basel II framework were also adopted in Solvency II.
❏ There are capital requirements for credit risk, market risk and operational risk. The latter risk type in particular was "new" to the banking industry.
❏ Multiple options allow companies to choose the approach that best fits their business. Advanced companies can use internal models whereas other companies may use a standardised approach. Internal models are more likely to produce lower outcomes than those of the standardised approaches. This provides an incentive for firms to improve their risk management frameworks.
❏ There is increasing reliance on internal models for all three risk types in Pillar I, which aims to align companies' own incentives for proper risk management with the supervisory objectives. Ultimately, this could avoid regulatory arbitrage; overall, it improves

the risk measurement, as internal models generally measure the risk more accurately. The internal models are calibrated on a 99.9% VaR and a one-year time horizon.

As we have seen, most of these revolutionary items were also included in the Solvency II framework, and sometimes were even taken a step further in the insurance industry. An example is the modular approach under Pillar I of Solvency II.

The Basel II standardised approach for credit risk refines the previous approach of 1988. The risk weights (0%, 20%, 50%, 100%) take into account the clients' credit ratings (Table 9.1). In addition, companies have the option to apply the internal ratings-based (IRB) approach. Here, companies use internal risk models to estimate the client's ratings by using historical default rates and by taking into account the client's characteristics (such as financial information). The rating is expressed in the probability of default (PD).[3] Chapter 4 examines the relation between the rating and PD. Other important credit variables are loss given default (LGD) and exposure at default (EAD). See Panel 9.1 for an example. There are two forms of the IRB approach: the IRB foundation, where banks estimate their own PDs per customer and use supervisory estimates for LGD and EAD, and IRB advanced, where banks estimate all three parameters themselves using internal models. In both IRB foundation and IRB advanced approaches, Basel II prescribes the formula that leads to the capital requirement based on the input from PD, LGD and EAD.

Table 9.1 Credit risk weights in Basel II standardised approach

Lending counterparty	AAA to AA− (%)	A+ to A+ (%)	BBB+ to BBB− (%)	BB+ to B− (%)	Below B− (%)	Unrated (%)
Sovereigns	0	20	50	100	150	100
Banks	20	50	100	100	150	100
Corporates	20	50	100	100	150	100
Retail mortgages	35	35	35	35	35	35

It is important to distinguish between expected loss (EL) and unexpected loss (UL). The EL is the long-term average credit loss that should underpin the credit rate. In insurance, this would probably be called the best-estimate credit loss. The UL would be the worst-case deviation from the EL. This is the basis for setting the capital requirement.

PANEL 9.1: THREE CREDIT VARIABLES: PD, LGD AND EAD

Peter, an account manager at a large bank, is discussing a new loan of €3 million with a client. To determine the PD, Peter analyses his client's annual accounts and also takes into account qualitative information such as the client's market position, strategic plans and other credits. The bank's rating system provides a PD of 0.05%, which is roughly equivalent to the A+ rating of Standard & Poor's and the A+ rating of Moody's.

Without collateral, the company's loss in the event of the client defaulting would be relatively high. An LGD of 100% would be potentially on the high side, as recovery processes would be likely to return some money. Assume that, without collateral, the LGD equals 50%.

The EAD is equal to the amount of the loan, ie, €3 million. If the bank provided additional credit facilities to the client – for instance, €0.5 million – then the EAD would be €3.5 million. This is because it can be assumed that a client will use its credit facility when it is in a phase of financial turmoil shortly before defaulting on the loan.

The EL in this case is calculated by multiplying the three credit variables PD, LGD and EAD:

$$EL = PD \times LGD \times EAD = 0.05\% \times 50\% \times 3.5 \text{ million} = €875.00$$

This amount forms the basis for the credit-risk premium in the credit rate calculation.

Should the client provide collateral to the bank, the LGD would change, as would the EL calculation. For instance, the client would provide a small office building (value: €2.0 million) as a collateral. At default, the bank would at least recover this value. In addition, one could expect that work-out processes would recover 50% of the residual value of the loan, which is 50% of €1.5 million, ie, €0.75 million. Hence, the LGD would be 21% (which is (€2.0 + €0.75 million) / €3.5 million).

Hence, the EL would be:

$$EL = PD \times LGD \times EAD = 0.05\% \times 21\% \times €3.5 \text{ million} = €367.50$$

The UL would be partly based on the EL combined with statistical models.

Larger banks have used Basel II as an opportunity to upgrade their rating systems and implement ratings that are much more quantitatively grounded. Data infrastructures have also been rebuilt and lending processes redesigned. As an example: traditionally banks' lending processes were identical irrespective of the risk of the client. During the Basel II implementation phase, banks redesigned their processes so that low-risk clients were processed much more quickly, with less heavy credit analysis, credit reports and, of course, lower capital requirements. While Basel II was in one sense a stick to hit banks with, many banks have indicated that they intended to perform these upgrades anyway. As such, Basel II has had an enormous impact on banks, resulting in €150 million projects for large, internationally active banks. For many of these banks, the benefits include the fact that capital requirements are better aligned with the underlying risk drivers of the companies. Larger banks mostly expected decreasing capital requirements, for instance, because they have major mortgage portfolios (mortgages are generally assumed to have a low risk profile).

The market risk requirements have remained the same compared with the 1996 Amendment, so this does not pose major changes for banks in their trading business. The same holds for the structure of the eligible elements of capital, ie, the structure of Tiers 1, 2 and 3.

The introduction of capital requirements for operational risk, however, has proven to be quite a challenge. While, in one sense, banks have always been exposed to operational risk, the complexity of the trading businesses and some large losses due to errors and frauds have set the tone for a new way of looking at this risk. However, measuring it is not as straightforward as measuring the other risk types (Chapter 5 has already explained the reasons for this in detail). Initial attempts to measure operational risk assumed that capital requirements for operational risk would be simply derived by probability distributions based on historical operational risk losses. However, in practice it appeared that information on operational risk is most often not available in data systems. For example, historically losses due to fraud were not separately recorded. In addition, in many cases errors in systems and processes had led to higher credit losses. Hence, operational risk was hidden in the regular credit loss databases. Another specific characteristic of operational risk is that it is very specific to the management and internal control practices of the bank. It can also be influenced to a large extent by the bank itself. This explains the problems in measuring such a complex risk type as operational risk.

Ultimately, Basel II includes three options for the operational risk capital requirement. First, the basic indicator approach sets a plain capital requirement as a percentage of the average gross income. Second, the standardised approach is more refined and includes different percentages for different business lines. Before being allowed to apply the standardised approach, however, banks need to satisfy certain supervisory criteria that prove they have proper operational risk management. Examples include clear allocation of responsibilities, proper risk identification processes and regular management reporting. The third option is called advanced measurement approaches (AMA), which basically gives banks the freedom to develop an approach that uses internal and external loss data and qualitative elements. The basic idea is that prescribing a measurement methodology is, by definition, inappropriate because operational risk is so specific to the bank. Therefore, the AMA provides greater freedom for companies to design their own specific risk measurement framework. In any case, Basel II led many banks to develop operational risk frameworks, including measurement methodologies.

Pillar II aims to address the risks not covered in Pillar I – most obviously, interest rate risk in the banking book. This is done in a more qualitative way, except for those banks that have a large interest rate mismatch position. Additionally, Pillar II requires banks to have an internal assessment of the total risk profile, the internal capital adequacy assessment process (ICAAP). For large banks, this will be largely based on the internal economic capital framework, whereas for smaller banks more qualitative assessments will be included. Most importantly, the ICAAP emphasises the explicit responsibilities of the executive board for risks and risk management. This is similar to ORSA as a part of Pillar II in Solvency II.

The major consequence of Basel II is that risk management has become increasingly important. Banks' internal risk management practices have received an enormous boost and banks have made massive efforts to align their risk management with best practice. As a result, the banking system has become more stable as capital is allocated to where the risk is. By using risk models, a common standard for risk measurement has become available to the capital markets which, in turn, allows banks to better trade risks. Of course, this is what happened in the early 2000s and allowed all kinds of complex risk vehicles to be traded on the capital markets. As we saw during the crisis, the complexity of the structures turned out to be too high to be properly understood. In this sense, the positive impetus of Basel II also has negative consequences.

There are fears that larger banks will push the smaller banks out of the market. After all, building internal models requires a significant upfront investment. The internal models will support banks when it comes to applying portfolio management techniques. While banks have managed their lending processes from a portfolio perspective from the outset, the new quantitative techniques will certainly provide an impetus for active portfolio management. Most importantly, this will result in an increasing drive for return optimisation and diversification effects. It is generally accepted that increased portfolio sizes result in diversification benefits. Potentially, smaller banks cannot benefit from such diversification because their portfolios are smaller, by definition. At the same time, financial markets have started to provide innovative risk management instruments such as credit derivatives. Although credit derivatives received quite some negative attention during the crisis, they could very well be beneficial for portfolio optimisation because they diversify and reduce credit risk. However, during the crisis, financial institutions provided credit derivatives assuming that the market would hardly draw on them. This turned out an expensive assumption (see Panel 6.2). Once the dust settles over the next few years, we can expect markets to continue to design innovative structures that really transfer risks in such a way that it is more transparent for investors and regulators. Thus, those banks that are not extremely well diversified can "buy" diversification benefits on the capital markets. While this is, in one sense, a new phenomenon, it is also fair because smaller and larger banks both have a *raison d'être*.

Another consequence of banks having a better view of the true risks of their transactions is that they will better price the risk in the credit rates. Traditionally, credit rates included only a few credit grades, whereas the methodology of PD often includes a significant number of credit grades. Differentiation in the credit rates will be the result. There have been concerns about the consequences for small- and medium-sized entitites (SMEs), which often rely entirely on bank financing. While the higher risk profile of SMEs compared to large corporates cannot be denied per se, the importance of SMEs in an economic system must also be recognised. SMEs often produce more than 90% of a country's GDP.

THE FINANCIAL TURBULENCE AND BASEL III

And then came the financial crisis... Banks faced extremely turbulent times during the entire financial crisis (the financial crisis and the lessons learned were described in Chapter 6, which also discussed the growth of securitisation in the banking industry and how liquidity problems caused a financial meltdown). Although there is an economic business rationale for securitisation, it was in practice often used to circumvent regulation, which is known as regulatory arbitrage. In addition to securitisation, many other off-balance-sheet transactions were designed and used to exploit certain loopholes in regulations. Decreasing capital requirements seemed to be a dominant reason.

During the crisis, banking supervisors urged banks to increase their capital base. Although obviously after the fact, banking supervisors responded relatively rapidly by issuing an amendment to the existing framework, which evolved into the Basel III framework. Although the name might suggest that Basel III replaces Basel II, it actually should be considered an amendment. This was also the case in the transition from Basel I to Basel II. Basel I developed the concept of capital quality, by designing the tiering structure. Basel II did not re-discuss that part, but in fact endorsed the prior agreement. Now Basel III includes new elements without reiterating the three-pillar structure and the credit models, for instance.

First of all, during the crisis banking supervisors became aware that insufficient attention had been paid to the impact of risks on the financial industry as a whole. Prior to the crisis, banking supervisors focused on individual institutions only, implicitly assuming that whenever a risk occurred only that bank would be hit while other banks would remain sound. In capital market risks, banks all face the same market circumstances, although some banks are hit more severely than others. New areas of work by banking supervisors includes policymaking on how to address systemic risk – for instance, by differentiating between supervisory approaches to systemic banks and non-systemic banks. A potential upgrade of the supervisory framework is to develop a joint view on systemic banks and contingent capital structures in order to bail out banks in financial problems. Especially relevant is the international approach for large banks. We saw during the crisis that problem solving with more than one national supervisor appeared to be more difficult than expected. However, supervisors will have to face the fact that banks are increasingly global players.

The new elements of Basel III will now be discussed.

Increased quality and quantity of capital base

The new framework includes a stronger focus on the amount of common equity as a part of capital requirements. Traditionally, within the total 8% rule, banks were allowed to cover only 2% of their risk-weighted assets with common equity and the rest with other capital instruments. The new framework includes a restriction for banks to use hybrid structures or subordinated debt to qualify as regulatory capital. Under Basel III, Tier 3 capital is abolished, implying that short-term subordinated debt does not qualify to cover capital requirements an longer. This increases the quality of the capital buffer.

In addition, banks are required to hold more capital than before, hence the quantity of capital also increases. Rather than focusing on the 8% rule as a total, now banks are required to hold at least 4.5% of their risk-weighted assets in common equity (shares, retained earnings). Furthermore, banks are required to hold an additional "capital conservation buffer" of 2.5% in common equity, with the aim of avoiding procyclicality – the phenomenon that solvency requirements could worsen a potential crisis. The capital conservation buffer can be used to absorb losses while still being able to operate above the bare minimum level. In addition, a national countercyclical buffer is introduced to ensure that sufficient earnings are retained during periods of excessive growth. This buffer is nationally organised.

Risk coverage

Minimum capital requirements for complex capital market products have been introduced, such as securitisations and re-securitisations (CDOs of CDOs). This includes more detailed credit analyses of complex products. In addition to the regular VaR analysis, banks are now required to perform even more stressed analyses on their trading portfolio. In the trading book, credit risk has been more rigorously included, by focusing on downgrading risk and default risk.

❏ Leverage: the Basel II framework did not include any measure on total leverage of the bank, whereas in practice leverage increased enormously prior to the financial crisis. Basel III includes a new, non-risk-based maximum of total leverage, which will serve as a floor to the risk-based capital requirements in Pillar I. Although it is not yet finally set in stone, initial ideas seem to be that the maximum leverage will be that 3% of the total on- and off-balance-sheet assets will need to be held in Tier 1 capital.

❏ Liquidity risk: new requirements for liquidity risk are included in the framework. Two new ratios are introduced: the Liquidity Coverage Ratio (LCR), which focuses on short-term stresses, and the Net Stable Funding Ratio (NSFR), a longer-term structural ratio (both will be discussed below).

❏ Additional Pillar II guidance to strengthen supervision: a number of guidance papers were published in key areas. Examples are liquidity risk management, (fair) valuation practices, stress-testing, corporate governance and compensation issues as a response to the public debates about the bonus-driven nature of the banking industry.

❏ Additional Pillar III guidance to strengthen market discipline: the Basel Committee aims to supplement the existing disclosure rules in a number of areas, although these details are by no means final. For instance, more disclosure is required in off-balance-sheet securities. Also, banks will need to provide more detail on the composition of their capital base and the remuneration policy for directors.

Liquidity risk in Basel III

As indicated above, liquidity risk is an important new element in Basel III. Solvency monitoring alone has proven to be insufficient in preventing significant crises. Although liquidity has never been off the regulatory agenda, the focus has been to address solvency measures. However, we have seen that once liquidity risk has had an impact, it can be massive. Therefore, the Basel Committee now explicitly works on liquidity measures, and banks are expected to have a monitoring system in place to address liquidity risk. In addition to the new liquidity ratios (as defined below), banking supervisors aim to focus more than before on the liquidity mismatch position and funding concentration. As we will see, liquidity risk impacts both the assets and the liabilities on the bank's balance sheet.

The LCR identifies the amount of high-quality, liquid assets that can be used to offset net cash outflows under an instant stress scenario. This is to address the liquidity risk of short-term liquidity problems. A large liquidity mismatch is a sign of this risk. The instant stress scenario consists of:

❏ a three-notch downgrade of the bank (eg, AA+ to A+);
❏ a loss of the retail deposit base (a 7.5% or 15% decrease, depending on the stability of the deposits);
❏ a loss of wholesale funding (7.5, 15, 25, 75 or 100% decrease, depending on the funding type);
❏ increase of market volatility impacting collateral values;
❏ clients drawing on unused credit facilities; and
❏ an increase of collateral calls related to derivative transactions.

Definition:

$$LCR = \frac{high\ liquid\ assets}{net\ cash\ outflows\ over\ 30day\ period} \geq 100\%$$

The LCR determines the amount of available liquidity on the balance sheet. The net cash outflows are stressed under the scenario described above. There is no definite list of qualifying assets (not yet anyway), since such a list tends to get outdated. However, the proposals include criteria for assets to be considered of high quality and to be liquid. The most important criteria is to have low credit and market risk and to be relatively easy to value, also without a deep liquid market. Historically, we can see that, during a crisis, market participants "flee to quality": they tend to switch asset portfolios towards liquid currencies, government bonds, and potentially also gold. Ideally, qualifying assets should be eligible as collateral to receive funding from central banks. The following assets are suggested: cash, central bank reserves, marketable securities under certain criteria and government/central bank debt. Interestingly, assets from other financial institutions do not qualify, so as to avoid liquidity problems from spilling over from one bank to another.

Definition:

$$NSFR = \frac{available\ stable\ funding}{required\ stable\ funding} > 100\%$$

The objective of the NSFR is to provide incentives for banks to achieve a longer-term funding base, rather than only short-term funding – which could create liquidity problems. The available stable funding is determined by weighting the liabilities of the bank by percentages. For instance, capital receives 100% weighting, whereas less stable retail deposits receive 70%. The required stable funding is determined by weighting the assets by similar percentages. For instance, cash receives a 0% weighting while short-term retail loans receive 85% weighting.

Capital requirements under Basel III

As mentioned, banks' capital ratios will change in order to have both higher levels of capital and higher quality of capital. The tiering structure was already designed in 1988, and amended in 1996 with Tier 3 capital. This consisted of short-term subordinated debt and could only be used to cover market risk. Basel III abolished the Tier 3 capital element and required even higher capital requirements for market risk. Basel III will continue to have two quality levels of capital: Tier 1 and Tier 2. The definitions will remain identical as under Basel I in 1988, but the requirements on the limits will differ. In addition, the sub-classification of Tier 2 into higher and lower Tier 2 capital will be abolished in order to simplify the framework. Tier 2 is subordinated debt with a maturity of five years or more. The capital conservation buffer is a new element that serves to avoid procyclicality and to provide an additional safety net. This new capital requirement partially resembles the structure of MCR and SCR in Solvency II, in the sense that banks may be allowed to breach the capital conservation buffer in certain circumstances. It allows the supervisors to intervene gradually. The capital conservation buffer is required to be covered by common equity. Figure 9.2 highlights the changes from Basel II to Basel III. Under Basel II, banks were required to hold 8% of risk-weighted assets in capital, of which 50% was to be covered by Tier 1 capital. Of this Tier 1 capital, 50% was to be common equity. Hence, only 2% (50% times 50% of 8%) of the total capital requirement was common equity: issued stock and retained earnings. This 2% will be increased to 4.5%, and another 2.5% conservation buffer will be added as well. This means that, in total, 7% (4.5% + 2.5%) of risk-weighted assets are covered by common equity, ie, capital of the highest quality.

The higher requirements will be gradually implemented using certain steps for each requirement. The implementation phase starts in 2013, and the aim is that Basel III will be fully implemented by 2019.

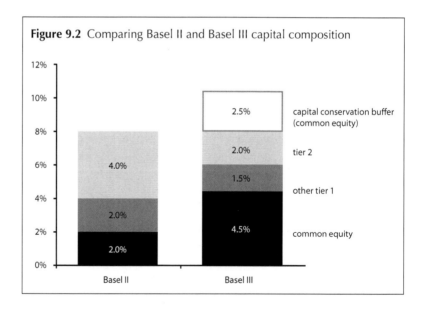

Figure 9.2 Comparing Basel II and Basel III capital composition

In 2009, the Basel Committee estimated that large banks would need a significant amount of capital to meet the new requirements. A quantitative impact study indicated that almost €600 billion is required by about 94 large banks in the sample group of 263 banks in order to comply with the new 7% rule for common equity. Smaller banks are likely to be already higher capitalised due to the specific nature of their risk portfolio. Introducing new requirements immediately would force large banks to increase capital levels or de-risk portfolios. This could potentially lead to effects in the real economy because lending could be limited. To prevent this, a long transition phase has been chosen. From 2018, all elements of Basel III should be in place. Before then, a parallel run will start from 2013. During the parallel run, Basel II will be in force, but banks will need to be preparing for Basel III. Disclosure requirements are planned to be in force as of 2015. Liquidity measures will start to be effective in 2015 with the LCR being mandatory, while the NSFR will be in force from 2018 onwards. This leaves the banking supervisors sufficient time to fine-tune the exact formulas and parameters of the framework. In order for this calibration to be most successful, banks will provide data from 2011 onwards.

COMPARING THE BANKING AND INSURANCE FRAMEWORKS

Banks and insurers are not identical. However, interesting parallels can be drawn between the two frameworks. Comparing Basel III and Solvency II is relevant for four reasons.

First, financial conglomerates that combine banking and insurance within one group are exposed to both regimes. Large gaps between the two regimes make the supervisory process extremely complex because financial conglomerates have to comply with both regimes.

Second, if one certain risk is treated more favourably under one regime, there is an incentive for companies to transfer their risk exposure from one regime to another. This does not fundamentally change the risk exposure in the financial system, but it does decrease the minimum capital levels required to absorb this type of risk. This kind of arbitrage is most obvious for financial conglomerates, but it can be expected that investment banks will offer transactions to perform this as well. Thus, the arbitrage mechanism becomes available to pure banks and pure insurers as well. However, the experience from the financial crisis is that arbitrage can amplify existing risks. Therefore, we can assume that supervisors will look into complex transactions in a much more detailed way than before to identify potential arbitrage.

Third, different treatments of the same risk also mean unfair competition for services from banking and insurance institutions competing for the same funds. An example is mutual funds and unit-linked insurance. Therefore, clients are also impacted by differences in regulatory regimes.

Fourth, in many countries banking and insurance supervisors are combined in the same entity. For instance, the Financial Services Authority (FSA) in the UK supervises both the banking and insurance sectors, and needs to be aware of potential similarities and differences between the two frameworks. Another interesting issue is how pension funds are supervised. In some jurisdictions, pensions are not under the same supervisor and hence could also face different regimes. In a number of western countries, however, pensions are supervised by the same entity as banks and insurers.

With Basel II in banking almost finalised by the time that the Solvency II for insurers debate really took off, Solvency II has built upon the Basel II experience. Many risk methodologies have been developed in the banking industry and then imported by insurers at a time when the methodologies were more mature. Important similarities are the three-pillar structure, the option for companies to use standardised approaches or internal models and the structure of eligible elements of capital (Tiers 1, 2 and 3). Insurers have been able to use the experience in risk modelling and methodologies and VaR. This is also reflected in Solvency II. The changes in Basel III have not been incorporated in Solvency II, but it seems that insurance supervisors typically consider the Basel III updates applicable for banks only. Liquidity risk is considered to be fundamentally different for banks than for insurers. However, the increase of capital levels in Basel III could potentially impact insurance capital levels as well. At the time of writing, there did not seem to be an identical initiative to increase the 99.5% level for the SCR in Solvency II.

Some important differences between the two regimes now follow.

❏ Solvency II includes all important risk types in Pillar I, whereas Basel III addresses interest rate risk in Pillar II. Basel III includes liquidity risk in Pillar I, which is entirely absent in the Solvency II framework. This might not be problematic because insurers do not create as much liquidity as banks.

❏ Basel III is calibrated on a 99.9% VaR, whereas Solvency II is calibrated on 99.5% VaR. Both include a one-year time horizon. This might create incentives for market participants to bring certain risks to insurers rather than banks. However, market practice is to consider insurers as slightly more risky than banks, which contradicts this initial principle. Potential but implicit reasons for this are that insurers are less prone to runs than banks (liquidity creation) or that some risks are included implicitly in Basel III, where they are explicitly calculated in Solvency II.

❏ Solvency II addresses technical provisions in addition to the capital requirements, while Basel III focuses on capital requirements only. This is because the banks' beneficiaries are depositors. Bank deposits are less exposed to solvency risks than technical provisions in insurance. Also, deposits callable on demand are easier to value than insurance technical provisions. In addition, banking credit loss provisions are less dominant than technical provisions in insurance.

❏ Liquidity risk is a central element of Basel III, although it is not so dominant in Solvency II. Although banking and insurance supervisors recognise the different function of banks and insurers and the lower interconnectedness of insurers, this does not say that liquidity risk is unimportant for insurers. A potential reason for less attention to liquidity risk in Solvency II might be that other technical issues have received more priority in Solvency II, such as the valuation of technical provisions and the calibration of other risk types in the SCR.

❏ Basel III is based on consolidated supervision, whereas Solvency II is based on solo-entity supervision. This is especially relevant for international groups. Group supervision for insurance is possible, but at the time of writing much still needs to be done at the solo level.

❏ Basel II has led companies to fundamentally redesign their lending processes, and hence it has had an impact on the core processes of the banks. Solvency II, on the other hand, is likely to change insurance companies' strategies for risks, but without having to completely redesign the core underwriting and investment processes. This means that the impact of Solvency II on insurance clients may be less than the impact of Basel II and Basel III on banking clients.

However, we will see if this will turn out to be true, since insurance products might still change after the introduction of Solvency II.

❏ Although the tiering structure is comparable between Basel III and Solvency II, the composition of the tiers differs enormously. An example is that insurers are allowed to use contingent liabilities to cover capital requirements under certain circumstances. This concept does not exist in banking. The requirements as laid down in Basel III focus on the composition of capital levels (see Figure 9.2) are very different from that of Solvency II.

❏ Finally, Basel III is intended to be a proposal and not a legally binding document. Jurisdictions across the globe will have to implement the proposals into law, which they might or might not do (completely). Solvency II is a regulatory framework, hence a law. In Europe, the requirements will be binding but, for other jurisdictions, they will serve as an example. For instance, some Asian insurance supervisors have been looking into the possibilities of applying Solvency II in their countries.

CONCLUSIONS

This chapter has described the banking framework. As shown, the banking industry has been developing from a period of deregulation and increasing globalisation since the 1980s. This increased the need for harmonised supervision and resulted in the first Basel framework. Basel II could be considered a major revision of the framework that resulted in more risk awareness. Basel II, however, did not prevent an unprecedented crisis from happening, which is the reason for Basel III. Basel III increased the quality and quantity of bank capital and included liquidity risk in the framework. Although more comprehensive and a good step forward, it remains to be seen whether this revision will be able to prevent massive future crises.

Companies that have the ability will ultimately succeed in evading regulation if it is beneficial to them. The key objective is to install a system that allows supervisors to receive warning signals and then act upon them. This holds for banks as well as for insurers. It is therefore vital that bank supervisors understand the inherent risks within the individual banks, as well as the banking system. This is also extremely relevant for insurers. We have seen that banking and insurance compete for the same funds, clients and risks. Over time, insurers have been lagging behind banks when it comes to innovative solutions of risk financing. An area in insurance where this is slowly developing is alternative risk transfer (ART, see Chapter 3). Without claiming that this a key risk, the insurance industry could learn from the Basel III framework in order to prevent crises from happening here.

1   Initially, the Basel Committee consisted of the supervisors of the G10 countries plus Luxembourg – however, it has been significantly extended. The Basel Committee is hosted by the Bank of International Settlements (BIS), which is why Basel II is sometimes also referred to as BIS2.
2   Historically, banks commonly distinguish the banking book from the trading book. The banking book comprises the process of (long-term) lending funded by (short-term) savings and other deposits. Interest rate risk is mainly caused by the mismatch in duration between assets and liabilities. The trading book business is often much shorter and also involves proprietary trading, eg, in interest rate options.
3   Also called expected default frequency (EDF). However, the use of the term PD in Basel II has caused important convergence in the terminology.

10

Management Control

It is the objective of management of an organisation to influence its members in such a way that the objectives of the organisation are reached. This is called management control. For financial institutions, developments in the field of management control are closely related to the developments in the field of risk management and economic capital, as described in the previous chapters. This chapter discusses the concepts of management control, and performance measurements such as embedded value, RAROC and capital allocation. Based on a consecutive series of examples, this chapter will specifically discuss how these concepts can be applied in the area of management control.

WHAT IS MANAGEMENT CONTROL?

Management control is defined as the process by which managers influence other members of the organisation to implement the organisation's strategy. An example of this control is the yearly establishment of budgets. On this basis, some business units can grow and others will have to cut back. In order to control, management needs information on the state of affairs within the organisation. Managers need to know to what extent the objectives of the organisation are being achieved and in what fields there is a need for measures. Often, the board of directors disposes of a staff department that collects, interprets and reports this information periodically.

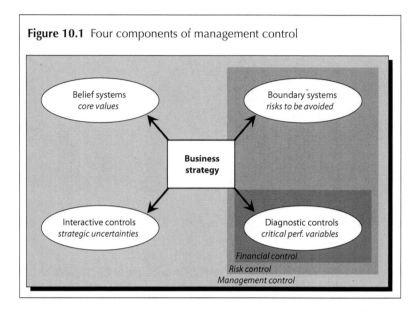

Figure 10.1 Four components of management control

There are two views of the management control concept. The first view defines management control as all actions of management in order to control the remaining members of the organisation to en- sure that the objectives of the organisation are achieved. For this purpose, several instruments are available stimulating initiatives to handle strategic uncertainties, and mission statements or codes of conduct in order to anchor the key values in the daily business of all employees of the company. These are all tools that managers can use to align the activities of the organisation with the ultimate ob- jective of the company. In addition, there are financially orientated instruments such as budgets. There is a relationship between "risk control" and "financial control" (see Figure 10.1). Risk control indi- cates what risks the organisation accepts and those it rejects, such as a limit system or also a code of conduct. Financial control focuses on the determination of financial performance measurement in or- der to reach the objectives of the organisation.

In the second view, management control is defined as gathering and interpreting information on the basis of which the management can steer the remaining members of the organisation. Management control retains the activities of a staff department called business control, performance management or management control that gathers, aggregates, interprets and reports information. It involves both financial control and risk control. This chapter will expand in particular on the duties of the controller; in other words, the focus will be on the latter view of management control. The reader might be confused about the role of the controller in comparison the role of the actuary, risk manager or similar functions. We will see in Chapter 11 that these roles converge heavily.

The controller of the insurance company reports on the state of affairs within the company on a monthly or quarterly basis. In the past, such management reports were particularly financially oriented. Gradually, however, non-financial and qualitative information has also entered the reports, for instance information on the market share per product (group), customer satisfaction. Within this framework, the balanced scorecard (BSC) method has gained popularity.

As has been seen in all previous chapters, risk management is an important factor for an insurer and hence for the management control system. The risk profile is expressed in terms of minimum capital buffer or capital requirement (or the internal or external capital requirement). Naturally, the capital requirement is compared with the current capital (see also Figure 2.4). Simultaneously, the return is an important factor for an insurer. For a long time, the return has been expressed in terms of monetary amounts (euros or dollars), but this chapter will also describe a method for expressing the return in terms of a percentage of the risk profile. Thus the balance between return and risk is charted. This is called the RAROC indicator (see page 244). These three approaches are important for the management control of an insurer (see Figure 10.2).

A system of indicators is an appropriate instrument for management control. With an indicator, management is able to judge the relevant facts in a quantitative and concentrated way. However, the danger of indicators is that there are so many that it can be hard to see the wood for the trees. In addition, it can be difficult to determine the cause of a particular indicator's underperformance. Why was the result in the non-life unit lower, for instance? In order to gain a clearer insight into the relationships between cause and effect, a systematic and well-arranged classification of indicators is important. The so-called Du Pont system can be helpful in this regard.

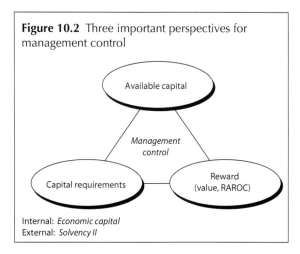

Figure 10.2 Three important perspectives for management control

Available capital

Management control

Capital requirements

Reward (value, RAROC)

Internal: *Economic capital*
External: *Solvency II*

An important aspect of indicators is that they should provide the right incentive. If, for instance, the most important indicator is premium income, managers will aim to increase it. This can, perhaps, come at the cost of high claims or high operational expenses. If, however, the key indicator is profit, then managers will aim to maximise that (ie, taking into account costs and claims). This chapter will show how a system of indicators could provide incentives to balance risk and reward and thus add real economic value.

MANAGEMENT CONTROL AND ECONOMIC CAPITAL

In Chapter 2, economic capital was defined as the necessary minimum capital buffer to cover the unexpected losses and decreases in value due to the various risk categories within a chosen period of time (often one year) and with a given confidence interval. The confidence interval is based on the internal rating objective of the insurance company. It was observed that a minimum amount of capital (economic capital) is apparently required to absorb the decreases in value caused by risks.

A minimum amount is necessary to be able to operate. Too much capital, however, is too expensive. There is an optimal amount of capital, although its precise calculation is difficult. Chapters 3, 4 and 5 described how the measuring methods for the different risk categories result in the amount of economic capital. Economic capital, however, is not only used to optimise the equity capital position of the balance sheet.

In practice, each insurer holds a surplus above the calculated economic capital. Apparently, economic capital is not used subsequently to align the present capital exactly with the bare minimum. The economic capital concept is mainly used in four applications.

1. As a measurement method: through economic capital, all risks are brought into one denominator as the basis for a consistent measurement method, enabling risks to be compared mutually. On this basis, policy considerations can be made, for instance in order to "exchange" part of the catastrophe risk for a market risk, or vice versa.
2. For risk limits: management can use economic capital in order to establish risk limits for departments or entire business units. In practice, the insured value is still used in non-life insurance in order to establish limits. In asset management (ie, the investment process of insurers) companies often work with the exposure per rating category, sector or country. In the future, economic capital can probably gain a position here. Then the department in question can establish how the limits will be allocated. Should many items with a low-risk profile be insured, for instance, or fewer items with a slightly higher risk? This way, risk limits can easily be applied by everyone.
3. For performance measurement: risk plays a big part in the evaluation of profitability. Significant return often involves a higher risk and less return involves a lower risk. For a good performance evaluation, profitability has to be adjusted for the risk run. For that purpose, so-called risk-adjusted performance measures (RAPM) are designed, based on economic capital. RAROC (risk-adjusted return on capital) is the most well-known term.
4. For capital allocation: management allocates capital to the business units periodically, for instance during the annual establishment of the budget. In this process, economic capital plays a central part.

In these four applications, the economic capital is an important instrument for the controller. The applications are classified according to their advancement. Capital allocation on the basis of economic capital, for instance, is not possible without a form of performance measurement (RAPM), which is not possible without clear risk limits and measurement methods for each type of risk. Many large insurers are introducing these applications.

When capital allocation is implemented at a level of individual policies, we speak of risk-based pricing. The perfect place for that is profit-testing by the actuary or controller. When developing a new product (or when fundamentally changing existing products), an analysis is made of the return over the entire term. Risk costs are included therein. In the past, the traditional solvency requirement (based on Solvency I, see Chapter 7) played a part. Nowadays, however, the risk costs of the economic capital are used as the basis. This way, controlling based on economic capital is completely anchored at the level of the individual products.

Although the measurement methods for the various risk categories are far from perfect, the expectation is that the economic capital concept will be introduced in most of the large and medium-sized insurers. The reason is that most supervisors encourage the larger companies to apply the most advanced approaches, within Solvency II in particular. If these approaches are chosen, it would be a waste to do this only for supervisory purposes. It is also better to "harvest" the benefit in terms of a better controlling system. Moreover, Solvency II (as well as other supervisory regimes) requires companies to actively use the outcomes of the models to steer the business. This is the so-called use test (see Chapter 8). Performance evaluation and capital allocation in the context of management control form part of that, this allows efficient use of capital.

MANAGEMENT CONTROL AND VALUE

For a very long time, there has been a preference to look at the profit when establishing the return. The accounting profit, that is. However, the profit is not a good measurement for performance. Firstly, some products have an unstable pattern of premium and benefits. An annuity, for instance, has one premium payment, but several benefit payments in the future. The profit in a year is distorted by these long-year effects. Secondly, the sale of life insurance in particular is coupled to acquisition costs that have to be earned during the entire period. Therefore, the increasing result in the following years is not a profitability result of those years, but rather a logical consequence of actions from the first year. It is well-known that the best way to increase the accounting profit is to sell less products and thus cut acquisition costs. Thirdly, the risk is not expressed well in the profit, for instance, it is not clear what the risk profile is, what reinsurance contracts are in place and what the investment portfolio consists of. Besides, the profit can be distorted by the "coincidence" of existing risks not ending up in high, unexpected claim payments in a certain year. All these reasons indicate that profit is not a good performance measure.

In the life industry, embedded value was developed to overcome these shortcomings. The embedded value is the net present value of all future profits (after taxes) that are related to the life insurance portfolio. The cash flow is calculated for each year of the term of the insurance policy: premiums minus the change in technical provisions, minus benefit payments, minus operational costs, minus capital costs,[1] plus investment return and minus taxes. The expected mortality rate and an expected surrender percentage (also called the lapse rate) are taken into account. This cash flow is discounted, with a discount rate where the risk is taken into account.

The calculation of the embedded value of an entire portfolio requires the necessary calculation power and technical systems. Embedded-value software actually derives the cash flow pattern of all policies from the production system.

It is common to distinguish value in force (VIF) and value of new business (VNB). Obviously, VNB is the most relevant indicator in the context of management control. The company can actively influence the VNB by steering the new production, whereas existing business is fixed and hence is VIF. Another benefit of VNB is that it is easier to calculate because it involves fewer products. This does not, however, imply that VIF is an irrelevant indicator, because mortality rates and other business variables can change over time. These have an impact on the VIF of an existing portfolio.

The traditional embedded value does not sufficiently take into account the risk, as a long-term expected investment return is included. Fluctuations and the current position of the financial markets are not sufficiently taken into account. Besides, the costs of the solvency requirement are not based on the risk. Often old (crude) Solvency I requirements are used. In addition, insufficient attention is paid to interest rate guarantees. In order to take this better into account, European embedded value (EEV) has been developed, in which guarantees and other embedded options are explicitly valued and thus expressed in the embedded value. Also, the discount rate is different from traditional embedded value.

Market-consistent embedded value (MCEV) is the latest variant of embedded value. This is entirely in line with the fair-value principles discussed in Chapter 7. There are not many insurance companies that can calculate MCEV for all life products at present. This is because MCEV requires that all risk models are in place and it is computationally more complex than traditional embedded value. The expectation however is that this number will gradually increase in the following years. However, MCEV is a logical evolution from EEV. The guidance on MCEV is also more detailed than the guidance on EEV in order to clarify how calculations should be done and how risks are to be taken into account. The guidance of the CFO Forum is principle-based and companies have to interpret it before applying it to MCEV calculations.

Table 10.1 An evolution of embedded value in life insurance

	Embedded value	European embedded value	Market-consistent embedded value
Discount rate	Fixed interest rate	Risk-free plus risk margin (could differ per product portfolio)	Risk-free rate (swap rates, potentially with inclusion of liquidity premium)
How risk is addressed	Implicit in prudence and in discount rate	Included in the discount rate	Non-hedgeable risk reflected in CoC method (one single CoC rate)
Required capital	Solvency I regulations	Economic capital model (confidence level undefined)	99.5% economic capital model
Options and guarantees	Not valued	Most valued	All valued

Within the non-life business, too, profit is not a good measure for the true performance, although it is not as bad as in the life business. This is visible in the run-off results for instance. In a certain year, the profit can decrease by setting extra prudent provisions that are only available many years later in the form of run-off results. Additionally, the profit is volatile, for instance, when incidentally heavy storms or other claim events take place. The principle of fair value can handle that better. The fair value of a portfolio only changes through a structural change of the claims expectations. Finally, the time effect of the claim payments is not taken into account in the traditional profit. This is especially relevant for long-tail claims such as asbestos and third-party liability. Fair value actually takes this adequately into account. This also has repercussions on the profit.

Table 10.2 Fair value in non-life insurance

	Traditional	**Fair value**
Discounting	No discounting	Risk-free rate and taking into account MVM
Parameters	Prudent parameters	Realistic assumptions
Observation period	Looking only at current accounting year	Taking into account all future years of run-off period
Risks addressed	Incidentally high peaks due to volatility	Risk on average basis and structural change in risk parameters
Required capital	Traditional risk measures	Economic capital

For both the life and non-life industries, fair value is a good performance measure, which does justice to the long duration period of products as well as to the risks involved. Thinking in terms of value is gradually gaining a foothold. We already noticed that in the life industry embedded value is being reported in the management control cycle. Many insurers are improving the embedded value systems in the direction of European embedded value or MCEV.

PANEL 10.1 HYPOTHETICAL CASE STUDY – HOLLAND INSURANCE GROUP (HIG)

A fictional insurer, HIG, operates through three business units: non-life, life and health. Some of HIG's key features are: the non-life business unit is a multiline non-life insurer through both commercial and retail products; the yearly premium turnover is €1.5 billion; reinsurance is used to cover risks, especially as the portfolio is slightly concentrated. The life business unit focuses on private life insurance, traditional products (annuities) and unit-linked products, where the investment risk is actually on the account of the client. The health business unit focuses on medical cost insurance. It has gone through turbulent times because of internal reorganisation. The total 2011 premium income is €700 million, resulting in a profit of €14 million.

The calculation of results (see Table 10.3) shows that, in 2011, HIG made a total pre-tax profit of €274 million. Table 10.3 shows that the non-life business unit made the biggest contribution. The embedded value of the life business unit amounted to €1.5 billion at the end of 2011. During 2011, the embedded value increased by €100 million, mostly on the account of VNB of €90 million. The remaining €10 million was due to a change in VIF, especially because of a change in lapse rates. This will be looked at again when the RAROC is determined.

The balance sheet of HIG is shown in Table 10.4. The technical provisions for the life business unit are divided into traditional and unit-linked technical provisions to indicate that the latter category consists of liabilities for risk of policyholders.

Table 10.3 Profit and loss account for HIG (2011, € millions)

	Non-life	Life	Health	Group
Premium income	€ 1,500	€ 1,000	€ 700	€ 3,200
Reinsurance	€ 120	N/A	N/A	€ 120
	€ 1,380	€ 1,000	€ 700	€ 3,080
Investment returns	€ 135	€ 500	€ 49	€ 684
Claims/benefits	€ 900	€ 700	€ 630	€ 2,230
Contribution reinsurance	€ 45	N/A	N/A	€ 45
	€ 855	€ 700	€ 630	€ 2,185
Operational costs	€ 450	€ 200	€ 105	€ 680
Change tech. prov.		€ 550		€ 550
Result	€ 210	€ 50	€ 14	€ 274
Change embedded value		€ 100		

Table 10.4 Balance sheet for HIG (at end 2011, € millions)

Assets	Balance sheet		Liabilities
Equities	€ 5,400	Capital	€ 2,100
Bonds	€ 8,600		
Private loans	€ 1,400	Tech. prov.	€ 10,555
Mortgages	€ 350	Life	€ 7,220
Real estate	€ 725	Non-life	€ 2,535
Liquid assets	€ 280	Health	€ 800
Other	€ 900	Unit-linked	€ 5,000
	€ 17,655		€ 17,655

At the end of 2011, the risk management department made the economic capital report (see Table 10.5). The total economic capital of the group amounts to €3.7 billion. We see that two components together determine well over 70% of the economic capital: non-life risk and market risk. The non-life risk is high due to the concentration of catastrophe risk in the portfolio. The market risk is high due to the equity risk and the interest rate risk. The life risk is relatively low as the life business sells products with both longevity and mortality risk. These offset each other for a great part. The credit risk for the life business unit is slightly higher than for the other business units due to the corporate-bond portfolio and private loans. The credit risk of non-life consists of bonds (€30 million) and credit risk on reinsurers (€20 million). The business risk for the business unit Health is relatively high due to changes in plans for privatisation of the health insurance system.

From now on, the return is also taken into account and the balance between return (value) and risk (economic capital) will be explicitly examined.

Table 10.5 Economic capital per business unit (2011, € millions)

	Non-life	Life	Health	Group	%
Non-life risk	€ 1,200			€ 1,200	32.5
Life risk		€ 200		€ 200	5.4
Health risk			€ 300	€ 300	8.1
Market risk	€ 300	€ 900	€ 300	€ 1,500	40.7
Credit risk	€ 50	€ 60	€ 30	€ 140	3.8
Operational risk	€ 50	€ 60	€ 40	€ 150	4.1
Business risk	€ 60	€ 60	€ 80	€ 200	5.4
Total	€ 1,660	€ 1,280	€ 750	€ 3,690	100

RAROC

The economic capital and value are both measures expressed in monetary amounts such as euros and dollars. Thus the height of the risk or value can be seen in absolute numbers. In order to compare large and small business units with each other properly, it is also good to have a relative performance measure, expressed in terms of a percentage. Besides, it is preferable to have a performance measure that observes the relationship between return and risk. Moreover, a high risk profile is not that bad if a business unit obtains a high return from it and, vice versa, a low return is not terrible either when there is barely any risk involved.

For a long time, investors have used the economic measure return on capital (ROC), also called return on equity (ROE). ROC measures the profit as a percentage of capital[2] and indicates how much profit is obtained with a certain amount of capital. The ROC/ROE indicator compares the relative return of two business units with a different volume.

$$ROC = \frac{accounting\ profit}{equity\ capital} \times 100\%$$

In the previous sections and chapters, it was discussed that the risk is not expressed well in the accounting profit. To look at the relationship between return and risk, a RAPM is required. There are different forms of RAPM, all with splendid acronyms such as RAROC or RORAC. The essence of these measures is that the return and/or capital is adjusted in one way or another for the risk taken. The indicators differ by the extent that the numerator or the denominator is adjusted or both.

$$RORAC = \frac{accounting\ profit}{economic\ capital} \times 100\%$$

$$RAROC = \frac{fair\ value\ profit}{equity\ capital} \times 100\%$$

$$RARORAC = \frac{fair\ value\ profit}{economic\ capital} \times 100\%$$

For the indicators RAROC and RARORAC, fair value is used as

a profitability measure. There, the long-term expectation of non-life claim amounts and mortality expectation of the underwriting risks are included. The slightly less advanced RORAC focuses on the accounting profit. As previously discussed, this contains some features that are not in line with the economical principles.

Usually, the term RAROC is used when actually RARORAC is meant. The remainder of this chapter will actually speak of RAROC when pointing to the performance measure where the numerator and denominator are both adjusted for the risk. The idea behind it is that RAROC does not stand for "risk-adjusted return" on capital, but actually for the risk-adjusted version of ROC. RAROC actually implies risk-adjusted "return on capital".

Two versions of RAROC can be distinguished, for two different applications. Firstly, there is the one-year version of RAROC used in performance evaluation. The one-year RAROC indicates the balance between risk and return during a particular year. As the period of the management control cycle often lasts one year, the one-year RAROC looks at that period of one year. It is the fair value change as a percentage of the economic capital in one year.

$$RAROC_{oneyear} = \frac{fair\ value\ profit}{economic\ capital} \times 100\%$$

Secondly, the lifetime version of RAROC balances return and risk over the lifetime of the product. This is used when setting premium rates, such as, for example, profit-testing by the actuary. Lifetime RAROC is very efficient for observing the return over the entire lifetime of a portfolio or even on the level of individual products. This is significantly relevant as the return is not constantly spread over the years, as was already seen on page 238. In a very stable portfolio, the two versions of RAROC will not differ too much from each other. Lifetime RAROC is the total fair value of a product/portfolio as a percentage of the total economic capital (net present value).

$$RAROC_{lifetime} = \frac{total\ fair\ value}{NPV(economic\ capital)} \times 100\%$$

An important form of management control in many companies is the annual budget cycle. Business units within the organisation present their plans to the executive board for approval before the beginning of the accounting year. These plans and prognoses are judged on the basis of return, risk, feasibility and the extent to which the plans fit into the entire strategy of the organisation. As a result, budgets are established. In a certain way, the business units are controlled on the basis of net profit or, in the case of cost centres, costs. The expectation is that RAROC will gradually gain a more important position in the budget cycle during the coming years.

PANEL 10.2 RAROC FOR HIG (CONTINUED)

Panel 10.1 ended with an overview of the risk profile in terms of economic capital for the fictional insurer HIG. In order to determine the RAROC (one year), the risk management department has adjusted the result for the risks to calculate the change in fair value (Table 10.6). The non-life business unit receives a deduction of €50 million on the result for the risk of incorporating the potential effect of an enormous catastrophe. In the budget cycle, a potential catastrophe is not taken into account, but it is in RAROC. The expected loss is taken into account rather than the maximum volume of a catastrophe. Assume that an extreme storm with a loss of €500 million occurs once every 10 years, then the deduction is 1/10th of €500 million, ie, €50 million. The RAROC is 9.6%. In the life business unit, they start from the increase in embedded value of €100 million in 2011 as proxy for the increase in fair value. That is not quite the same, but for the executive board it is acceptable as temporary alternative. The RAROC of life is 7.8%. The result of health is not adjusted. The short-term contracts ensure the result concords with the increase in fair value. The RAROC of health is 1.9%. The RAROC of the group is 7.4%. The executive board considers that too low. Later, it will be shown how it can improve the return along with the business units.

Table 10.6 RAROC per business unit (2011, € millions)

	Non-life	Life	Health	Group
Result/ embedded value	€210	€100	€14	€324
Adjustments	(€50)	N/A	N/A	(€50)
Change in fair value	€160	€100	€14	€274
Economic capital	€1,660	€1,280	€750	€3,690
RAROC	9.6%	7.8%	1.9%	7.4%

SYSTEMATIC REPRESENTATION OF RAROC

The beginning of this chapter emphasised that management control consists of a system of indicators and that the controller needs to classify these in order for the management to control the company properly. The Du Pont system is a model whereby all financial indicators from a balance sheet and profit and loss account are combined in a useful and practically relevant representation. In the Du Pont method, the return on investment (ROI) indicator is unravelled in the underlying indicators, which in turn are broken down to the lowest level possible. This way, the controller gains an insight into why the ROI might fall short of expectations. Based on this, management can take action. The management reports state the aggregated indicators (left-hand side of the diagram), but the management takes action by means of the detailed components (right-hand side of the diagram). The importance of the Du Pont model is its useful structure rather than the exact specification of the indicators.

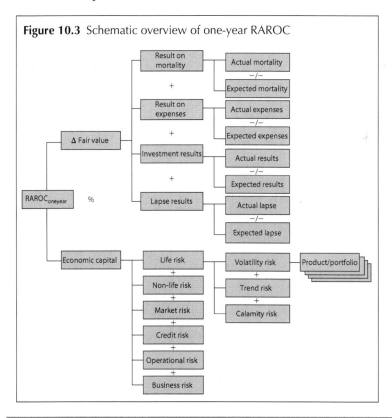

Figure 10.3 Schematic overview of one-year RAROC

The Du Pont system can also be applied to RAROC. Just as there are two versions of RAROC, here are two Du Pont figures. In both cases, "something with economic capital" in the denominator and a "fair-value type" component in the numerator can be seen. The one-year RAROC contains the changes in the fair value during that year. Figure 10.3 elaborates on an example from the life business, in which the result is divided into components, stemming from the analysis of the embedded value. The denominator of the RAROC calculation is the sum of the economic capital of all risk categories.

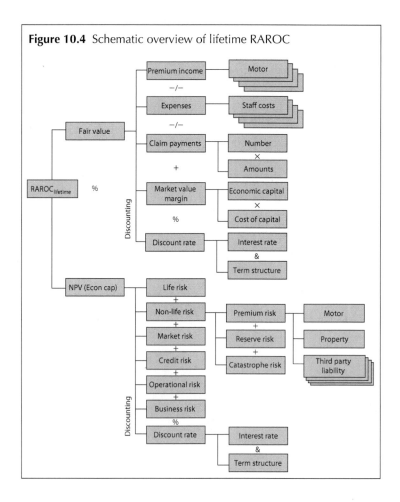

Figure 10.4 Schematic overview of lifetime RAROC

The lifetime RAROC uses the net present value method to determine the numerator (total fair value) and the denominator (economic capital over the entire term). As this is the sum of many amounts, it cannot easily be introduced in a Du Pont diagram. Therefore, Figure 10.4 explicitly mentions the discounting process. The discount rate is determined by the yield curve. Figure 10.4 is a non-life example, but it is of course equally applicable to life insurance.

THE PHENOMENON OF DIVERSIFICATION

Diversification arises when different activities complement each other, in the field of both return and risk. As such, for instance, commercial non-life insurance and pension products complement each other, not only from a commercial point of view but also due to the risk profile. If there is a heavy storm, pensioners do not necessarily live longer. With catastrophes there is more need of money, which causes interest rates to rise. This is beneficial for a pension fund. Besides, in extreme circumstances, the financial markets can become very unpredictable and this requires precautions. Diversification indicates how activities complement each other effectively in terms of risk.

The diversification phenomenon plays a major part in the economic capital concept. The total risk in well-diversified institutions is relatively low in comparison with the sum of the risk of individual activities. As economic capital is an indicator of the total risk, it also applies that the total economic capital is lower than the sum of the economic capital per entity or per risk category. The "surplus" of economic capital that actually arises on group level can be seen as the reward for the diversification in terms of economic capital. This surplus is called the diversification benefit. In many insurance companies, the diversification benefit is in the range of 40-50% of total economic capital.

The diversification effect is calculated by using correlation factors. Correlations are statistical measures assessing the extent to which events could occur simultaneously. They are most often expressed as a variable between 0 and 1. A correlation factor of 1 implies that certain events will always occur simultaneously. Hence, there is no diversification effect and two risks identically add up. Risk managers tend to say that such risks are perfectly correlated (ie, they have a high correlation factor), meaning that these two risks do not actually diversify at all. A correlation factor of 0 implies that diversification effects are present and a certain diversification benefit exists. Correlation factors are likely to be represented in the form of a matrix as can be seen below (Panel 10.3). The calculation of the diversification benefit implies a mathematical operation called "matrix multiplication".

PANEL 10.3 DIVERSIFICATION BETWEEN THE COMPONENTS OF THE NON-LIFE RISK FOR HIG (CONTINUED)

The risk manager of HIG has calculated the economic capital for non-life risk per component. The premium risk is €300 million, the reserve risk €200 million and the catastrophe risk €900 million. The effect of diversification (the diversification benefit) is calculated through the so-called correlation matrix (Table 10.7). This happens through the mathematical operation of "matrix multiplication" which will not be discussed in detail here.

Suffice to say here that the correlation matrix (cf Table 10.7) shows that premium risk and reserve risk diversify better than premium risk and catastrophe risk because the correlation factors are 0.25 and 0.70, respectively. The lower the correlation factor, the greater the diversification benefits. It can also be concluded that the matrix is symmetrical, with the numbers below and above the "diagonal" being identical. The diagonal by definition always includes the number 1.

The diversification benefit here amounts to €200 million, whereby the total non-life risk results in €1.2 billion (see Table 10.8).

Table 10.7 Correlation matrix for HIG

	Premium risk	Reserve risk	CAT risk
Premium risk	1.00	0.25	0.70
Reserve risk	0.25	1.00	0.25
CAT risk	0.70	0.25	1.00

Table 10.8 Calculation of diversification for non-life risk (€ millions)

Risk type	Economic capital
Premium risk	€200
Reserve risk	€300
Catastrophe risk	€900
Total	€1,400
Diversification benefit	€200
Total economic capital	€1,200

Within the economic capital, a difference is made between three types of diversification. Firstly, there is the diversification within a risk category. For instance non-life claims do not arise simultaneously for all clients: not all houses burn down simultaneously and not all cars crash on the same day. Therefore, the total economic capital for non-life risk is much smaller than the sum of the economic capital per client. The same applies for life risk, market risk and operational risk.

In addition, not all equity investments fall simultaneously and equally in value (market risk) and it is extremely improbable that a big fraud, theft or IT problem would take place simultaneously (operational risk). In other words, also risks diversify between risk types. In Chapter 2, it was shown that risk pooling is one of the key activities of insurers. All these cases are examples of diversification within single risk categories. Although the concept is very obvious, it is not at all simple to determine the exact volume of diversification benefits. Correlation factors can be hard to calculate exactly.

Figure 10.5 Three kinds of diversification

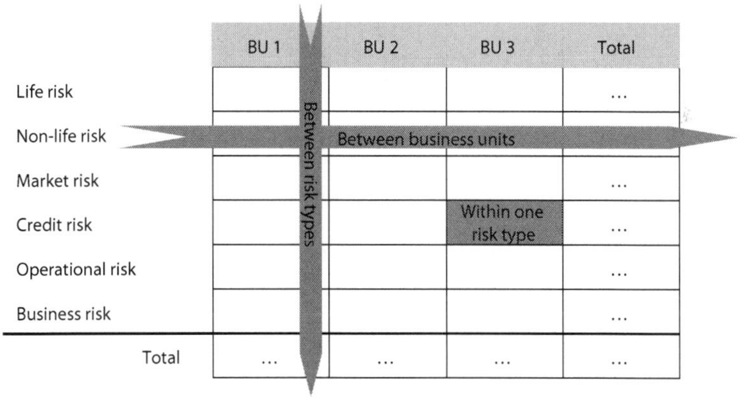

	BU 1	BU 2	BU 3	Total
Life risk				...
Non-life risk		Between business units		
Market risk				...
Credit risk			Within one risk type	...
Operational risk				...
Business risk				...
Total	...	...	...	...

Secondly, there is diversification between business units, but within one risk category. It is already known that business premises and residential properties will not necessarily burn down simultaneously. As such non-life risk in property insurance will diversify between the business lines corporate and retail underwriting. Often, the business units are organised along product lines, for instance corporates or private individuals. In fact, this form of diversification is a special form of diversification within one risk category. In practice, economic capital calculations are often made per business line. Then the risk manager has to determine the diversification between business lines explicitly. A special case is international diversification for companies with similar business lines in multiple countries.

Thirdly, there is diversification between risk categories. For example, it can be distinguished that there is a very small probability that both a big system breakdown (operational risk) and extreme losses on the account of credit risk will take place. As it is mathematically impossible to prove exactly how high the diversification factor has to be, rules of thumb are generally applied for the diversification between risk categories.

In the calculation of economic capital, the diversification within one risk category of the business units is often determined first. Then, the risk manager aggregates the total of all business units together, per risk category (horizontal arrow in Figure 10.5). Finally, he aggregates the business units (vertical arrow in Figure 10.5) in order to determine the total economic capital.

In the economic capital concept, each merger or acquisition also needs to be evaluated for its possible impact on the total economic capital at group level. Will this increase or decrease when a new business unit is acquired? In that case, what will happen to the RAROC afterwards? The new unit will also change the turnover and profit of the group. Thus not only the performance of the new business unit has to be considered, but also the risk profile of the entire group and the changes in the diversification.

DIVERSIFICATION AND ECONOMIC CAPITAL

The concept of diversification introduces the problem of different versions of economic capital. When there is a difference between the total economic capital of the insurer as a whole and the sum of the economic capital of the units, which version of the economic capital should be taken into account? The sum of the economic capital of all business units or the diversified economic capital at group level? Furthermore, how should the diversification benefit be handled? Three possible versions, each with their own pros and cons, can be distinguished:

❏ undiversified economic capital;
❏ diversified economic capital; and
❏ marginal economic capital.

In allocating the economic capital to the business units, the choice might be to ignore the economic capital benefit flowing from risk diversification within the group. This is called undiversified economic capital, where each business unit is judged by its own merits. Although, in the first instance, this seems a logical approach, problems arise because of a surplus of economic capital at group level due to diversification. What needs to be done with this surplus?

The first option is establishing a type of diversification unit ("corporate centre") at group level. This unit manages the diversification benefit of the group and can invest it, for instance according to an agreed risk profile. In this variant, the RAROC of most business units is not so high, because the risks included in the business units' economic capital ultimately disappear at group level.

An alternative is to return the diversification benefit to the business units on the basis of a determined allocation key. The business units benefit from belonging to a group. They are evaluated (in terms of RAROC, for instance) on the basis of the diversified economic capital. The costs of the economic capital turn out lower than the actual risk profile in the business unit, which is reflected by a higher profit or lower rates for clients. The advantage here is that the sum of all units concords with the economic capital of the group. The disadvantage is that the economic capital of a determined business unit partly depends on the composition of the entire group. However, a problem arises if one of the group's businesses changes its risk profile. Such a change will be only partly reflected in the economic capital of that specific business unit but, as a consequence, the entire diversification effect changes: the economic capital and the RAROC of all other business units change too, even though those business units changed nothing themselves.

When all business units fully incorporate the economic capital into the prices that are charged to the client, the group as a whole can handle lower prices better than undiversified competitors. The insurer can pass on the diversification benefit totally to the client. There is nothing left in terms of profit margin, although it could produce higher volumes and reach a higher market share.

The marginal economic capital is determined by calculating the economic capital of the group and then taking out one business unit. Consequently, the economic capital of the group will decrease by a certain amount, which is the so-called marginal economic capital of the respective business unit. If this exercise is applied to each business unit within the group, an overview of the marginal economic capital is gained. The total of the marginal economic capital is generally less than the total economic capital of the group. As a result, a part of the economic capital is not allocated to the units, resulting in a relatively high RAROC for all business units. As such, the marginal economic capital method is especially applied in strategic decisions such as the acquisition or sale of portfolios or entire business units.

As is becoming clear, each version of the economic capital has its pros and cons. In practice, we see a mix of the first and the second approach in the insurance industry. Parallel to the first method, a "kitty" is created at group level in order to manage the diversification benefit, for which the executive board is responsible. This also does justice to the activities of the board, which actually manages a portfolio of different activities (private and commercial non-life insurance, life insurance, pensions and the like). The income of this portfolio is, on the one hand, the profit from the individual activities and, on the other hand, the diversification benefit of the portfolio. If a business unit does not accomplish sufficient diversification, the executive board could decide to reduce these activities. Naturally, at the moment of making such decisions, the board will analyse how much the respective activities contribute to the achievement of the long-term objectives.

An entirely different and very pragmatic method of dealing with diversification effects is to calibrate the business units at a lower rating than is aimed for at the group level. When, for instance, an AA rating is preferred at group level, the executive board can choose to settle the business units on the basis of an economic capital based on an A rating. It is assumed that the diversified economic capital with an AA rating is exactly equal to an undiversified economic capital with an A rating. This solution has been especially developed from a pragmatic point of view.

PANEL 10.4 HANDLING DIVERSIFICATION (CONTINUED)

In Panel 10.1, it was seen that the total economic capital of the three business units is €3.7 billion. The risk management department has investigated the diversification effects. Consequently, the economic capital decreases by approximately 45%, due to non-life risk and market risk partially offsetting each other. Normally, equity prices and non-life claims are not exactly related to each other. The diversification effect in these two risk categories is also the largest. If the diversification effect is included, the RAROC at group level increases to 13.5% (5,274/2,030), which is higher than each business unit would have reached separately if diversification were not taken into account (cf Panel 10.2).

The diversification benefit is proportionally allocated back to the business units. This method implies that the unit with the highest stand-alone economic capital receives the highest diversification benefit. Total undiversified economic capital was €3,690 and the non-life business unit contributed 45% to that (1,660/3,690*100=45%). Therefore, the non-life business unit receives 46% of the diversification benefit: €747 million (45%*1,660=747). The executive board uses the principle of diversified economic capital. As a consequence, economic capital decreases most in the non-life business unit (see Table 10.9). The RAROC of all business units also increases (see Figure 10.6). Only the health business unit still performs under the hurdle rate.

Table 10.9 Economic capital and diversification (2011, € millions)

	Non-life	Life	Health	Diversification	Group
Non-life risk	€1,200			€620	€580
Life risk		€200		€70	€130
Health risk			€300	€70	€230
Market risk	€300	€900	€300	€750	€750
Credit risk	€50	€ 60	€30	€50	€90
Operational risk	€50	€60	€40	€50	€100
Business risk	€60	€60	€80	€50	€150
Total	€1,660	€1,280	€750	€1,660	€2,030
Diversification benefit	€747	€576	€337 ← ⌐		
Diversified economic capital	€913	€704	€413		€2,030
Value	€160	€100	€14		€274
RAROC	17.5%	14.2%	3.4%		13.5%

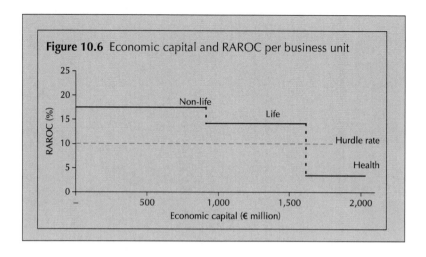

Figure 10.6 Economic capital and RAROC per business unit

ECONOMIC CAPITAL AND BALANCE SHEET OPTIMISATION

Until now, we have used the economic capital outcomes in the context of management control, ie, with the aim to encourage business
units to obtain the organisation's objective. Economic capital can
also be used to optimise the balance sheet. After all, the economic
capital is the minimum amount of capital required to survive in
adverse circumstances. And as indicated in Chapter 2, this requirement is to be brought in line with the available capital on the insurers balance sheet. This is similar to the activity of the supervisor,
comparing the available capital level to the SCR under Solvency II.

In Chapter 8, we already mentioned the existence of multiple
types of capital on the balance sheet. Capital can be in the form of
regular issued shares, retained earnings, but also hybrid capital can
serve to absorb losses. Hence, hybrid shares also count as capital.

Most often insurers will try to remain well above the minimum
capital level in order to avoid breaching the minimum level. There
are many reasons for this. First, it is a strong signal to investors and
rating agencies that the company has sufficient capital levels. Second, in times of stress it is most often difficult to raise additional
capital and also to decrease the risk profile. This is because in market
stresses, investors normally have a low appetite for additional risk
assumptions. And also, liquidating a risky portfolio can be hard (and
potentially highly loss-making) in times of market stress. In order

to avoid having to raise capital in difficult times, insurers have the option to set up contingent capital. This means that well in advance the insurer agrees with investors to draw on a limit that can serve to help the company through the difficult period. This can be in the form of subordinated loan, but also in the form of regular equity capital. Mutual companies may have similar agreements with members. Members normally may be more loyal to the company than regular shareholders to stock-listed companies. Also, mutuals have less other ways to issue capital than through members.

Balance sheet optimisation involves the following steps:

❏ determining the total risk appetite: how much risk will the company want to assume as a total and the relative proportions of each risk type;
❏ analysing current economic capital outcomes, including the relative risk position;
❏ determining the availability of capital levels; and
❏ if required, assessing whether capital levels are in line with economic capital outcomes and determine a migration strategy.

In addition to raising capital, an insurer can also optimise the balance sheet by hedging certain risks. Market risks can be hedged using derivatives such as equity options, interest rate swaps, and interest rate options. Most insurance companies have already used interest rate derivatives to lengthen the duration of their assets when there was a duration mismatch with the liabilities. Another ways to hedge risks is by using reinsurance as described in Chapter 3. When determining the reinsurance strategy, most insurers with economic capital models use the outcomes actively.

Although economic capital is a key input for balance sheet optimisation, it is not the only one. Other relevant parameters are the required capital by the supervisor and the required capital by the rating agencies. In many cases, the economic capital determined by the insurer will be lower than the regulatory capital. In that case, of course the SCR is the binding factor and the company will even operate with a margin above SCR for safety reasons.

> **PANEL 10.5 BALANCE SHEET OPTIMISATION FOR HIG (CONTINUED)**
> As indicated in Panel 10.1, HIG's capital on the balance sheet is
> €2,100 million. At the same time, Panel 10.4 indicated that HIG's total
> economic capital amounts to €2,030 million. Let us assume here that
> the regulatory capital and the required capital by the rating agencies is
> lower. This implies that HIG has only €70 million of capital in excess of
> the requirement, which is only 3%. The risk management department
> has raised this issue during an executive board meeting. This is quite a
> bit lower than the executive board desires.
>
> After this analysis by the risk management department, the executive
> board decides that it would like to decrease the total capital requirement
> in the future while at the same time investigating options to attract more
> capital. It decides that over time, the company would need minimum
> 30% of excess capital. However the executive board agrees to set this
> as a long-term goal and decides to ask the risk manager to investigate
> potential future actions. We will see in Panel 10.8 how this will be
> turned into actions in the next year.

ECONOMIC PROFIT AND THE HURDLE RATE

The controller uses the economic capital and the RAROC to evaluate and compare the performance of the group's various business units. However, achieving a positive RAROC alone is not sufficient for the controller. In exchange for the risk there is a return, but a certain amount of economic capital is also required as a buffer in order to cover unexpected losses. The insurer has to set aside this capital buffer and cannot use it to generate other return. The costs of this capital also have to be included when judging the total return. There is a kind of minimum RAROC.

Insurers use the so-called hurdle rate to adjust the return for the costs of the capital buffer. This hurdle rate indicates the minimum RAROC that an activity has to produce in order to compensate for the costs of the economic capital. Only when RAROC exceeds the hurdle rate, does a business unit really add economic value. This concept is called economic value added (EVA) or economic profit (EP). The economic profit is the RAROC minus the hurdle rate multiplied by the necessary economic capital.

Economic profit = Economic capital x (RAROC – hurdle rate)

If a unit outperforms the hurdle rate, then the economic profit is positive and economic value is added to the organisation. The income adjusted for risks is higher than the costs of the capital underpinning those risks. If it performs under the hurdle rate (EP negative), this activity destroys the economic value. Therefore, the EP is a supplement to the performance measurement tools of economic capital and RAROC in the controller's toolkit.

PANEL 10.6 ESTABLISHING THE HURDLE RATE

Although the EP concept seems clear, its practical application is not at all that simple. Establishing a hurdle rate is a special and complex process. For instance, what is the cost of capital? Through the capital asset pricing model (CAPM), it is possible to determine the cost of capital on the basis of the volatility of the share price. For insurers not quoted on the stock market, rules of thumb are available. For composite financial institutions, it is difficult to apply CAPM only to the insurer. The share price is actually a reflection of the entire group and not separately of the insurance units.

In addition, there is a question whether each entity would have to meet the same hurdle rate or whether the management should establish different hurdle rates for different entities. The economic capital concept, including its derived applications, tries to bring all risks into one denominator. Therefore, in principle, all business units should have the same hurdle rate. Management can then allow some units to destroy economic profit (EP) for strategic interests of a specific activity. A bright, new, promising activity will probably only be able to create a positive economic profit after a few years, due to the usual start-up problems. For business units whose products are especially meant as a cross-selling vehicle for the needs of other units, management can allow a negative economic profit.

In fact, the EP is in line with the embedded value, or rather its modern versions, such as market-consistent embedded value and fair value. Both indicate how much value has been created by taking the risks. Market-consistent embedded value bases the value on discounting a series of cash flows. Part of these cash flows is a risk charge derived from (preferably) economic capital. Thus this risk charge is consequently discounted. EP applies the same principle. However, it applies the risk charge later in the calculation process by using a hurdle rate as described. Having the economic capital and the fair value available, EP can be calculated faster, which might make it seem less reliable and precise to some. However, the principles underlying EP and market-consistent embedded value are identical.

PANEL 10.7 RAROC AND THE HURDLE RATE FOR HIG (CONTINUED)
The executive board applies a hurdle rate of 10%. The RAROC of the non-life business unit is the highest at 17.5%. The health unit performs well below the hurdle rate and therefore destroys value (the EP is negative). The HIG group as a whole does create value, as its RAROC exceeds the hurdle rate at 13.5%. Total EP is positive at €71 million.

Table 10.10 RAROC and EP per business unit for (2011, € millions)

	Non-life	Life	Health	Group
Economic capital	€913	€704	€413	€2,030
RAROC	17.5%	14.2%	3.4%	13.5%
Hurdle rate	10%	10%	10%	10%
EP	€69	€30	(€27)	€71

CAPITAL ALLOCATION

Within an insurer, the total amount of capital is limited. As capital is a scarce resource, the amount of risks that can be taken also has to be considered to be scarce. In other words, the return and risks involved need to be balanced. The insurer prefers to focus as much as possible on the risks that produce a relatively high return, while other risks are reduced when possible.

In order to express this, capital allocation within an insurer's management control framework is applied. The available economic capital is allocated to the business units that can develop activities with it (capital allocation). Note that this involves the imaginary distribution of capital (economic capital) among the business units based on the risk profile, in order for these units to develop activities. That is different from the actual investment of physical capital in activities. However, it is possible to actually recapitalise units on the basis of their economic capital, but it is not strictly required for the principle of capital allocation. The economic capital concept actually assumes that capital within an insurance group can be transferred if necessary. Capital allocation can be a paper exercise.

Each business unit uses its allocated economic capital as the basis for its activities. It is ensured that the total risk is restricted to a maximum of the allocated economic capital. The allocated economic capital is, therefore, also the basis for the risk reports and performance reports, for instance through RAROC.

Although, in theory, it is possible in one year to allocate the capital completely differently compared with the previous year, this does not happen in practice. The insurer actually has a robust long-term strategy. Therefore, the insurer has more or less bound itself to its markets and existing or new clients. Market parties will find the organisation unreliable if they jump to motor insurance one year and decide to define a completely new key activity the following year. In practice, the largest part of the capital will have a fixed allocation key. For the remainder, it is possible to anticipate market developments and the general state of the economy.

Allocation mechanisms

Different mechanisms are possible for allocating the available economic capital. Firstly, management could establish the allocation without the business unit having any influence on it (ie, top-down decisions). Management chooses an allocation that fits well within the strategic plan. A non-optimal allocation can be chosen, should there be strategic reasons for it. A second option is for the business units to trade economic capital with each other in a kind of internal market, whereby RAROC acts as the price indicator in establishing transactions between business units. The great advantage here is that a maximum RAROC is reached if all business units achieve the result they had previously expected. The natural question is to what extent the result of this allocation fits in with the long-term strategy of the organisation. It is actually difficult in a competitive internal market to express long-term strategies for the price in terms of RAROC.

The third allocation mechanism is a hybrid in which the management and the business units jointly establish the allocation. This is a process of negotiation, whereby the management can take the interests of all parties into consideration and simultaneously supervises the long-term strategy. Based on several general principles, an allocation key is established in collaboration with all involved parties. This is the process that takes place in most insurance companies.

PANEL 10.8 ECONOMIC CAPITAL ALLOCATION AT HIG (CONTINUED)
The executive board wants to make less economic capital available in 2012. In total, it wants to allocate only €1.8 billion economic capital to the business units. This means that all business units must present a plan to restrict the risk profile. The plans are as follows.

❏ The non-life business unit focuses on prevention and the reinsurance policy. Through prevention, the economic capital decreases by €30 million. This involves €10 million in costs. A higher reinsurance coverage frees up €200 million of economic capital. The reinsurance premium increases by €15 million.

❏ The life business unit takes measures to decrease the operational risk by €10 million. The cost of this is €5 million. This decision is strictly speaking not "profitable" in terms of RAROC (or rather: "value-generating"), but aims for future efficiency benefits. Life also hedges a large part of the equity risk, causing a drop in the economic capital of €100 million. This causes this result to decrease by €10 million. The most important change is a planned volume growth of 10%. As the RAROC exceeds the hurdle rate, the EP increases with the volume. The risk manager calculates that both the result and the life risk increase by 10%.

Table 10.11 Economic capital allocation per business unit (2012, € millions)

	Non-life	Life	Health	div.	Group
Non-life risk	€970			€610	€390
Life risk		€240		€70	€170
Health risk			€300	€70	€230
Market risk	€300	€800	€300	€720	€680
Credit risk	€50	€60	€30	€50	€90
Operational risk	€50	€50	€40	€50	€90
Business risk	€60	€60	€80	€50	€150
Total	€1,430	€1,210	€750	€1,590	€1,800
Diversification benefit	€715	€552	€323		
Diversified economic capital	€715	€658	€427		€1,800

❏ The health business unit focuses particularly on cost control. €10 million is saved through an efficiency programme, which increases the RAROC to 5.6%. This is still under the hurdle rate, but due to the strategic interest of the health market, the executive board finds this RAROC acceptable.

The RAROC of the HIG group as a whole increases to 14.9%. The EP is €89 million, an increase of 25% for 2012. The measures taken by the non-life business unit do not add value, because the economic Profit remains €69 million. However, the executive board still considers these measures desirable in order to limit HIG's total risk exposure (ie, the total economic capital consumption).

Table 10.12 Economic capital, RAROC and EP (2012, € millions)

	Non-life	Life	Health	Group
Result	€185	€105	€24	€314
Profit adjustments	(€45)	N/A	N/A	(€45)
Changes in fair value	€140	€105	€24	€269
Economic capital	€715	€658	€427	€1,800
RAROC	19.6%	15.9%	5.6%	14.9%
EP	€69	€39	(€19)	€89

With the decrease in the amount of economic capital compared to 2011 from €2,030 million to €1,800 million, the executive board has achieved a step in attaining an 30% excess capital on the balance sheet. At the same time, the 2011 profit now serves as retained earnings as part of capital on the balance sheet. In total, HIG made a profit of €274 million in 2011 (see Panel 10.1). This means that capital for the 2012 opening balance sheet is €2,374 million (€2,100 in 2011 plus €274 profit). Now that HIG has an economic capital level of €1,800 million and an available capital level of €2,374 million, there is a 32% excess capital (2,374/1,800*100% = 132%).

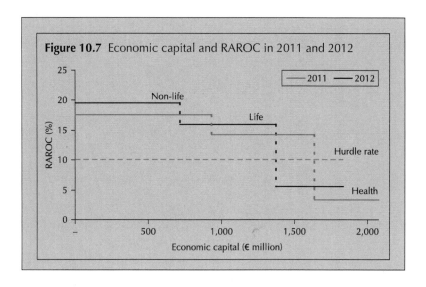

Figure 10.7 Economic capital and RAROC in 2011 and 2012

RAROC ASSUMPTIONS

The concept of RAROC is based on a number of assumptions of which management needs to be well aware. The backgrounds of the calculation results are of great importance in order to interpret the outcomes well. This is particularly important because the calculations are complex exercises, and could cause management to lose sight of the wood because of the trees.

Explaining the models in a clear and simple way is a difficult job for some risk managers or actuaries and, conversely, managers sometimes may find models useless. It is important, though, to understand the models well before the results can be applied in a meaningful manner. A key criterion of a good risk model is the extent to which management can understand its outcomes: are they logical and sensible from a business perspective? Although this might be of dominant importance, this section emphasises a number of different assumptions in the concept of RAROC.

A number of key assumptions are made in the process of the risk calculations and economic capital models. There is a clear separation between two kinds of assumptions. Firstly, there are simplifying assumptions that make it possible to create statistic models. An example of this is the simplification of correlations in the risk model calculations. In general, the modellers can ground each hypothesis with a statistical analysis. They have probably already made sensitivity analyses in which they assess the consequences of each assumption. Questions arising in such analyses are for instance: what would the total economic capital be if all the correlations were 10% higher than currently estimated? Secondly, there are conceptual assumptions on the risk phenomenon of risk within insurers. These assumptions are as follows:

All possible deviations of the profit are explained by one of the known risk types

The risk manager assumes that the company exclusively makes its return by taking risks. When there is a negative profit (loss), this is explained by the fact that one of the assumed risks materialised. To explain profit fluctuations that are not driven by well-known risk types, new risks have been created (for instance, operational risk, then business risk). Therefore, this hypothesis is workable in practice. However, the question is whether the contrary also applies: are extreme returns always explained by taking exorbitant risks? Management has to be aware that the risk is not the only explanatory factor of return.

All risks can be included in the prices

According to this assumption, compensation is received for the risk taken, ie, taking extra risks is rewarded by additional returns. This occurs for market risk and non-life risk. Management consciously assumes a position for a certain risk and wants to receive compensation in return. This involves the valuation of financial risks in particular. It is more difficult to explicitly include operational and business risks in a tariff. The client will not want to pay for this tariff when the insurer makes many operational mistakes. In judging RAROC figures, the management has to be aware that compensation cannot be received for all risks. Therefore, it is not always that simple to judge the RAROC figures of fee-based business units (eg, asset management) that cannot assume financial risks.

All known risk types can be quantified on the basis of an objective statistical model

Within the economic capital method, VaR types of measurement methods are the starting point. In this measurement method, it is often assumed that losses from the past serve as a model for future losses. For the "new" risk categories such as operational risk and business risk, in particular, this assumption is difficult to maintain as the sector lacks sufficient data to validate this hypothesis. Besides, not all (negative) effects of risks are measurable, such as reputational damage and opportunity losses. This makes complete and adequate quantification difficult in some cases.

There is a causal connection between the economic capital and the possible appearance of losses

This implies that if the economic capital changes, the expected loss will increase or decrease. In the case of non-life risk, this means, for instance, that the economic capital decreases when preventative measures are taken towards the client. It does not really apply to operational risk. In many financial institutions, the economic capital is mainly based on loss data. When an incident occurs, measures are taken to reduce the probability of repetition in the future. This, however, cannot be reflected in the economic capital for operational risk because the model is based on historical data. This is also valid for the underwriting risks. Changes in the claim payment procedure or in the claim systems could decrease volatility of the claims. However, this materialises only after a certain period of time in economic capital, since the calculations are based on historical data. The reverse is also true. Imagine a company with two product systems selling the same products. Would all products be in the same system, the volatility would be lower just simply due to the law of large numbers. This should be reflected in a lower economic capital outcome. In practice however, no material change has occurred in claim payments or processes. Potentially the operational risk profile has changed, but not the underwriting risk profile.

For some risk categories, doubts can be placed on the validity of these assumptions. The non-financial risks (operational risk and business risk), in particular, are not the direct consequence of assuming a commercial position. The issues connected to these assumptions were often previously raised but then ignored in the practical elaboration of the RAROC concept. However, the entire financial industry will have to find a solution for these issues in the near future for the concept of economic capital to be fully used in the companies' management control cycles.

MANAGEMENT CONTROL CYCLE

All applications within the economic capital concept have already been discussed in the above sections of this chapter. The question now is how to apply the economic capital concept within the management control cycle. In the first sections of this chapter, it was shown that management control aims to influence the members of the organisation to contribute to the entire organisation's objective.

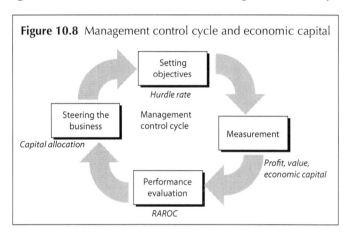

Figure 10.8 Management control cycle and economic capital

The typical management control cycle consists of the following steps (see Figure 10.8):

❏ setting objectives;
❏ performance measurement;
❏ performance evaluation; and
❏ taking measures.

The first step is establishing the objectives. Management informs the other members of the organisation of the objectives. These objectives are often established by mutual agreement. With the establishment of the objectives, the long-term strategy of the respective business units, the market circumstances and other remaining items that can be of influence are considered. In the insurance environment, as was elaborated in this chapter, the first objective is to establish the hurdle rate. This is complemented by the objective of value (or EP) to be achieved, or RAROC. With that, the management indicates the lower limit and preconditions for the future performances of the respective business units.

In the second step, the output of the business units is measured. In the traditional situation, the return in particular was looked at in terms of profit. Here, the added value and the risk profile will gradually gain importance, when the economic capital and value are included.

The third step in the management control cycle is performance evaluation. The output measured in the second step is assessed and evaluated. As the risk run is an important explanation for the level of the achieved results, RAROC will be used in the performance evaluation. A couple of insurers already publish the composition of the economic capital and achieved RAROC in their annual reports. The expectation is that gradually more insurers will follow this example, especially with Solvency II in sight. Embedded value has been a component of life insurers' annual reports for years, although improvements can be expected in the context of market-consistent embedded value and fair value.

The last step in the management control cycle is taking measures towards the business units. Many control mechanisms are used, such as qualitative control and budgets, but capital allocation will also become a more important mechanism for insurers. Management allocates a certain amount of economic capital to each business unit, which is free to operate to a certain extent. Some units will be restricted in their movements, while the capital allocation for other units will leave space to grow. Management can thus express in which direction it wants to steer the organisation, with the achievement of the long-term objectives of the organisation as the final objective.

During the annual budget process, objectives are settled for the coming accounting year in terms of profit and growth, although the capital allocation can be adapted at the same time here. Then, during the entire year, the output of the business units is measured. The controller reports these figures each month or quarter to the executive board. In this report, not only will the profit be determined (measured), but how well the obtained results concord with the agreed objectives (performance evaluation) will also be judged. If necessary, the objectives will be adjusted or steered by taking other measures. A continuous process is in place here, whereby activities from each step will be performed simultaneously.

In the near future, the RAROC concept and all its related applications will gradually play a more important part in financial institutions' management control cycles. The concept offers possibilities for mutually comparable but different activities, where the risk profile is to be taken into consideration. However, it cannot be assumed that the Holy Grail has been found. Restrictions are clearly attached to the use of RAROC and value. This is due to the assumptions that lie at the foundations of the concept as well as the assumptions and limitations of the statistical calculations of the economic capital because of deficient historical data.

Controlling organisations is a complex matter that cannot be expressed in only one figure. Therefore, the management will have to continue using a spectrum of qualitative and quantitative variables, as has been discussed. However, the introduction of RAROC and value-based measures can be seen as a step forward especially from the financial perspective.

FINANCIAL CONGLOMERATES

Nowadays, it is common to combine insuring and banking under one roof. Around 1990, the abolition of rules led to a wave of mergers between insurers and banks. The terms referring to such combinations are "all-finanz institutions", "bancassurance", "assurfinance" and financial conglomerate. Well-known European examples traditionally have been Allianz, Groupama and ING, but Aegon and Aviva also have banking activities, albeit significantly smaller compared to their insurance operations. We will see below that Allianz, ING have taken initiatives to decrease the interconnectedness of their banking and insurance operations. However, the advantages of financial conglomerates are:

❏ larger financial strength and cross-selling possibilities;
❏ economies of scale in the back offices leading to cost efficiency; and
❏ risk-spreading due to maturity structure and diversification effects.

For a long time, the maturity structure was an important argument for combining insurers and banks. After all, insurers have life insurances of a long duration and banks have mortgages of a long duration. This neutralises the consequences of fluctuations in the interest rate. Nowadays, insurers and banks both use derivatives in order to cover the effects of interest fluctuations. In particular, swap markets have become significantly liquid and efficient. This implies that the maturity structure might a less important driver for financial conglomerates.

The combination of non-life insurance and lending also causes great diversification effects. Suppose that a corporate client takes out both insurance and a loan with a financial conglomerate. If a large-scale event occurs (for instance, a storm), there are two possibilities: the company receives a claim payment from its insurance and is able to repay the credit, or the company receives no claim payment and remains in default on the loan. However, both situations do not take place simultaneously. If an insurer and a bank are not combined, neither of them can take this into account, although a combined financial conglomerate naturally can. As such, diversification is an important argument for financial conglomerates and justifies the reasons for intermediates described in Chapter 2.

The various financial crises in the 2000s have also highlighted the fact that insurers can be fragile and prone to financial market crises. The financial crisis of 2008 and later (see Chapter 6) has been a wake-up call for many financial market participants. Rating agencies started to become more alert to financial conglomerates' sensitivities to financial crises. This has resulted in an initial movement for companies to disintegrate. Fortis in Europe was an interesting example in 2008, but that was also driven by a near-failure and bailout by the three national governments of the Benelux. Other examples are Allianz that sold its Dresdner bank to Commerzbank and ING that considered separating its banking and insurance activities.

For financial conglomerates, especially, the economic capital framework is an important management controlling instrument. All the applications discussed earlier in this chapter apply. The framework allows financial conglomerates to measure the different risks of the various activities in a consistent way. At group level, the credit and insurance risks can be partially offset. Naturally, with the economic capital, consistent performance measurement and capital allocation can also be applied. Therefore, the economic capital principle is also an important instrument for financial conglomerates.

CONCLUSION

Chapters 3, 4 and 5 discussed how the economic capital is calculated. This chapter elaborated on the application of the results. The importance of risk as a component of management control was discussed. Through examples, it was seen that economic capital can assume an important position in management control, for instance through capital allocation and RAROC reports. The same applies to value (embedded value, fair value, EP) as a performance measurement in the management control cycle.

A key achievement of the economic capital framework is that it provides a common risk language, a common denominator for risk and return. We have seen that many assumptions in the calculations were stressed during the financial crisis (Chapter 6). A potential response is to either reject the concept of economic capital completely or to increase capital levels based on these stressed calculations. A more viable alternative is to continue using the current assumptions as a common language. This will improve acceptance of the outcomes. Balance sheet optimisation will continue to be done conservatively with the objective that the insurance company will need to withstand extreme crisis situations.

Not all insurers are ready to introduce all applications completely. The expectation is that the larger companies will take great steps forward in the coming years. Solvency II has already been an impetus for this and this will continue to be the case over the coming years. This implies that, on the basis of the reports of controllers and risk managers, more people, departments and functions will gradually familiarise themselves with all concepts evolving around the economic capital control framework.

---

1   This is often the old Solvency I requirement, but some insurers apply the economic capital.
2   This book prefers the term ROC, as in financial institutions it is not unusual to also add the subordinated debt capital to the overall capital amount and use that as well as a buffer to cover risks.

11

Organising Risk Management

Risk management within the insurance industry has developed strongly over the last few years. The financial crisis that begun in 2008 has contributed towards insurers becoming more aware of some important risks. However, this development has been ongoing since the early 2000s. In professionalising risk management, insurers have partly followed the route taken by banks, with a number of financial conglomerates such as ING and Allianz leading the way.

In previous chapters, we have looked in detail at the various risk categories that were identified in Chapter 2 and insurance regulation, of which Solvency II is the most predominant. It was also explained in Chapter 10 how economic capital outcomes can be used in the framework of management control. All these applications have been relatively technical and quantitative in nature. However, this chapter will look at risk management from an organisational perspective, firstly by looking at the major theme of corporate governance, focusing on how to structure a countervailing power for all levels in an organisation. Such a countervailing power will improve the quality of decisions. The framework of three lines of defence is also a way to structure this within the company. This chapter will also examine the function of the chief risk officer (CRO), risk management departments and dedicated risk management committees.

CORPORATE GOVERNANCE
Over the last few decades a number of major scandals have oc-

curred, most of which have been much discussed in the media. Many of these scandals were caused by an inadequate balance of power in the executive board. Corporate governance is how a company is managed, and details how it ensures that the company makes well-balanced decisions. For instance, it should monitor if the CEO has too much power without being challenged or criticised. As a result of the scandals, regulation was developed in a number of countries. In some countries, this was carried out by the regulator, while others involved self regulation developed by the industry in the form of codes of conduct.

Corporate governance is an extremely wide and important topic, and really deserves an entire book to itself. However, this book on risk management would be incomplete if it did not pay any attention to it, especially in the context of our debate of the financial crisis in Chapter 6. Therefore, we briefly touch upon it in this chapter, since adequate corporate governance is a key element of a risk organisation. It is worth emphasising that corporate governance relates to the position of the company towards its shareholders, but similarly to the position within the company internally.

The problem of corporate governance is laid down in agency theory, which explains that agents can have different objectives from that of principals giving agents money to reach the principals' objective. In one way, the principal would like to monitor the behaviour of the agent without having to do all the work themselves. The same is true for shareholders that give the executive board of a company the freedom to manage their funds with the objective of maximising the value of the stock. Or the supervisor monitoring the behaviour of insurance companies with the ultimate objective of protecting policyholders.

One of the ways to address corporate governance is to have a non-executive board that supervises the behaviour of the executive members. This is common practice in most insurance companies. After some scandals, a number of corporate governance codes emerged regarding the way non-executive members should monitor executive members of the board. The most important issue is that sufficient countervailing powers are installed within the executive board, such as a strong chief financial officer (CFO) and chairman of the board. This relates to sufficient quantity and quality of countervailing powers. For instance, the role of the chairman of the board is to challenge the proposals and decisions of the CEO. However, sometimes the chairman of the board has proven to be too friendly to the CEO and agreed to all proposals as long as profit was generated, although we now know that high profit and high risk can go hand in hand.

Many corporate governance debates focus on the variable income of executive board members. This was also true during the financial crisis. Indeed, academic research proves that variable income is an important source of risk – risk of fraud that is. Of course, variable income related to the firm's financial performance is an incentive to increase the financial results of the company and hence to increase the return of shareholders. This incentive needs to be balanced in order to avoid the CEO misstating the results in their own favour. When the most powerful person in a company is subject to fraud risk, who will identify such fraud and mitigate the risk? This is essentially a core task of corporate governance and the responsibility of mitigating this risk lies with the non-executive members of the board of directors. Again, it is key that the CEO is challenged on their decisions and proposals.

Although incentive setting in CEOs compensation packages (and for the other executive members of the board) may seem simple, it can be extremely complex. For example, academic proof regarding the effectiveness of bonuses has not yet been provided. Potentially, compensation in terms of stock options and shares may be more effective because they are related to the long-term value of the firm rather than short-term profit. In the context of insurance, this book has sufficiently addressed the fact that profit is an extremely bad indicator of performance. The key issue for corporate governance is to encourage intrinsic motivation of the executive members of the board to perform.

Someone recently pointed out to me the dilemma of the successful CEO. A successful CEO increases the performance of the company and is rewarded for that by shareholders. And potentially, with much media attention, this gives them status. With increasing status comes increasing power. This power needs to be countervailed in order to remain in control. The dilemma of the successful CEO consists in the fact that an increase in their power seldom goes in parallel with an increase in countervailing power. This is a key risk and central to corporate governance.

A large failure in the UK triggered the formation of the Cadbury Committee on corporate governance, and it issued the first major code for stock-listed companies. A number of other failures led to improvements in the Cadbury Code, and also outside the UK. The Sarbanes–Oxley (SOX) regulation in the US is the best -known example, but most countries have their own equivalent (albeit more principle-based than SOX). There is a difference between strict rule-based regulation such as SOX and more principle-based regulation. Principle-based regulation gives freedom to the companies on how they implement the regulation. Companies can set up their own systems in a way that they feel is most suitable. Some codes of conduct are based on the principle of "comply-or-explain". This means that companies are expected to implement the particular code except when they feel that it does not fit their specific situation. In that case, they have to explain to stakeholders why they have done so and how a different measure is implemented in the spirit of the original code. Mostly, this explanation is offered in the annual report. This leaves freedom for the companies to adapt the implementation to their own needs – and it basically forces them to think in the spirit of the original code.

PANEL 11.1: SARBANES–OXLEY
The main catalyst for the SOX act was the collapse of Enron in 2001, with fraud and misrepresentation of the financial results being the main reasons for this collapse. While the SOX regulation was being prepared for approval in the US Senate, WorldCom collapsed – another historical fraud case that shocked the world. The official name of SOX is the "Public Company Accounting Reform and Investor Protection Act", passed in 2002.
Seven important provisions of SOX.

❑ Audit regulation: a central US institute (Public Company Accounting Oversight Board) oversees the functioning of audit firms in order to prevent conflicts of interest by accounting firms.
❑ Auditor independence: it is prohibited to influence the auditor if that could lead to misrepresentation of the financial statements. Also, in order to remain independent, the company needs to change audit firms or audit partners regularly to be approved by the company's audit committee.

- ❏ Corporate responsibility: the CEO and CFO of stock-listed companies are personally accountable for the financial statements, as well as their accuracy and reliability.
- ❏ Enhanced financial disclosures: companies will need to disclose more information, including off-balance-sheet items and risk information. This is in line with updated IFRS requirements.
- ❏ In-control statement: The most visible aspect of this personal accountability is the "in-control" statement, signed by the CEO and CFO. This element of SOX is explained in section 404 and is frequently cited. In the in-control statement, management assesses the quality and effectiveness of the internal control system. In practice, this leads to intensive documentation on the effectiveness of the controls in order to prove that a particular item on the balance sheet is correctly presented.
- ❏ IT: internal controls are preferably automated. As a result, many companies adapted IT systems in order to prove the effectiveness of internal controls.
- ❏ Penalties: concrete penalties are described in SOX for fraud and so-called white-collar crimes. This follows the personal accountability of the CEO and CFO for the financial statements. Also, SOX aims to legally protect whistleblowers.

The SOX regulation received both criticism and praise. The main reasons for the criticism was the administrative burden for companies that needed to comply with, and the rule-based nature of the regulations. The main reason for praise was that it created a clear sense of urgency for companies that corporate governance is a serious business. Also, financial statements have improved significantly after 2002. Whether this is due to SOX or due to general awareness after the scandals is debatable.

Corporate governance can be formalised through certain codes of conduct and legal regulations, and the level of corporate governance can be measured. Relevant indicators are include the number of audit committee meetings, the presence of a financial expert in the audit committee, the number of board positions of each non-executive member and the separation of roles of the chairman of the board and the CEO. Nearly every insurance company now presents corporate governance in their annual reports. This chapter in the annual report explains the compensation packages of the executive board members and how the non-executive members supervise the executive board, as well the roles of different the board members.

Although these formal corporate governance measures are relevant, academic research has shown that formal indicators are unrelated to the occurrence of fraud. Here is where the debate becomes interesting – how then can sufficient countervailing powers be installed in order to prevent fraud? The relation between the CEO, the CFO and the chairman of the board are extremely important. Due to corporate governance regulation, these three persons can be held personally accountable for any misstatement of the financial results.

In addition, the audit committee has a monitoring role in risk identification. The accountant will have to sign off the financial results of the firm and, as such, they have an important role. What the scandals showed was that accounting firms were hesitant to approve any exception from the standard interpretation of the accounting rules. This is because accountants can now also be held personally accountable in some cases. At the same time, the initial overreaction after SOX seems to have faded away, and accountants have now returned to being more client-oriented. Another key role for accountants is to remain a countervailing power to the company by remaining sufficiently independent and to verify the accuracy and reliability of financial statements.

For stock-listed firms, the corporate governance of institutional investors is crucial. These are sophisticated parties that are able to evaluate company performance and the strategic choices of the firm. We saw in the period leading up to the financial crisis that some hedge funds took this role a bit too aggressively and forced companies to present higher results than were realistic. However, generally, corporate governance is relevant for institutional investors – this is of especial interest for insurance companies, as they are themselves large institutional investors.

PANEL 11.2: WORLDCOM
WorldCom, which was set up in 1983, was the second largest phone operator in the US until its failure in 2002. Mergers and acquisitions were an important source for growth, especially in the 1990s, when it carried out a large takeover of telecom giant MCI. In 2002, an investigation of the internal auditors led to restatements of its financial accounts and the conviction of its CEO. In the period before 2002,

WorldCom had misstated earnings significantly and incorrectly capitalised costs as assets. Both could be considered fraud. Due to misstating earnings and costs, the profit was presented as too high. By capitalising costs, the total assets of the firm increased, which in turn increased equity. The CEO also held capital, so this fraud also boosted his personal capital. In total, the WorldCom fraud amounted to roughly US$11 billion.

One of the underlying reasons for the WorldCom fraud was that the growth strategy through acquisitions depended on an increase in stock value. This created enormous inverse incentives for the company, especially when the markets decreased and merger alternatives also shrunk. In addition, the large amount of stocks held by the CEO created conflicts of interest. Analysis of the WorldCom case showed that the CEO was able to present false information to investors and to the non-executive members of the board. In doing so, he was insufficiently held back by colleagues such as the CFO and the company's financial controller. By the way, many employees in the financial departments were aware of this and apparently did not sound the alarm bells. All in all, countervailing powers failed to prevent the fraud from continuing within WorldCom.

Culture was key in allowing the fraud to continue for so long. The culture within WorldCom was based on the strong belief that the promises made to the shareholders should be met at all costs. There was also an atmosphere where employees felt insufficiently safe to ask questions, or even raise objections. In other words, countervailing power failed throughout the organisation. The institutionalised countervailing power of audit failed as well. A report on WorldCom found that some senior employees had never even heard of internal audit.

The external auditor should also have discovered the fraud, but failed to do so. Audit firm Arthur Andersen apparently did not sufficiently check the effectiveness of WorldCom's internal controls, and WorldCom also withheld detailed financial information from Andersen. An accounting firm should have never accepted this – again countervailing power.

Non-executive members of the board did not notice the fraud due to the influence of the CEO over the board. Members of the board hardly had any involvement in the company apart from attending board meetings. Furthermore, they hardly met other WorldCom employees outside the presentations during the board meetings. The boards discussions and decisions seemed to be steered by the CEO.

An interesting conflict of interest occurred when the CEO granted a leasing agreement for an airplane to the chairman of the compensations committee. This was done without notifying the other board members, even when this fact should have actually been disclosed to the public.

HISTORICAL DEVELOPMENT

In the 1990s, the risk management field was heavily disintegrated and spread over various departments. The certified actuary had an important role in the calculation and determination of the technical provisions. The statutory accounts need to be certified by the actuary, making them a key player in the debate. The mathematical competence of the actuary makes their role crucial for analysing certain underlying patterns in claim payments (an initial step towards modern risk management). By determining the technical provisions, the actuary ensured that sufficient (implicit) prudence was in place to absorb any setbacks in the benefit payments. The risk models used for that purpose were less advanced than they are nowadays. Briefly, the risk models at that time aimed to estimate the expected value of the claim payments, while today's models also focus on potential fluctuations around that expected value. Prudence was sometimes added in a very crude way. For instance, in the case of non-life insurance, prudence was included by not discounting technical provisions for most products.

In addition, actuaries or risk managers in the investment department were responsible for the performance of ALM studies (see Chapter 4). Traditionally, these were not always fully based on cash flows from the insurance business. A so-called "asset-only" approach was employed, meaning that only the market and credit risks of the investments were considered. This aimed to limit investment losses while at the same time ensuring sufficient investment returns. The traditional balance between fixed income and equity in the investment portfolio dates from those days when investment was an activity performed relatively in isolation from underwriting.

Within the underwriting or reinsurance departments, portfolio analysis was carried out from a risk perspective, although it was definitely not a structural activity. Credit risk from reinsurers was limited by spreading the reinsurance contracts over a wide range of reinsurers, although seldom based on credit risk policies. Rather, logic and commonsense was the basis for such decisions.

Since then, much has changed. Actuaries have evolved into risk managers that run quantitative risk models. The outcomes of those risk models play a key role in the decision-making process of the business (as we explained in Chapter 10).

For the area of management control, a parallel development can be drawn. It has already been shown that, around the mid 1990s, controlling was oriented especially towards finance and administration. The controller was actually the bookkeeper, and ensured that the annual accounts were drawn up and certified by the chartered accountant. As such, certain measures needed to be in place to ensure that the annual accounts were reliable and reflected underlying truth. To that end, the controller made reconciliations between the general ledger and product systems, for instance. They were also interested in the risk of errors in the core processes because this could influence the accuracy of the annual accounts. Logically, the technical provisions and investments form a large part of the balance sheet as part of the annual accounts. Therefore, the sensitivities in these items were also an area of focus. However, in practice, many controllers have always considered the P&L statement more important than the balance sheet statement.

Nowadays, the qualitative and non-financial aspects also play a part in the responsibilities of the controller. The administrative tasks of the controller have therefore moved into the background. Over the years, the controller has taken a much more proactive position and delivers advice on various aspects within the company to its management. The controller has evolved from an administrative employee/accountant to a financial/strategic management advisor, and can sometimes be seen as the financial conscience of a management team or executive board. This involves the management control role as described in Chapter 10: supporting decision-making by managers. As such, a group-wide "helicopter view" has become a minimum requirement.

For both professions, actuarial and controlling stereotypes exist to describe the typical actuary and typical controller. Both are professionals in the deepest sense of the term. This implies that they both have a technical and quantitative expertise to a very detailed level. For example, both understand accounting rules well enough to estimate the impact of certain developments. At the same time, this technical expertise makes their work hard to understand for laymen and managers, especially with communicative skills mostly being not as well developed as in commercial departments. This makes actuaries and controllers sensitive to the following classical stereotype: being right without being heard while advising managers.

A key challenge lying ahead for both professions (or actually they are gradually converging into one and the same profession) is to master the competence of communication. How should technical details be explained to decision-makers in such a way that the advice is understood and adopted? Empathy is an important step for both the risk manager and the controller. Decision-makers often have a wide array of concerns on their mind. To that end, it is important how the risk manager and the controller convey the message effectively. Building a good working relationship is often more important than to be technically right and complete.

Within the framework of economic capital and RAROC, the striking the balance between risk and return has gained an important position in both the actuarial and controlling professions. For the controller following old financial standards, it is no longer sufficient to establish what return has been achieved. Often major risks lie beneath extraordinary returns, of which a controller must be aware. On the other hand, the actuary does not simply have to sound the alarm bell when a major risk occurs, as this will probably be compensated by sufficient return. Intensive co-operation between the controller and the risk manager is imperative here because the controller largely determines the numerator of the RAROC fraction and the risk manager determines the denominator. It can be expected that gradually more risk management and control tasks will be integrated. The two worlds of control and risk management are gradually converging (see Figure 11.1).

Indeed, it has become increasingly obvious that the activities of risk management and controlling are converging. For instance, embedded value (as explained in Chapter 10) was once a topic for just actuaries but is now included in regular management reporting. However, a separate actuarial embedded value report exists to describe the technical details and the technical sensitivity analysis. Of course, it would be more coherent to include these sensitivities in the general management report, such that managers could understand the wider context of the outcomes. In practice, we see that it is also a political issue: the controlling department writes the monthly management report and the actuarial department writes the embedded value report. If these elements were included in only one report, what department would then be the owner of the report? Despite the silliness of such considerations, unfortunately we see that this can happen within insurance companies.

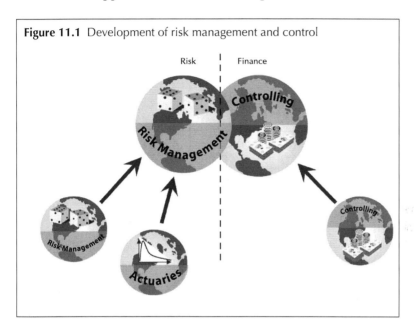

Figure 11.1 Development of risk management and control

INTERNAL RISK GOVERNANCE

Ultimately, the responsibility for risk management rests with the executive board. This has always been the case, but has become more visible with the introduction of a number of risk frameworks. However, a structure is required for this to work in an efficient and effective way. After all, the executive board has to delegate tasks so that it can bear that overall responsibility.

In Chapter 5, we identified three lines of defence within the organization, to clarify roles and responsibilities in the risk management framework. Originally, the principle of three lines of defence was designed in the area of operational risk, partly to clarify the differences between the operational risk manager and the internal auditor. However, the principles can be applied equally well in other risk areas and, as such, it is a useful framework of reference in organising risk management. A discussion of these three lines of defence now follows.

❑ General management: the decision makers are managers themselves, and they are the first line of defence. Managers are responsible for the entire organisation, its outcomes and its risks. To that
end, managers have to determine their own risk appetite, the risk
limits and to monitor compliance to these limits. Also, managers
have the responsibility to put risks into the wider perspective of
the organisation. Although risk is obviously important, it is by no
means the only perspective. After all, the most risk-averse organisation could well be the one that does not dare to sell any products.

❑ Risk management department: general management is likely
to appreciate advice on a wide array of topics in their decision-
making. Risk management is one of the advisory bodies. For
each decision, risk management can evaluate the relevant risks
and the impact on the total risk profile of the company. However,
for this to be efficient, it is also useful to draft risk policies so that
the rest of the organisation has guidance on what risks to accept
and what risks to avoid. Examples are investment policies, underwriting guidelines, business continuity management (BCM)
policies, liquidity management policies and credit risk exposure
limits. As indicated in Chapter 5, developing a risk measurement
methodology (ie, economic capital) is a key responsibility of the
risk management department in its second line of defence role.

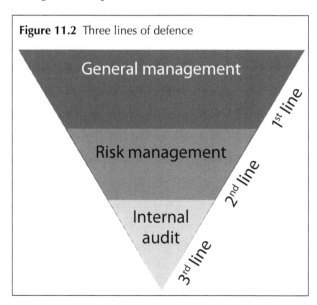

Figure 11.2 Three lines of defence

General management

Risk management

Internal
audit

1st line

2nd line

3rd line

❏ Internal audit department: internal audit monitors whether the organisation complies with the risk management policies – they are the third line of defence. Internal audit carry out investigations on-site and, as such, internal auditors know the business to a good level of detail. In order to be independent, internal audit needs to have a certain distance from the operational processes of the company. In addition to their monitoring role, internal audit may advise the second line of defence how to draft their policies to better capture the entire risk profile. Since risk models have become more important for insurers, internal audit has become involved in the evaluation of the risk models of the risk management department. This requires them to have sufficient understanding of the risk models, but also a level of understanding of what processes are required to produce adequate risk models.

The three lines of defense framework clearly points out the key responsible level for risk management: general managers have the end responsibility to implement the required measures. Problem solving is the responsibility of general managers. The risk management department is only the support function, although it also looks at the risk dashboard to warn general managers of potential risk areas. However, when things turn badly unintentionally, the risk manager often has just a big a problem as the general manager. After all, it is the role of the risk manager to identify risks. Unidentified risks should be a core concern of the risk manager.

This framework is relevant at a holding level, but it is of course equally applicable at the business unit level. We often see that a company has a risk management department at a holding level and a similar set-up within the business units. Often, risk managers within the business units have two "bosses". They report hierarchically to the business unit management, but there are frequently functional lines to the holding level's risk management department. The benefit of this is assurance that group risk policies are implemented at the lower levels. For instance, functional reporting lines ensure that the local risk manager has adequate tools available to implement the policy. An additional benefit is that the group risk department is more likely to design relevant policies. Holding level departments may have a great deal of oversight but less detailed knowledge of the relevant risks in the business units. A dialogue between the holding and the business units promotes relevance and consistency.

RISK MANAGEMENT DEPARTMENTS AND THE CRO

With the increasing importance of risk as a key business variable, companies are also in the process of changing the allocation of resources to risk. One of the areas where this is most visible is the appointment of a CRO. Over the last 5–10 years, most of the larger insurance companies appointed CROs and more companies can be expected to follow suit. Some insurers have simply renamed the chief actuary as the CRO. Such a name change also typically includes a changed or new function. When a CRO is appointed, they are also given responsibility for group-wide risk management departments. In previous years, these departments were mostly oriented towards the implementation of risk management (ie, they were project-based). Over time, they tended to move towards professional risk management functions, including policymaking and advising line management and executive bodies on important pieces of policy such as reinsurance and ALM. However, the responsibility of the CRO is not identical for each company. With the strong position of the actuary, some insurers decided to keep the chief actuary as the primary responsibility for underwriting risks. The CRO in these companies could be either responsible for just operational risk or, in some rare cases, also for investment risks. It is obvious that in insurance companies without a clear CRO, the allocation between responsibilities is hybrid and potentially unclear – which is a risk in itself!

The position of the CRO differs from company to company. In some cases, the CRO reports directly to the executive board. The most logical direct reporting line for the CRO is to the CFO, but this is not always the case. In others, the CRO holds a board position. For both cases, however, it is obvious that a close link with the CFO is essential. As indicated above, there is a natural tension between risk and control. These natural tensions should be brought under the responsibility of one person (such as the CFO) or body (eg, the board), but the creation of unproductive barriers should be avoided. Close cooperation between controllers and risk managers should be the foundation underlying proper risk management.

The advantage of the CRO reporting into the CFO is that risk and return can be addressed consistently – ie, by one person. The CFO is likely to have a financial director as another direct report, and the

CFO can combine these two views into a coherent perspective. Also, risk has a clear impact on accounting (for example, IFRS4-Phase II – see Chapter 7). The role of the CFO is also to challenge the business of improving performance and act as a watchdog. This equally well requires one coherent view of risk and return.

The advantage of the CRO as a board position is that risk receives sufficient attention. It is of utmost importance that risk awareness exists at all levels in an organisation, including the top level. With the CRO on the board, it is ensured that complex products or strategic decisions are evaluated according to the level of risk.

As an illustration, Table 11.1 provides an overview of the position of a number of CROs in some major European insurers. Academic research shows that complex and highly leveraged firms are more likely to appoint CROs onto the board. The role of the CRO in such insurers is to explain the risk profile to investors and other stakeholders. In banking, wholesale banks tend to appoint CROs at board level more often than do retail banks. Wholesale banking is considered more complex. The parallel with insurance is that reinsurers are also more complex than retail insurers. We can see in Table 11.1 that all reinsurers in the sample have appointed a CRO at board level, whereas the CRO of retail insurers reports into the CFO.

CROs could have an important strategic role in either position, both at board level and as a direct report of the CFO. What we see in practice is that some CROs as direct reports are heavily involved in strategy development and play a strong advisory role in a wide range of ad hoc topics. This is a strategic involvement at the top level. Other CROs focus on implementation of policies and, for instance, Solvency II compliance. Although this is important, it is a less strategic role.

The CRO is ultimately the second line of defence. As in management control, the role of the CRO is to function as a countervailing power to business line decision-makers. To that end, they should challenge the business managers and executive board on how risks could be addressed more effectively. They should also challenge them to identify risks that remain unseen. As in the general management control framework, the risk management cycle includes risk objective setting, risk measurement, risk evaluation and taking risk measures (see Figure 10.8).

Table 11.1 Risk governance in annual reports

Company	CRO position	Risk committee
Aegon	CRO reports to CFO	Non-executive risk Committee and executive group risk and capital committee
Allianz	CRO reports to CFO	Non-executive risk committee, two executive committees
Aviva	Not disclosed	Group Alco and operational risk committee
Axa	Not disclosed	Three separate committees
Eureko	Not disclosed	One overarching executive committee
Agea	CRO reports to CFO	Non-executive committee, executive insurance risk committee
Generali	Not disclosed	Non-executive internal control committee and executive group risk committee
ING	CRO in board	Seven separate committees
Munich Re	CRO in board	Group risk committee and global underwriting and risk committee
Prudential	CRO in board	Multiple committees
Swiss Re	CRO in board	Group risk and capital committee, group products and limits committee
Zurich	CRO in board	Non-executive risk committee, two executive committees

Another development is the installation of a central risk management department that oversees all group risk exposures and provides aggregate risk reports to the management board. Often the risk department is headed by the CRO. The insurers that we know mostly organise the risk management department along the lines of the risk types. This is because the risk managers all have their technical expertise in a certain risk area rather than across business lines. The size of the risk management departments varies from company to company, also depending on the level of centralisation in the insurer. When insurers are very decentralised, it is more logical to have a strong risk management department in each business unit, whereas more centralised insurers have larger risk management department at the group level.

An important task of the risk management department is to ensure that the risk profile of the group is within the limits of the company's risk appetite. To that end, a framework of policies and procedures is often developed, along the lines of the risk types that we used in Chapters 3, 4 and 5 of this book. Each policy determines:

❏ how the risk is measured;
❏ what the maximum risk exposure is;
❏ how the risk profile is reported and to whom;
❏ who decides on overdrafts;
❏ how the risk is managed and by whom; and
❏ what tools exist to manage the risk.

In any case, it is of the utmost importance that risk management departments work closely with the financial departments. For instance, this is key during the process of calculating economic capital where financial and risk data are required to run the risk models. In practice, it appears to be more complex to align timelines of economic capital calculations of the risk management department to the year-end closing of the controlling department, as an example. However, it is also obvious that this is improving over time.

In addition to working with the controlling department, other departments are crucial counterparts of the risk management unit. First of all, general management is a key here because they are the first line of defence. Also, risk managers advise general management on how to improve the risk profile in such a way that long-term value is created. With value creation as the core financial indicator, general management will potentially need to update compensation schemes throughout the organisation. Hence, controlling and risk management will jointly need to set up a system to measure value creation up to the lowest organisational level possible in such a way that individual employees can be rewarded along the lines of the value created.

Second, the marketing department is a counterpart because they need to be aware of the risks that are sold by the company. Potentially, certain distribution channels are more profitable in terms of value than others and the risk manager can support the required analyses to bring this insight to the decision-makers. Also, the marketing department needs to be aware of the product criteria that carry a high economic capital in order to be able to generate value-creating new business. Depending on the organizational structure of the insurance company, new product development is done in the marketing department or in the underwriting department. In any case, the risk manager should ensure that decision-makers are able to distinguish between good and bad risks.

Third, claims management departments need to be empowered to implement prevention in such a way that it decreases economic capital only when that creates value. Prevention does not only decrease the level of the claims, but it often also decreases volatility of claims, and hence economic capital. To that end, economic capital analyses with the risk manager and the controller are the first step in this process.

Finally, the risk manager will logically liaise with the reinsurance and investment departments. Since these activities are an important way to steer the total economic capital profile, the risk manager often already has regular contacts with these departments. Investment departments or the capital department are also commonly the relevant authorities for discussing the restructuring of the balance sheet with ART instruments (see Chapter 3). Since optimising the balance sheet is important as well, the risk manager will liaise with these departments to ensure balanced decision-making on this issue.

Many risk management departments that we have seen work within a definite routine. They build risk models, report the outcome of the models periodically and work with the business to improve model outcomes and improve the risk model itself. What receives relatively little attention are emerging risks: risks that are not identified yet. How can companies become aware of risks it does not yet know of? This may seem a highly unstructured question, but in practice risk assessment tools exist to monitor the external environment and to raise specific issues. Potentially, this is an area where the insurance industry could gain from insight.

RISK MANAGEMENT COMMITTEES
In addition to the risk management department and the function of the CRO, insurers often set up special dedicated risk management committees. These are multidisciplinary management com-

mittees, consisting of both executive and lower level managers. In some cases, there are also non-executive risk committees set up as part of the non-executive (supervisory) board. For instance, this is the case for Aegon, Swiss Re and Aviva (see Table 11.1). The executive board committee on risk management in most firms consists of the CRO, CFO and a number of business unit risk officers and financial officers. Often investment, ALM and reinsurance expertise is also represented in the committee. Although technical expertise is represented, the risk management committee is a first-line body because it supports the executive board. Most of the time, it has received decision-making authority from the board.

The reason to set up multidisciplinary committees is twofold. First, it is an opportunity to discuss the topics at a sufficient level of detail with technical experts from both group and business unit level. This ensures that certain perspectives of the risk profile are not overlooked. Second, it is also a way to receive sufficient buy-in and commitment from group level to implement decisions in business units. Sometimes risk management committees are merely for information sharing. Other committees have decision-making authority derived from the responsibility of the executive board. Typical examples of decisions made by committees are the annual investment plan and the reinsurance renewal strategy.

There are multiple ways to install multidisciplinary committees. Some insurers have one single risk management committee that addresses all risks in a coherent way. Other companies have multiple risk management committees, such as one committee for each risk type. An ALM committee, for instance, operates under the mandate of the executive board to manage the investment strategy, asset allocation, mismatch position and market and credit risk positions. An underwriting risk committee, on the other hand, focuses more on underwriting risk (including life and non-life) and manages underwriting risk in the group and the reinsurance strategy. Thus, the organisation of these committees follow the major risk types.

Another option is to install a higher-level risk management committee, which would be mandated by the executive board to approve all the major risk policies, including investment and reinsurance strategy. The major advantage here is that risks are addressed coherently. To ensure sufficiently grounded decision-making, it is essential that the members of the committee are highly skilled, including in technical aspects.

The advantage of one overarching committee is that coherence between various risk perspectives is ensured. However, at the same time, it would be challenging to deal with all risk aspects that need to be addressed with a sufficient level of detail. Multiple dedicated committees ensure the latter issue can be resolved. In either structure, it is important that governance is in place and that the risks are discussed in a multidisciplinary way.

In addition to the risk committees organised along the lines of risk types, some insurers have set up a new product committee to approve all new products that are issued by the insurer. This ensures that business units comply with new product criteria. More importantly, however, is that products drive much of the risk profile of the organisation. When new products are launched, they automatically force the company into a certain risk. Ensuring that new products are healthy in terms of risk profile is a means to prospective risk management.

CONCLUSION

This chapter has described the way in which risk management can be effectively organised. Adequate risk management requires a proper risk organisation. The three lines of defence described here are central for allocating responsibilities regarding risk management. In organising risk management, it is important to keep in mind that risk and controlling are closely related. As such, the two (or more) departments that perform these activities should be aligned and organised in such a way that co-operation is facilitated. The key theme should be to pursue co-operation rather than isolation.

Appointing a CRO is one of the ways in which risk management can be organised. The responsibilities of the CRO include challenging the business to assume risks in a balanced way. We have seen that insurers have made different choices in the exact positioning of the CRO, be it on the board or reporting to the CFO. In our examples, we have seen that the more complex the risk profile of an insurer is, the more likely the CRO is an executive board member rather than a direct report of the CFO. In addition to appointing a CRO, companies have installed risk management committees to ensure multidisciplinary perspective in decision-making processes relating to risk.

Within the executive board there should be sufficient counter-vailing power to ensure that the rationale behind all decisions is challenged at all times. This ensures balanced decision-making. While it is important at all levels of the organisation, it is of utmost value at the highest level (the executive board). This key element of corporate governance seems simple, but can be extremely com-plex. The most visible element discussed here are the CEOs com-pensation packages, which are also the issue that has grabbed to most media headlines. As history has shown, formalised corporate governance is not sufficient to avoid debacles. Soft elements should ensure that the countervailing power actually materialises.

12

Conclusion

Risk management is at the core of the insurance industry. This has been the case since its foundations and will continue to be so in the future. However, we have seen that the explicit focus on risk management has increased during the first decade of the 21st Century, with new methodologies for measuring risks being developed – which has also given way to new risk management tools to actively manage risks and alter an insurance company's risk profile. In addition, the financial crisis and the advances in Solvency II have created a momentum for insurance companies to address risks.

This book has described the seven major risk types and the respective ways to manage and measure them. In the context of underwriting risk, the cash flow projections are key to determining the value of an insurance portfolio and performing simulations. In life, the embedded-value tools are the most logical way to derive cash flows, whereas in non-life the loss triangles are being used. In both cases, cash flows are used to apply simulations based on the underlying risk profile. While the tools may differ, the methodology underlying the valuation of the liabilities and the risk models is exactly identical. This may be counterintuitive for those who consider an actuary to be either life or non-life but never both. However, the modern way of looking at value and risk is creating consistency in the methodologies for both risk categories. In the context of the investment risks, it was seen that the economic balance sheet is central to risk management analyses. This captures the interaction between assets and liabilities that is so central to investment risks. Companies use scenarios to assess the various investment risks, such as interest rate risk and equity risk. Chapters 3 and 4 also showed how risk management instruments relate to measurement outcomes.

Economic capital is the predominant risk measurement technique. Although the calculation of economic capital can sometimes be complex, the underlying concept is relatively easy to understand: an insurance company needs a buffer to absorb risks. In addition to a sole measurement methodology, the concept of economic capital allows companies to address the risks in a coherent manner. Because risks are measured consistently, they can then be mutually compared – for instance, by comparing the risks of various portfolios or business units. In these kinds of comparisons, the risk is traded off against the return made on each activity. Only if risks and rewards are balanced can a company create long-term value. The concept of economic capital allows companies to make these assessments in the management control framework. Thus, the risk management instruments can be applied in management control as a tool with which to better steer the business.

USING THE OUTCOMES

This book has argued that the concept of economic capital is not only an ex post measurement tool, but that it can be of much value in a management control framework. In management control, economic capital is applied to address issues of strategic importance to the company, such as pricing, budgeting and capital allocation. It can be expected that the new quantitative information and techniques will feed into the management control cycle. The major advantage of using economic capital and risk management information in this cycle is that such information aligns management incentives with the objective of the company better than traditional profit information does, by managing the balance between risk and reward.

Around the year 2000, insurance companies started producing heavy embedded-value reports in addition to their regular annual financial reports. Those companies had actually began to use embedded value in their internal reporting cycles some years before that. A few years from now, it is expected that the regular internal reporting cycle will include – in addition to the monthly underwriting returns – the market-consistent embedded values and the economic capital positions. Obviously, RAROC will also form the core of management reporting. It can also be expected that the current separate embedded-value reports will be integrated in the regular annual report and accounts.

Fair value (or embedded value) could be a relatively new concept for some managers. In life, many decision-makers have at least heard about it, stemming from the initial versions of embedded value in the 1990s. However, its actual use has differed significantly between companies. Some have used it actively, while others treat the embedded-value outcomes as "for information" in their board meetings. The latter companies will pick up over time and understand the concept of value actively. For instance, insurers will better understand the relation between value and interest rates. Fair value in accounting regulations (IFRS4 phase II) will also enhance that process.

Solvency II will support the risk-based decision-making even further, since the use test will require companies to show the supervisors how internal models are used in decision-making processes. As a result, regular reporting is a sine qua non. Solvency II also requires companies to make multi-year forecasts of capital requirements in the ORSA. Insurers will make these economic capital projections in the light of their strategic plans. Again, it is of crucial importance to embed the calculations and reports in the day-to-day processes of the company so that managers can use the numbers to steer the business at all hierarchical levels of the organisation.

CHANGING THE INSURANCE INDUSTRY

In Chapter 1, we quoted the concern of managers that risk managers would start taking over the business by being too dominant in the decision-making process. Of course, the issue really is how will the new risk management methodologies change the insurance industry? Will using economic capital outcomes have an impact on strategic decisions?

With risk and return being better aligned, some products will change. We have already indicated that the high guarantees in life products are extremely expensive. These insights are likely to lead to change over time. We can already see this in mature markets such as western Europe, where traditional life insurance with guaranteed returns is getting less attractive. Less mature markets, such as in southeastern Europe, still have a long way to go. However, Solvency II will force companies in these markets to value guarantees. Also, these markets are dominated by western insurance groups with a great deal of knowledge and expertise on guarantees. The focus should be on how to change the market sentiment regarding risk and return. In less mature but growing markets, clients and insurance agents are extremely powerful. Over time, however, we can expect to see a decrease in the use of guaranteed products.

Another area that is high risk is non-life, where catastrophe risk is high. Depending on the structure of the product and the geographical area, liability could be long-tail but less volatile than short-tail products such as motor or property insurance. We can therefore assume that the values of these products are likely to change over time. It remains to be seen whether market forces are sufficiently strong to change the actual premium of these products. After all, motor products are considered to be a cross-selling product. If clients buy a motor product, they are also likely to buy other products with the same insurer. The means by which the exact distribution of price increases and decreases is to be achieved remains to be seen. It also depends heavily on the exact portfolio composition of each individual insurer and the situation in each region. After all, catastrophe risk is a very regional phenomenon, depending on flooding, earth quakes, storms, etc.

New to non-life insurers is also the fact that long-tail products are dependent on interest rates. So far, we have seen few non-life products with a premium structure that depends on interest rates. Clients find it logical that banking products do change with interest rates (cf mortgages, savings accounts), but less logical that liability products depend on interest rates. However, the value of a liability claim does heavily depend on the interest rate. How this will work out in the future is as yet unclear since the liability is only recognised when a client reports a claim – which might be independent of the date of the sale of that product. This is an area that insurers will still need to work on.

All these potential price changes should be placed in context. As indicated, financial aspects are not the only relevant aspect in determining the price of an insurance product. Cross-subsidising, marketing issues and competitiveness are also important areas. However, the change in pricing means that economic capital and fair value makes the reasoning explicit rather than implicit. It is crucial that risk managers play an important role in making these strategic decisions happen. They can support managers in providing the relevant and necessary insights. However, the actual decision is made by general managers, not by the risk manager.

SUPERVISION

We have seen how supervisors have endorsed the modern risk management principles in their supervisory regulations and practices. Solvency II is high on the agenda of supervisors all over Europe, but also outside the European borders. It serves as an example for many regulators across the globe.

Not all supervisors are ready for Solvency II, nor are the insurers themselves. Also, supervisors are now in the process of getting to grips with the new advanced techniques for measuring risks. The findings from the various quantitative impact studies (QISs) in the Solvency II context have provided supervisors with a wide array of background, just as insurers have gained experience. While supervisors may find the new "state-of-the-art" calculations more complex than the traditional reports, they are very positive about the new insights that this gives them, as has been seen in the countries that have already upgraded their national supervisory frameworks. However, much work will still be required before Solvency II comes into force. Are supervisors already sufficiently able to approve internal models before the implementation date? Are supervisors able to absorb and digest all the information in the new extensive reports that they will receive under Pillar III? Are supervisors adequately aligned to co-ordinate supervision of international groups? All these issues are works-in-progress. In addition to the efforts of the supervisors themselves, there is a clear role for companies to clearly communicate and explain their approach to supervisors.

The major advantage of the regulatory developments, such as Solvency II, is that supervisory requirements are closely aligned with insurers' internal risk management activities. Firstly, this is more efficient because companies will be able to cut down on duplication of work. Secondly, it is more effective because a company that follows its internal risk management principles will automatically reach supervisory objectives. Regulatory arbitrage will be avoided.

With the successes of the insurance industry in the context of Solvency II, and also Basel II and III in the banking industry, supervisors in other industries, such as pension fund regulators, may well follow suit. Some of the methodologies used in the life insurance business can be transferred to pension funds. However, the specificities of pensions need to be addressed, such as government rules and the role of the sponsoring company. There are already some ideas for developing a Solvency II-type framework for pensions. At the same time, we must be aware that pensions are even more nationally regulated than insurance. This will pose challenges for the industry in the further development of an updated supervisory framework.

Another area where new risk management techniques were being implemented at the end of the 2000s is the energy industry. In the process of the privatisation of national energy suppliers, companies have started to trade energy on the global energy markets. This involves facing similar risk positions to those of financial institutions. It also involves similar techniques, such as VaR. While supervision is still in the process of being developed, there is a clear role for supervisors as delegated monitors on behalf of individuals buying energy for their economic activities. Supervisors might be able to benefit from the lessons learned in the banking and insurance industries in their work to develop supervision for energy companies.

FINANCIAL CRISIS

We saw in Chapter 6 that the chain of financial crises has disrupted significantly the financial markets. Although the impact has not been as great as during the great crash of the 1930s which prompted the Great Depression, it is still one of the most dominant crises in financial history. Financial crises come and go, and this will continue to be the case. It is well known that financial markets have a short-term memory in the sense that they hardly learn from past crises. At least, not permanently…

Risk management is key to withstand a financial crisis. Will the new risk models be able to prevent future crises? This is an interesting and logical question. Despite its simplicity, this question is difficult to answer – especially since financial market participants tend to repeat their mistakes. Therefore, let us derive some sub-questions. First, will risk models be able to identify trends that might predict the advent of a new crisis? The answer to this question might be negative. Economic capital models in themselves are based on historical data and hence are insufficiently forward looking to identify hazardous trends. This implies that human expertise is required to identify these trends. This leads us to the next sub-question.

Second, will the new risk management techniques support risk managers in identifying trends in the market? The answer to this seems to be positive. Risk managers are much more focused than before on the outside world and use their tools to extrapolate trends towards the future. Scenario analysis and stress-testing can be used to identify potential weaknesses that need to be addressed. This could be weaknesses for individual companies but also vulnerabilities in the market as a whole. The new focus of regulators on financial stability will support this development.

Third, will the concerns of risk managers be sufficiently heard by decision-makers? This can only be guessed at. We mentioned above that the financial markets have a short-term memory – in times of prosperity, decision-makers find it hard to take such concerns seriously. It is viewed as pessimism rather than realism. Also, there is the phenomenon that companies would rather be in a financial crisis jointly with competitors than to step out of the booming phase of a crisis before the tide turns and run the risk of missing a part of the extraordinary returns of the boom phase. So, it is key for risk managers to communicate their messages effectively. In the years prior to the subprime crisis, various economists pointed out the risks without being paid any notice. The challenges lying ahead for risk managers are to effectively convince decision-makers of the inherent risks before the boom busts.

Fourth, will companies be able to better withstand a crisis with the risk models available? The answer to this question could be positive. Economic capital models are increasingly used throughout the financial industry, not the least due to new regulation (Solvency II and Basel III). This means that once a new crisis hits the financial markets, more capital is available and capital is better allocated to the areas where the risks are. Non-regulated companies will continue to be a problem – for example, hedge funds. Also, we have seen that, during the crisis, the appetite for risk decreased and companies were required to hold more capital for the same risks. However, with a continuing focus on capital in relation to risks, we can expect that capital will be better available to the companies that need it.

This is a rather ambiguous answer to the key question of whether risk models will be able to prevent future crises. If there is no clear answer, why do we need all those models? Economic capital provides an extremely useful risk language. It allows us to translate different risks into one number and then to compare risk and return. This is a key characteristic of economic capital that should be exploited to the full. By using economic capital and value throughout the organisation, insurers ensure they are ready for the next financial crisis by continuously balancing risk, return and available capital.

RISK MANAGEMENT INNOVATIONS

A greater focus on risk management opens the door to more innovative instruments such as ART. Although Chapter 3 touched upon instruments such as weather derivatives, catastrophe bonds and securitisation, the possibilities are numerous. With more risk management information becoming available all the time, it can be expected that further innovative products will be developed by the capital markets and offered to insurance companies. The first signs are already visible in the context of long-term interest rate risk products, catastrophe protection and securitisation. However, the market for the last two in particular is less deep. This can be expected to change over time because capital markets have a better risk absorption capacity than do individual counterparties, such as reinsurance firms. Also, capital market solutions for longevity are starting to arise. In the UK, a number of life insurers and pension funds have issued capital market instruments to hedge life risks. This is not feasible for all companies, since a certain scale is required. The increasing understanding of risks and the transparency in the value of insurance liabilities might open doors for smaller companies to trade these risks as well. Once a better understanding of the risks spreads throughout the financial markets, life securitisation might also become available in countries with less deep financial markets.

Two phenomena will enhance this development. First, consistent reporting requirements such as those in Solvency II will create increased transparency, which fosters investors' trust in the market. IFRS4 phase II will support this development since Solvency II and IFRS will be much more aligned than the traditional system. Despite this, it remains to be seen to what extent IFRS and Solvency II will be identical. Second, better information in the context of risk management and economic capital will increase the understanding of market participants, who will become more aware of the risks of the products and therefore be more willing to invest in them. As a result, once-illiquid underwriting risks should gradually become more liquid and have a market price.

These ART developments will not make traditional reinsurance redundant. On the contrary, reinsurance companies will always be there to absorb specialised risks that cannot be transferred to the capital markets very easily. They will also remain important for smaller companies that do not have the sufficient portfolio size to use ART techniques. To that end, they will continue to play the important role of risk mitigant in the insurance industry.

LANGUAGE PROBLEM OVERCOME?

If risk management and economic capital are so strategically important to the insurance business, a prerequisite is that these concepts are extremely well understood by a wide audience within the insurance firm. Although it may seem rather obvious, it is good to emphasise this because the individuals who normally do the complex calculations may not have the communication skills to explain the concepts to other staff. Communication and clear explanations of the concepts are key to implementing risk management within the company and truly embedding it in the day-to-day operation of the business.

In writing this book, the aim was to bridge the gap between the technical nature of the calculations and the wider strategic importance of the concepts (in Chapter 1, this was even called a language problem). It is hoped that this book has achieved that objective for readers.

Selected Bibliography

Allen, F. and A. M. Santomero, 1999, "What Do Financial Intermediaries Do?", *Journal of Banking and Finance,* **25**, pp 271–94.

Artzner, P., 1999, "Application of Coherent Risk Measures to Capital Requirements in Insurance", *North American Actuarial Journal,* **3(2)**, pp 11–25.

Artzner, P., *et al,* 1999, "Coherent Measures of Risk", *Mathematical Finance,* **9(3)**, pp 203–28.

Association of British Insurers, 2007, "A Guide to the ICA Process for Insurers" (available at www.abi.org.uk).

Babbel, D. F., *et al,* 2002, "Fair Value of Liabilities: The Financial Economics Perspective", *North American Actuarial Journal,* **6(1)**, pp 12–27.

Banks, E., 2004, *Alternative Risk Transfer: Integrated Risk Management through Insurance, Reinsurance and the Capital Markets* (Chichester: John Wiley & Sons).

Basel Committee on Banking Supervision, 2004, "International Convergence of Capital Measurement and Capital Standards: A Revised Framework", www.bis.org.

Berd, A.M. (ed), 2010, *Lessons from the Financial Crisis* (London: RiskBooks).

Bernstein, P. L., 1998, *Against the Gods: the Remarkable Story of Risk* (New York: John Wiley & Sons).

Booth, P., *et al*, 1999, *Modern Actuarial Theory and Practice* (Boca Raton: Chapman & Hall).

Bryis, E. and F. de Varenne, 2001, *Insurance: from Underwriting to Derivatives* (Chichester: John Wiley and Sons).

Butsic, R. P., 1994, "Solvency Measurement for Property Liability Risk Based Capital Applications", *Journal of Risk Insurance*, December, pp 656–90.

Casualty Actuarial Society, CASACT, 2004, "Fair Value of P&C Liabilities: Practical Implications", www.casact.org.

CFO Forum, 2004, "European Embedded Value Principles", www.cfoforum.nl.

CFO Forum, 2009, "Market Consistent Embedded Value Principles", (available at www.cfoforum.nl).

Chapman, R. J., 2006, *Simple Tools and Techniques for Enterprise Risk Management* (Chichester: John Wiley and Sons).

Comité Européen des Assurances (CEA), 2007, "Solvency II – understanding the process", www.cea.eu.

Comité Européen des Assurances (CEA), 2011, Solvency II – Making it workable for all", www.cea.eu.

Comité Européen des Assurances (CEA), Mercer Oliver Wyman (MOW), 2005, "Solvency Assessment Models Compared: Essential Groundwork for the Solvency II Project", www.cea.assur.org.

Cools, K., 2005, *Controle is Goed, Vertrouwen nog beter* (Assen: Koninklijke van Gorcum).

Cowley, A. and J. D. Cummins, 2005, "Securitisation of Life Insurance Liabilities", *Journal of Risk and Insurance*, June, pp 193–226.

CRO Forum, 2005, "A Framework for Incorporating Diversification in the Solvency Assessment of Insurers", www.croforum.org.

Crouhy, M., *et al,* 2006, *The Essentials of Risk Management* (New York: McGraw-Hill).

Cruz, M. (ed), 2009, *The Solvency II Handbook* (London: RiskBooks).

Culp, C. L., 2002, "The Revolution in Corporate Risk Management: A Decade of Innovations in Process and Products", *Journal of Applied Corporate Finance,* Winter, pp 8–26.

Cummins, J. D., 2000, "Allocation of Capital in the Insurance Industry", *Risk Management and Insurance Review,* **3**, pp 7–28.

Doff, R. R., 2004, *Economic Capital en risicobeheer bij banken* (Amsterdam: Nibe-Svv).

Doff, R. R., 2006, *Risicomanagement bij Verzekeraars: Risicobeheersing, Economic Capital, Toezicht en Solvency II* (Amsterdam: Nibe-Svv).

Doff, R. R., 2009, "Solvency II Bij verzekeraars: Analyse Naar de Jaarrekeningen", *Maandblad voor Accountancy en Bedrijfseconomie,* *83, November, pp 364–72.*

Drzik, J., 2005, "At the Crossroads of Change: Risk and Capital Management in the Insurance Industry", *Geneva Papers,* **30**, pp 72–87.

Eling, M. *et al.,* 2009, "Minimum Standards for Investment Performance: A New Perspective on Non-life Insurer Solvency", *Insurance: Mathematics and Economics,* **45**, pp 113–122.

Federal Office of Private Insurance (FOPI), 2006, "The Swiss Experience with Market Consistent Technical Provisions – The Cost of Capital Approach", 24 February.

Federal Office of Private Insurance (FOPI), 2004, "White paper of the Swiss Sovlency Test", available at www.finma.ch.

Financial Services Authority (FSA), 2004, "Interim Prudential Sourcebook", www.fsa.gov.uk.

Financial Services Authority (FSA), 2007, "ICAS – Lessons Learned and Looking Ahead to Solvency II", www.fsa.gov.uk.

Swiss Financial Market Supervisory Authority (FINMA), 2006, "Technical Document on the Swiss Solvency Test" (available at www.finma.ch).

Froot, K. A. and J. C. Stein, 1998, "Risk Management, Capital Budgeting and Capital Structure Policy for Financial Institutions: An Integrated Approach", *Journal of Financial Economics,* **47**, pp 55–82.

Galbraith, J. K., 1997, *The Great Crash 1929* (New York: Mariner).

Hull, J.C., 2009, *Risk Management and Financial Institutions* (Boston, MA: Pearson Prentice Hall).

International Actuarial Association (IAA), 2004, "A Global Framework for Insurer Solvency Assessment", www.actuaries.org.

International Actuarial Association (IAA), 2007, "Measurement of Liabilities for Insurance Contracts: Current Estimates and Risk Margins", www.actuaries.org.

Johnson, L. D. and E. H. Neave, 2008, "The Subprime Market: Familiar Lessons in a New Context", *Market Research News,* **31(1)**, pp 12–26.

Kaas, R., *et al,* 2001, *Modern Actuarial Risk Theory* (Boston: Kluwer Academic Publishers).

KPMG, 2002, "Study into the Methodologies to Assess the Overall Financial Position of an Insurance Undertaking from the Perspective of the Prudential Supervisor", May.

Lelyveld, van, I., 2006, *Economic Capital Modelling: Concepts, Measurement and Implementation* (London: Risk Books).

Main, A. and A. Sufi, 2008, *"The Consequences of Mortgage Expansion"* (available at www.ssrn.com).

Matten, C., 2000, *Managing Bank Capital* (Chichester: John Wiley & Sons).

Mercer, Oliver, Wyman (MOW), 2004, "Life at the End of the Tunnel: The Capital Crisis in the European Life Sector".

Merton, R. C. and A. F. Perold, 1993, "Theory of Risk Capital in Financial Firms", *Journal of Applied Corporate Finance,* 3, pp 16–32.

Mikes, A., 2008, "Risk Management at Crunch Time: Are Chief Risk Officers Compliance Champions or Business Partners? (available at www.ssrn.com).

Morris, C.R., 2008, *The trillion Dollar Meltdown* (Philadelphia: PublicAffairs).

Myers, S. C. and J. A. Read, 2001, "Capital Allocation for Insurance Companies", *Journal of Risk and Insurance,* December, pp 545–80.

Nakada, P., *et al,* 1999, "P&C RAROC: A Catalyst for Improved Capital Management in the Property and Casualty Insurance Industry", *Journal of Risk Finance,* Fall, pp 1–18.

Pensioen- & Verzekeringskamer (PVK), 2004, "Financial Assessment Framework (FTK)", www.dnb.nl.

Ryan, S. G., 2008, "Accounting In and For the Subprime Crisis" (available at www.ssrn.com).

Saita, F., 1999, "Allocation of Risk Capital in Financial Institutions", *Financial Management,* Autumn, pp 95–111.

Saita, F., 2007, *Value at Risk and Bank Capital Management* (Elsevier: London).

Santomero, A. M. and D. F. Babbel, 1997, "Financial Risk Management by Insurers: An Analysis of the Process", *Journal of Risk and Insurance*, June, pp 231–70.

Schroeck, G., 2000, *Risk Management and Value Creation in Financial Institutions* (Hoboken: John Wiley & Sons).

Simons, R., 2000, *Performance Measurement and Control Systems for Implementing Strategy* (New Jersey: Prentice Hall).

Smit, R.C. and I. Walter, 2006, *Governing the Modern Corporation* (Oxford: Oxford University Press).

Soros, G., 2008, *The New Paradigm for Financial Markets* (Philadelphia: PublicAffairs).

Swiss Re, 1999, "From Risk to Capital: An Insurance Perspective" (available at www.swissre.com).

Swiss Re, 2005, "Risk and Capital: Some Thoughts on Risk Modelling in Insurance Companies" (available at www.swissre.com).

Taleb, N. N., 2007, *The Black Swan* (New York: Random House).

Tillaart, A. H. A. J. van den, 2003, "Controlling Operational Risk: Concepts and Practices", PhD Thesis, Twente University Netherlands.

Vaughan, E. and T. Vaughan, 1995, *Essentials of Insurance: A Risk Management Perspective* (Chichester: John Wiley & Sons).

Zaik, E., et al, 1996, "RAROC at Bank of America: From Theory to Practice", *Journal of Applied Corporate Finance,* Summer, pp 83–92.

Websites
Comité Européen des Assurances (CEA)
www.cea.eu

CFO Forum
www.cfoforum.org

CRO Form
www.croforum.org

EIOPA
eiopa.europa.eu

European Commission on Solvency II
ec.europa.eu/internal_market/insurance/solvency

Groupe Consultatif
www.gcactuaries.org

International Actuarial Association (IAA)
www.actuaries.org

International Accounting Standards Board (IASB)
www.ifrs.org

International Association of Insurance Supervisors (IAIS)
www.iaisweb.org

Basel Committee on Banking Supervision
www.bis.org/bcbs

Index

(page numbers in italic type denote tables and figures)

Pillar III 179–80, *179*, 196–9
  see also Solvency I; Solvency II
pooling principle 12
portfolio composition 42, 52, 298
portfolio limits *141*
premium risk 50, 56
  economic capital for *61*
premiums, investment of 16
private-equity risk 66
privatisation, in insurance industry 1–2
probability distribution 27, 27–8, 28–9,
    29, 30, 31, *31*, 32–3, *33*, 41, *46*, 47, 48,
    59–1
  and non-life risk 56, 59
probability of bankruptcy 32, 80
probability of default (PD) 80, 81, 217
Prudential 90
Public Company Accounting
    Oversight Board 276

Q
Quantitative Impact Studies (QISs) 153,
    172, 173–7, *176*

R
RAROC, *see* risk-adjusted return on
    capital
rating agencies 24, *78*, 78–80, 122
  see also individual agencies
rating ambition 32–3, *33*
RBS 119
real estate, as premium investments 16
real-estate risk, 66
reinsurance 19, 42, 53–5, 63, 75, 77–8,
    164, 201, 242, 257, 262, 280, 287
  contracts, categories of, *54*
  examples of 55
replicating portfolio 73
reserve risk 50, 56–9
  economic capital for *61*
retrocession 53
risk:
  calamity 41
  catastrophe 50, 59, 165

concept of, different definitions 20
credit-spread 66–7
currency 66
definition of 17–18
equity 66
inflation 66
for insurers 17–20
interest-rate 66
investment 63–85
  market 63–74; *see also* market risk
life 37–47
  components of 41, *41*
  controlling 42–3
  defined and discussed 18, 39–41
  economic capital for 45–7, *46*
  measuring 43–5
  and reinsurance 42; see also
      reinsurance; risk
  and securitisation 42
management, basic forms of *19*
model 41
modelling, deterministic and
    stochastic 48
non-financial 87–110
  business 102–9; *see also* business risk
  lapse and expense 105–6
  operational 87–102, 165; *see also*
      operational risk
non-life:
  components of 50, *51*
  controlling 51–4
  defined and discussed 18, 50–1
  economic capital for 59–62
  insurance products for 48–50
  insurance, fair value in 241
  and life insurance, minimum
      capital requirements for 142
  measuring 56–9
  prevention as control of 51–2
  parameter 41
  premium 50, 56
    economic capital for *61*
  private-equity 66
  real-estate 66